CW00952181

Praise for *The Marketing Agency Blueprint*

"When I was a Marketing VP, I paid a PR agency, an ad agency, and a digital agency. Each one focused on building long-term campaigns that targeted my company's prospects and interrupted them to pay attention to a message. I would not hire those agencies today. In the always-on 24/7 world of the web, buyers use search engines and social media to look for products themselves and at their convenience. At the same time, the lines between PR and marketing have blurred to be unrecognizable. It's time for a new type of agency, one built to take advantage of the communications revolution, one that helps companies get in front of buyers when they are ready and eager to engage. In his engaging *Marketing Agency Blueprint*, Paul Roetzer shows you how to transform your firm to thrive in the real-time world we live in today."

—David Meerman Scott,
Bestselling author of *The New
Rules of Marketing & PR*

"It's about time. There have been countless websites, books, and events for marketers to adapt to the current marketing revolution, but never one for agencies and service providers. Well, this is it. *The Marketing Agency Blueprint* is a must-read for any group or individual providing marketing services to clients."

—Joe Pulizzi,
Founder, Content Marketing Institute

"Paul Roetzer's *The Marketing Agency Blueprint* paints a clear picture for the inevitable transformation of twenty-first century marketers, and then lays out a succinct roadmap for others to follow. If your goal is not just to survive, but to thrive and gain a competitive advantage in the midst of new media realities, this may just become your new marketing bible."

—Dustin S. Klein,
Publisher and executive editor,
Smart Business Magazines & Events;
Coauthor/contributing editor,
The Benevolent Dictator

"I've worked with Paul for more than 10 years, and am continually impressed with his vision and drive. My faith in him and his agency led me to take a risk and evolve my marketing efforts. I am an old-school numbers guy, and the proof is in the results. What Roetzer presents in *The Marketing Agency Blueprint* is the future of the marketing services industry."

—**Kenneth Paine,**
CEO, Industrial Heat Sources and Hy-Tech Products

"Marketing has gone through a massive transformation. This creates a significant opportunity for agencies. Millions of organizations need help in navigating these new, fast-moving waters. *The Marketing Agency Blueprint* is a practical, insider's guide that should be required reading for anyone building the next-generation marketing services firm."

—**Dharmesh Shah,**
Cofounder and CTO, HubSpot

"Inbound marketing ranks among the most powerful, quiet trends of the last decade. Paul's experienced this change firsthand and writes eloquently and actionably on how marketers and businesses of all stripes can earn amazing returns by investing in the channels of search, social, and content."

—**Rand Fishkin,**
CEO, SEOmoz

"Paul Roetzer is a young lion of marketing who realized early on how technology and new media make the traditional agency model as dated as an episode from *Mad Men*. Roetzer champions marketing as an evolving discipline where value creation is the basis of success. He sees modern marketing as a marriage of talent and analytics. The result is cost-effective delivery of great marketing that can level the playing field between large and small competitors. His ideas are proven through practical application in the marketing agency he founded. Roetzer's book is a seminal view of how marketing services can and will be delivered in the future. It is a must-read for the next generation of marketing professionals—and the customers they serve."

—**Gary Christy,**
Brand Leader, Westfield Insurance

the
marketing
agency
blueprint

the
marketing
agency
blueprint

the handbook for building
hybrid pr, seo, content,
advertising, and web firms

paul roetzer

WILEY

John Wiley & Sons, Inc.

Published by John Wiley & Sons, Inc., Hoboken, New Jersey.
Published simultaneously in Canada.

For general information on our other products and services or for technical support,
please contact our Customer Care Department within the United States at (800) 762-
2974, outside the United States at (317) 572-3993 or fax (317) 572-4002.

Wiley publishes in a variety of print and electronic formats and by print-on-demand.
Some material included with standard print versions of this book may not be included
in ebooks or in print-on-demand. If this book refers to media such as a CD or DVD that
is not included in the version you purchased, you may download this material at
http://booksupport.wiley.com. For more information about Wiley products, visit
www.wiley.com.

Library of Congress Cataloging-in-Publication Data:

Roetzer, Paul, 1978-
The marketing agency blueprint: the handbook for building hybrid PR, SEO, content,
advertising, and web firms / Paul Roetzer.
    p. cm.
 ISBN: 978-1-118-13136-7 (acid-free paper)
 ISBN: 978-1-118-17688-7 (ebk)
 ISBN: 978-1-118-17689-4 (ebk)
 ISBN: 978-1-118-17690-0 (ebk)
 1. Marketing. I. Title.
 HF5415.R5665 2011
 658.8–dc23   2011032163

Printed in the United States of America

10 9 8 7 6 5 4 3 2 1

In memory of Mike and George.

And to my wife, Cheryl,
whose patience and unwavering
support have made it possible
for me to follow my dreams.

Contents

Foreword   Brian Halligan   xiii

Acknowledgments   xvii

Introduction   1
    The Origin   1
    The Opportunity to Emerge   2
    Causes for Change   2
    Accelerating Transformation   4
    The Value Imperative   5

Chapter 1 Eliminate Billable Hours   7
    Disrupt or Be Disrupted   7
    A Broken System   8
    The Power of Transparency   14
    The Move to Standardized Services and Set Pricing   15
    Value-Based Pricing   15
    Focus on Recurring Revenue   24

Chapter 2 Transform into a Hybrid   27
    Every Firm Is a Tech Firm   27
    Meet the Demand for Digital Services   34
    Understand Your Role in the Ecosystem   38
    The Art of Outsourcing and Collaboration   48
    Diversify Your Revenue Streams   50

Chapter 3 Think Talent and Team   55
    Great Teams Finish First   55
    A Players, the Draft, and Free Agency   57
    Hire, Retain, and Advance Hybrid Professionals   61

		Talent Evaluation and Professional Reviews	72
		Leaders Must Lead: The LeBron James Parable	75
Chapter	4	**Build a Scalable Infrastructure**	**79**
		Make Decisions That Fit Your Growth Goals	79
		The Realities of Costs, Funding, and Cash Flow	88
		Agility, Mobility, and the Cloud	91
Chapter	5	**Devise an Inbound Marketing GamePlan**	**95**
		The Shift to Inbound Marketing	95
		Origins of the Inbound Marketing GamePlan	96
		The Foundation: Brand and Website	99
		Audiences: Segment and Prioritize	104
		Objectives: Set Your Success Factors	107
		Strategies and Tactics: Take an Integrated Approach	109
		Does Inbound Marketing Really Work for Agencies?	116
Chapter	6	**Control the Sales Funnel**	**121**
		Agency Sales System Essentials	121
		People, Tools, and Processes	124
		Understanding the Buying Cycle	135
		Lead Generation	137
		Prospects and Lead Nurturing	139
		Conversions and Transitions	143
Chapter	7	**Commit to Clients**	**147**
		Build Relationships and Loyalty	147
		The Significance of Systems	152
		Prioritizing and Evaluating Accounts	159
		The Marketing Consultant Laws	161
Chapter	8	**Deliver Results**	**165**
		Become Measurement Geeks	165
		Use Analytics to Adapt	169
		Activate Builders and Drivers	172
		Unplug to Excel	180
Chapter	9	**Embrace Failure**	**185**
		If Your Model Is Broke, Fix It	185
		The Disruptor Advantage	186
		The Traditionalist Opportunity	186
		Spend Less Time Planning, More Time Doing	188

Chapter 10   **Pursue Purpose**   193
             Stand for Something   193
             The Purpose Pyramid: A New Planning Paradigm   194
             Fate, Destiny, and the Business of Life   199

Conclusion   201
             The Transformation   201
             Core Concepts   202

Resources   211
             Visit MarketingAgencyInsider.com   211

Notes   213
About the Author   219
Index   221

Foreword

When I started HubSpot in June 2006 with my business partner, Dharmesh Shah, our experiences with marketing agencies led us to almost entirely avoid working with them. In fact, we designed our original business model around selling our marketing software directly to end customers, and developed an internal marketing team that would not be dependent on agency assistance. Our decision to circumvent marketing agencies did not result from questioning their skills or capabilities, but rather from their failure to acknowledge the impending shifts in consumer behavior.

I felt as though many marketing agencies were, and still are, trying to cling onto the *Mad Men* marketing methodology. They want to sit in rich mahogany corner offices with 21-year-old scotch on ice, and brood over their grandiose and flowery advertisement campaigns. They rely too heavily on traditional outbound marketing techniques, such as television advertisements and cold calling, which allow them to safely distance themselves from the nitty-gritty operations side of marketing and direct contact with the end consumer. However, the detached Don Drapers of the marketing world cannot simply rely on creating deep and lofty brand awareness campaigns any longer.

Consumers have now assumed control over their purchasing processes. With the help of devices like DVRs, satellite radio, and caller ID, consumers no longer tolerate irritating outbound marketing efforts designed to interrupt their daily lives. Instead, they know what they want to purchase, and strongly object to businesses that try to force-feed them messages. With millions of Internet pages at their fingertips, consumers actively research their own product information online. They contribute to forums, follow industry thought leaders on Twitter, and even write their own blogs about products and services. By filtering the excessive marketing clutter produced by outbound techniques, the Internet has changed consumers' buying behaviors in ways we never thought possible.

Because of this dramatic shift, we believed that it was time for marketing agencies to concentrate on providing inbound marketing strategies to their clients. As Dharmesh and I explained in our book, *Inbound Marketing*, this involves creating an integrated online process that uses original content to provide educational and salient advice to consumers, helping them with their purchasing decisions.

These "hybrid" agencies—as Paul coins them—could help clients develop original content (blog posts, whitepapers, etc.) that would attract interested and engaged prospects, who would begin to associate and rely on those businesses as active thought leaders in their respective industries. This would significantly bolster the client's online reputation through indexed pages and inbound links, leading to an increased level of website traffic. With systems in place to track the progress of their inbound marketing campaigns, these agencies would be able to adapt strategy based on solid metrics to ensure improvements over time.

Agencies like PR 20/20 are the breaths of fresh air for which the marketing world has been gasping. Although he started his agency to specialize in traditional PR and marketing services, Paul possessed the foresight to see the inevitable shifts of the business world. He was brave enough to make the switch to an inbound-oriented strategy early, and executed it perfectly.

Unlike the mad men of today, Paul became the marketing Renaissance man; he understood that marketing consultants could not succeed as one-trick (or in this case, service) ponies, and that collaborations with companies like ours would lead to excellence. When he joined the HubSpot movement in October 2007, he voraciously consumed all things HubSpot. By 2008, Paul became one of our most adept product users, and PR 20/20 became the first agency to join our Value Added Reseller (VAR) program.

All of this work, driven by a hunger for knowledge and drive to innovate, added up to incredibly significant gains for PR 20/20. Starting as a one-man shop in late 2005, Paul now employs 10 dedicated employees. What is even more impressive is that, through testing its methodologies on itself, PR 20/20 grew revenue by nearly 500 percent in just four years; increased its average website visits from less than 1,000 per month to more than 8,000; boosted blog subscriptions by 1,400 percent; and has totaled 12,000 inbound links and more than 900 indexed pages.

In addition to these successes, the agency has also perfected its inbound marketing service offerings for clients. In 2010, PR 20/20 launched the industry's first service packages that bundled website development, brand marketing, search marketing, social media, content marketing, and public relations for a set monthly fee.

To truly drive change in the industry, Paul understood that it was necessary to educate and improve the marketing-services world at large. He became one of HubSpot's leading inbound marketing evangelists, and began speaking nationwide on topics including blogging, content marketing, social media, and inbound marketing strategy. With the help and support from agency partners like PR 20/20, the HubSpot VAR program now accounts for 20 percent of our sales revenue. Based on demand, we are forecasting that our revenue from agencies will be 40 percent by the second quarter of 2012.

We now take tremendous pride in working with savvy marketing agencies that not only purchase HubSpot for their clients, but also frequently for themselves. With more than 170,000 marketing agency contacts in the HubSpot database, we have high hopes that many more agencies will fully embrace the inbound marketing methodology, and believe that these agencies will be the next generation of Madison Avenue marketing all-stars. As Paul explains, these hybrid agencies will master a new kind of business model, where a sales team, software tools, refined business infrastructure, and new marketing processes all work in unison to support the marketing agency's core consulting services.

In a time when others were unwilling to accept the apparent shifts in the marketing services industry, Paul's commitment to changing the course of his agency, and the agency world at large, is incredibly commendable and truly impressive. This book is particularly special because you will read about Paul's personal experiences as a business owner and marketer, rather than try to decipher the ideological musings from some business scholar or analyst. No matter the maturity of your agency, Paul comprehensibly dissects his success so that you can replicate it.

All professionals in the marketing-services field should read this book because it clarifies the confusion around the roles and responsibilities of marketing agencies in an inbound marketing world. The marketing-services industry is at a turning point where an agency must choose whether to, as Paul states, "disrupt or be disrupted." So the question now is, which side will you choose?

—BRIAN HALLIGAN
CEO AND COFOUNDER, HUBSPOT

Acknowledgments

In 2005, at the age of 27, I became an entrepreneur in pursuit of a better way. My business partner, Larry Ondercin, believed in me enough to fund the startup phase, and four months later we hired our first employee, Christina Capadona Schmitz (@christinacs), who took a chance and bought into a vision when I was still working out of coffee shops.

We assembled an amazing team of highly motivated professionals, and created a culture that refused to accept traditional wisdom and conventional solutions.

The Marketing Agency Blueprint would not be possible without the entire PR 20/20 team—Christina, Keith Moehring (@keithmoehring), Laurel Miltner (@laurelmackenzie), Tracy DiMarino (@TracyDi Marino), Dia Dalsky (@DiaDalsky), Christy Hajoway (@ChristyBarks), Jessica Donlon (@JessicaDonlon) and Laura Pinter (@lipinter). Their work, commitment, sacrifice, and friendship mean the world to me.

The book also has been inspired by countless people, some of whom I know personally, and others whose work, writings, and teachings I have admired through the years. It would be impossible to recognize them all, but here are some of the entrepreneurs, professionals, authors, and teachers who have influenced my life, business, and writing.

- Chris Brogan
- Clayton M. Christensen
- Matt Cutts

- Rand Fishkin
- Jason Fried
- Malcolm Gladwell

- Seth Godin
- Peter N. Golder
- Robert Greene
- Brian Halligan
- David Heinemeier Hansson
- Mel Helitzer
- Tony Hsieh
- Steve Jobs
- David H. Maister
- Tim O'Reilly
- Daniel H. Pink
- Cassandra Reese, PhD
- Howard Schultz
- David Meerman Scott
- Dharmesh Shah
- Bradford Smart, PhD
- Jim Sweeney
- Gerard J. Tellis
- Fred Wilson
- Sergio Zyman

Introduction

We are on the cusp of a truly transformational period in the marketing-services industry. The old guard, rooted in tradition and resistant to change, will fall and new leaders will emerge.

The industry will be redefined by marketing agencies that are more nimble, tech savvy, open, and collaborative. Digital services will be ingrained into the DNA of every agency, and blended with traditional methods to execute integrated campaigns. Agencies will create and nurture diverse recurring revenue streams through a mix of services, consulting, training, education, publishing, and software sales. They will use efficiency and productivity, not billable hours, as the essential drivers of profitability. Their value and success will be measured by outcomes, not outputs. Their strength and stability will depend on their willingness to be in a perpetual state of change, and an ability to execute and adapt faster than competitors. The depth, versatility, and drive of their talent will be the cornerstones of organizations that pursue a higher purpose.

This is the future of the marketing-services industry. A future defined and led by underdogs and innovators. You have the opportunity to be at the forefront of the transformation.

THE ORIGIN

In February 2004, I came to a life-changing realization—the marketing-agency model was broken and had been for years. Although I was only four years into my career at that time, a number of contributing factors had become obvious to me:

- Billable hours were inefficient at best. Professionals were more worried about meeting hour quotas than delivering the level of

1

service and quality needed to produce measurable results for clients.

- There was little differentiation between firms, and a lack of innovation within the industry.
- Training and education were stagnant. Firms and universities were teaching the same systems, principles, and services that had been applied for decades.
- Request for proposals (RFPs) were a waste of time and energy, for both clients and agencies.
- Standard measurement systems, such as press clippings, impressions, reach, ad equivalency, and PR value were meaningless, and they had no real connection to bottom-line results.

The industry was ripe for disruption.

THE OPPORTUNITY TO EMERGE

Fast-forward to today, and many of the same challenges exist. Traditional firms—public relations (PR), advertising, search engine optimization (SEO), and web—are fighting to remain relevant by grasping for new services, such as social, mobile, and content, rather than focusing on what really matters, including pricing, technology, staffing, infrastructure, processes, and purpose.

As a result, there are unparalleled opportunities for emerging agencies and consultants to transform, disrupt, and thrive within the developing marketing services ecosystem.

The agencies and professionals with the will and vision to adapt and evolve will rise, and many traditional and digital-only firms will become obsolete.

CAUSES FOR CHANGE

The forces that are fueling transformation can be narrowed down to three primary catalysts—*change velocity*, *selective consumption,* and *success factors*—which we will explore throughout the book:

Change Velocity

The rate of change, continually accelerated by technology innovations, has created growing demand for tech-savvy, forward-thinking firms.

Tech-savvy forward thinking firms.

Specifically, trends and shifts in consumer behavior, business processes, software, data analysis, communications, and marketing philosophies have affected the need for evolved services and consulting.

Consider the impact and meteoric rise of cloud computing, virtualization, social networking, mobility, and group buying as examples. We live in a real-time world, which demands real-time agencies.

Although change velocity presents challenges, it also provides significant advancement opportunities. Technology has made it possible to create remarkably efficient agency management and client services systems that lower operating costs, while increasing productivity and profitability.

Agencies have access to a wealth of reliable software-as-a-service (SaaS) platforms in the areas of time tracking, project management, customer-relationship management (CRM), lead nurturing, website content-management systems (CMS), sales, accounting, data storage, campaign management, monitoring, analytics, enterprise social networks, virtual meetings, and communications. Not only does this reduce the barrier to entry, but it makes it possible for emerging firms to more quickly compete with, and usurp, slower traditional firms.

Selective Consumption

Selective consumption is the basic principle behind inbound marketing, the philosophy made popular by HubSpot, a fast-rising Internet marketing software company. In essence, consumers are tuning out traditional, interruption-based marketing methods, and choosing when and where to interact with brands.

They are conducting billions of Internet searches each month, downloading case studies and ebooks, opting into e-mail newsletters, watching online videos, listening to podcasts, following brands and professionals on social networks, joining online communities, posting product reviews, and reading blogs, and they are increasingly doing it all from their mobile devices.

As a result, business-to-business (B2B) and business-to-consumer (B2C) organizations in every industry are shifting budgets away from print advertising, trade shows, cold calling, and direct mail toward more measurable and effective inbound marketing strategies that cater to consumer needs.

Savvy firms are capitalizing on the shift by expanding and integrating their service offerings in the areas of search, mobile, social, content, analytics, web, PR, digital advertising, and e-mail marketing. They also are diversifying revenue streams and driving new business through affiliate relationships and value-added reseller (VAR) partnerships with marketing software companies.

Success Factors

Marketing campaigns are not about winning awards for creative, building the flashiest websites, gaming Google for higher rankings, generating mounds of media coverage, or negotiating the lowest cost per thousand (CPM) in order to interrupt the largest audience. The job of a marketing agency is to produce results that impact the bottom line. It's that simple.

Although traditional marketing firms rely on impressions, reach, advertising equivalency, PR value, and other arbitrary measurements of success, marketing firms now have the ability to consistently produce more meaningful outcomes—inbound links, search engine rankings, click-through rates, website traffic, landing page conversions, content downloads, blog subscribers, and leads—that can be tracked in real time and directly correlated to sales.

These success factors are how firms should and will be judged.

Success Factors

ACCELERATING TRANSFORMATION   *Results Driven Services*

I have spent more than seven years building a new agency model at PR 20/20 because I passionately believe there is a better way.

We have worked closely with technology companies such as HubSpot to develop more results-driven services and more efficient processes, drawn on the teachings of industry luminaries such as David Meerman Scott (@dmscott), and been influenced by the business models of innovative organizations such as Apple, Google, Salesforce, and 37Signals.

We are far from perfect, and we certainly do not have all the answers, but it is time we share what we have learned in order to accelerate change.

This is not a book about who we are, but rather what I believe we, as marketing agencies, have the potential to be. *The Marketing Agency Blueprint* presents 10 rules for building tech-savvy, hybrid agencies that are more efficient, influential, and profitable than traditional firms, and, most importantly, are capable of delivering greater results and value to clients.

The book explores lessons learned building PR 20/20, and draws on my own experiences working in a traditional marketing firm. It also integrates knowledge and resources from the leaders and innovators who are transforming the marketing-services industry.

Capable of delivering greater results & value to clients.

THE VALUE IMPERATIVE

The Marketing Agency Blueprint, with its supporting resources at www.MarketingAgencyInsider.com, is designed to help entrepreneurs build their agencies and futures, and stimulate a more open and collaborative agency ecosystem.

One of my favorite quotes, which has come to encapsulate my philosophy on business and life, is from Tim O'Reilly (@timoreilly), founder of O'Reilly Media, "Create more value than you capture."[1] That is exactly what I hope to accomplish with this book.

I encourage you to connect with me on Twitter (@paulroetzer), and join the Marketing Agency Insider community on Twitter, LinkedIn, and Facebook. Together, we can transform an industry.

- Website: www.MarketingAgencyInsider.com.
- Twitter: @AgencyIn.
- Book Hashtag: #AgencyBlueprint.
- LinkedIn Group: Search "Marketing Agency Insider."
- Facebook Page: www.Facebook.com/MarketingAgencyInsider.

chapter **1**

Eliminate Billable Hours

Inefficiency is the enemy of success.

DISRUPT OR BE DISRUPTED

Disruptive innovation can hurt, if you are not the one doing the disrupting. This term, coined by Harvard professor and bestselling author Clayton Christensen (@claychristensen), and commonly talked about in technology circles, is a very real issue for marketing agencies.

According to Christensen, disruptive innovation, "describes a process by which a product or service takes root initially in simple applications at the bottom of a market and then relentlessly moves 'up market,' eventually displacing established competitors."[1]

Disruptive innovation is already happening in the marketing-services industry, and it is going to change everything, including pricing and service models, measurement methods, tools and platforms, higher education, industry accreditation, marketing budgets, organization charts, and career paths.

Think about the firms coming up that have superior knowledge and capabilities in the high-demand areas of search, mobile, content, and social. Do you think the status quo is sustainable for traditional marketing firms? The upstarts and innovators may not immediately attack the core larger enterprise markets sought after by the big agencies, but before you know it, the collective ecosystem of emerging agencies will have built a diverse and collaborative empire that will shift the power in the industry. Then, it is only a matter of time.

SUPERIOR KNOWLEDGE & CAPABILITIES IN THE HIGH DEMAND AREAS OF SEARCH, MOBILE CONTENT & SOCIAL.

7

Whether you are an emerging agency seeking to disrupt or a traditional firm on the wrong end of the impending evolution, here are several things to remember about disruptive innovation:

- Disruptive business characteristics include: lower gross margins, smaller target markets, and simpler products and services.
- It often comes from the outside, and once you realize what is happening, it is probably too late.
- Success requires an uncommon tolerance for risk and a desire to embrace the unknown.
- Victory favors those who are bold and decisive in their actions.
- Traditional agencies that are slow to adapt will fail, and many existing industry experts will become irrelevant. This will be good for the industry.
- Unparalleled opportunities will arise for marketing agencies and professionals, and new career paths will be defined.
- The underdogs and innovators will become the leaders.

Pricing strategy is a key component to disruption. Agencies motivated to change will shift away from the inefficient legacy system of billable hours, and move to more results-driven, value-based models accessible to the mass market. This presents the opportunity for agencies and independent consultants to disrupt the industry with lower prices, and potentially higher profit margins.

A BROKEN SYSTEM

I started my career in the marketing industry at a traditional PR firm. In those days (1999–2005) we charged a flat rate of $125 per hour, and billed in quarter-hour increments. The flat rate meant that clients paid the same hourly rate for my work as they did for time logged by our most senior personnel. This was easier to track and report internally (when people actually completed their timesheets) than a tiered hourly rate, but from a client's perspective, I always struggled to understand how paying a junior associate and a senior executive the same $125 per hour made any sense. Where is the value in that?

Then again, I also never bought into the tiered-rate model. Even today I cannot comprehend how firms justify charging upward of $964 per hour for a senior executive's time, which, according to the 2009 American Association of Advertising Agencies (4A), was an average rate for large U.S.-agency chief creative officers.[2] Even more shocking to me is that there are corporations willing to pay those excessive fees.

This is the core issue of what I call the *salary-rate fallacy*.

The Salary-Rate Fallacy

A standard formula used by agencies to determine billing rates is to apply a salary multiple, commonly a factor of two or three. According to communications industry consultants StevensGouldPincus, the most profitable PR firms should target 35 percent of revenue for base salaries, and 50 percent of revenue for total labor costs, including salaries, bonuses, and freelance/outsourced labor.[3] So, in theory, if employees generate three times their base salaries in revenue, then firms will fall within target profitability ranges.

Firms may use variations when determining hourly rates, and take additional factors into account, but a simple salary multiple enables them to account for overhead expenses and employee compensation, while leaving room for net profit margins. Target net profit margins vary greatly based on agency size, growth rate, and life stage, but, most likely, they will fall in the range of 10 to 25 percent, depending on which benchmark report you reference.

In order to understand the deficiencies of this approach, let's take a look at an example of how an agency professional's hourly rate would be calculated using a 3× multiple.

In this scenario, we will assume the professional's *production rate*, or the time he is billable, is approximately 57 percent (or 100 hours per month). The remaining 43 percent of nonrevenue-generating time may be accounted for through administrative tasks, account management, business development, professional development, and networking. Here is how it breaks down:

Forty-seven weeks (number of work weeks in a year after accounting for five weeks of vacation, personal days, and holidays)

Forty-five hours per week (assumes five, 9-hour days)

Annual available hours = 2,115 (47 weeks × 45 hours per week)

Annual billable hours = 1,200 (assumes conservative estimate of 100 hours per month)

Salary = $150,000

Required Billings (3×) = $450,000

Billing Rate = $375 per hour ($450,000/1,200 hours)

Assuming there are 1,200 hours of billable work to be done in the year, this formula seems easy enough, and makes financial sense, at least for the agency. The problem is that the formula is completely agency driven. It is tied exclusively to outputs, not outcomes, and assumes that all agency activities—account management, client communications, writing, planning, consulting, creative—are of equal value.

Thus, the fallacy: A marketing agency executive making X ($150,000) per year is worth Y ($375) per hour. The fact is that the amount a professional is paid does not have a direct correlation to the quality or value of the services they provide, especially when you consider the impact of change velocity, selective consumption, and success factors, which were discussed in the introduction. And yet, we have an entire industry built on this pricing concept.

Maybe the executive's time is worth $375 per hour to build advertising creative or to consult on crisis communications situations, if that is what he built his career and salary on, but now client needs are rapidly evolving (change velocity). They are demanding different services (selective consumption) and measuring return on investment (ROI) in new ways (success factors).

Clients are willing to pay a premium for experience and knowledge they do not have, but the unfortunate reality is that young professionals, who have grown up in a digital world, may be more qualified to provide consulting and services in high-demand areas such as social media, SEO, and mobile. It is almost a reverse of how the industry has traditionally worked. Clients would pay for inefficiencies of junior account executives while they learned the craft and gained experiences, but the labor and hourly rates were cheap. Now clients pay for the inefficiencies of senior executives to learn the digital game, but their hourly rates are not coming down.

In addition, as costs increase to run and grow the agency, including rising employee salaries, there are only two obvious options to maintain or increase profits: (1) raise hourly rates or (2) demand professionals work more hours, neither of which creates greater value for clients.

The salary-rate fallacy is the core reason that billable hours are a broken system. Unfortunately for many traditional firms, it is the basis for their financial structure and incredibly difficult to change. Even for firms working off retainers, rather than project-based hourly rates, in order for the agreements to make financial sense, retainers still must be based on an estimated number of service hours using the hourly rate formula.

For example, if an agency has a $5,000 per month retainer, the number of hours that will be dedicated to the account each month could look like this:

Senior account executive ($300/hour × 5 hours)   = $1,500
Account executive ($150/hour × 10 hours)   = $1,500
Assistant account executive ($100/hour × 20 hours) = $2,000

TOTAL : 35 hours   = $5,000

If the agency exceeds its monthly allotment, they either absorb the losses or request more budget. The other, less desirable options are to push more hours to cheaper junior staff with less experience, record the time against other projects with available budgets, or make it up by shorting time spent on the account during the next month. In other words, traditional retainers do not really solve what is wrong with billable hours.

The Cost of Inefficiency

To further explore the challenges of the billable-hour model, consider the case of a press release. What do you think a press release is worth?

The correct answer, like any product or service in a free market, is whatever a client is willing to pay. However, in the traditional model, the cost comes down to two primary factors: hourly rate and the producer's efficiency. So let's examine the practical application of billable hours in an agency.

Scenario 1 Professional A is an assistant account executive and an exceptional copywriter who requires minimal oversight. She is assigned a press release that will be distributed on a national wire service. She completes a strong original draft that is reviewed internally with no edits, and it is then quickly approved by the client. As a result, the cost is relatively straightforward.

Hourly rate   = $150
Hours to complete =   3
Cost   = $450

Scenario 2 Now let's look at what happens to the price had Professional B, who also has an hourly rate of $150, been assigned the same press release. Although she wrote a few releases in college, this is her first real-world project. In addition to her raw writing skills,

Professional B is easily distracted. She is addicted to her Twitter stream and has e-mail alerts that pop up every two minutes, so she rarely focuses on her tasks for extended periods. As a result, she takes a bit longer than Professional A, and the quality is subpar, requiring multiple revision rounds before it even goes to the client for approval. The cost for the first draft:

$$
\begin{aligned}
\text{Hourly rate} &= \$150 \\
\text{Hours to complete} &= \underline{\quad 5 \quad} \\
\text{Cost} &= \$750
\end{aligned}
$$

However, we are not done yet. We also need to account for the one hour of a senior associate's time to edit and revise the original draft, 15 minutes to review the edits with Professional B, 30 minutes for Professional B to make the edits, and another 30 minutes for the senior associate to edit and approve the final version. Oh, and the senior associate's hourly rate is $250 an hour. So, the final cost looks like this:

Original draft ($150/hour)	= 5 hours or $750
Senior associate edit and review ($250/hour)	= 1.25 hours or $312.50
Professional B edits ($150/hour)	= 0.50 hours or $75
Senior associate final edit—Round 2 ($250/hour)	= 0.50 hours or $125
Total	= 7.25 hours or $1,262.50

There is zero added value for the release from Professional B, yet, the client pays nearly three times more for the exact same deliverable. The client is actually penalized, and forced to pay for the agency's inefficiency and professional development.

The model is broken.

Inefficiency Factors

There are countless factors that can affect a professional's efficiency, but distractions, time tracking, and motivation are three of the biggest culprits.

Distractions Marketing agency professionals are multitaskers. At any given moment, they are connected through an array of channels competing for their attention—Twitter, Facebook, Internet, TV, chat, e-mail, phone, text, Skype, Intranet—not to mention face-to-face time and meetings. In essence, they are always distracted or anticipating distraction, and, therefore, they are never performing at their peak and never achieving flow.

Yet clients are expected to pay full hourly rates when, in reality, professionals rarely are focused solely on the project at hand. I know if I were paying someone for their creative work, I would rather they spent 60 uninterrupted minutes straight on my project than 60 minutes over three hours with calls, e-mails, tweets, and instant messages in between. I will take efficiency with higher levels of creativity and attention every time.

Distractions lead to higher costs and lower quality.

Time Tracking Time tracking is not exact by any means. Although agencies and professionals may have the best of intentions for accuracy, it is easy to accidentally leave the meter running or even to forget to start the meter as you battle distractions and jump from one project to the next. As a result, it is common to estimate or round your time in logical increments. This means clients commonly pay for time that never happened. A five-minute phone call tracked as 15 minutes may not be a big deal once, but multiply that out over a 12-month campaign, and you are looking at hours of wasted time and money.

Plus, professionals responsible for billable-hour quotas certainly do not want to miss any client time, so they try to account for every activity, no matter how mundane. This time adds up and can eventually start to take valuable hours away from more meaningful and measurable work.

My experience was that, over time, clients would often avoid calling, or even stop keeping us in the loop on key strategic discussions because they did not want to incur the charges for us to have a chat or read and compose an e-mail. So agencies make a few dollars to fulfill billable-hour goals, but lose out on long-term opportunities. This is the type of shortsighted thinking that will doom agencies.

Motivation There is little motivation for agencies or their professionals to complete work more efficiently. The value of employees to an agency, and, therefore, their ability to advance and build wealth, is directly tied to how many hours they log and how many of those hours actually get billed to clients. As a result, professionals often are more worried about meeting hour quotas or staying within monthly retainer limits than they are with delivering the level of service and quality needed to produce measurable results for clients.

Going back to the press-release example, which professional looks better on paper based on the standard model? Professional A, who finished the release in three hours for $450, or Professional B, who took more than seven hours with the help of her supervisor for a cost of $1,262.50?

Well, if the client had the budget available to allow for the inefficiency, Professional B comes out ahead and the client never knows the difference.

Low-quality work should not cost the client more, but that is exactly what happens. Either that or the agency eats time as professional development, but that is not something most agencies are eager to do.

Just think what an agency could accomplish, and how much value it could bring to its clients, if it rewarded professionals for retention and growth of accounts, rather than how many hours they bill in a year.

THE POWER OF TRANSPARENCY

There is a certain mystery to billable hours and agency services. Clients are not always sure exactly what they are getting or what it costs. This works for agencies because billable hours are an imperfect mix of art and science, and as long as the agency produces results, clients are happy.

However, there are those times when things do not go so smoothly. Maybe the client anticipated a return on investment sooner, does not feel like the account is getting enough attention, or is just too demanding and unrealistic. There is also the possibility that the agency may have slightly overpromised to win the business and just cannot deliver to the expectation levels that were set.

All of a sudden, invoices are being scrutinized a little more closely. The client's chief financial officer (CFO) takes a keen interest in the growing monthly expense, and now the chief marketing officer (CMO) has to explain the value of the agency to his executive team. The problem is that he has no idea. After four months at $10,000 per month, he has invoices full of activities but nothing tangible to share with his bosses to justify the relationship. The mysterious nature of billable hours is not that much fun for either party at this point.

Now the agency team has to invest nonbillable (in theory) hours reviewing and explaining invoices, and scrambling to demonstrate some meaningful and measurable impact they have had. Even though both sides entered the engagement with the best of intentions, the relationship becomes tenuous, and time and energy that should be focused on producing outcomes is diverted to saving the account.

This scenario, which played out continuously over my first five years in the industry, was a primary motivating factor in my desire to create a different agency model. I became obsessed with the idea of making services tangible with clearly defined costs, features, and benefits, almost like buying a product off a retail shelf or signing up for a software service. My theory was that, if clients understood exactly what they were getting and agreed ahead of time what it was worth, then we could remove the mystery from the equation and focus on delivering value and results.

Transparency would build trust, remove the friction from the client-agency relationship, and make it simpler to sell services to the mass market. The problem was that the billable-hours model was the only one I had ever known. How would I build an entirely new financial model and productize a service business?

THE MOVE TO STANDARDIZED SERVICES AND SET PRICING

My solution was to standardize services, and apply set prices based on a number of variables. In essence, I believed it was possible to achieve economies of scale in the production and delivery of services, much like a manufacturing company does with products. If we could lower the cost of services over time by improving efficiency, then, in theory, we could increase profits, possibly even above industry benchmarks.

Set prices would enable us to bundle services into packages designed to fit specific market segments, such as franchise owners, and it would dramatically reduce time spent building new business and account development proposals. Plus, we would be able to make marketing agency services more affordable and effective to the underserviced market of small businesses in the United States and around the world. Everyone wins.

It seemed so obvious, but I had no idea how to actually build a financially viable business model. So I set out on a 21-month journey from February 2004 to November 2005 to make it happen.

VALUE-BASED PRICING

I took the approach that if you can define the scope, which is possible with nearly every marketing agency service, then you can standardize the service and assign a set price. Although some services, such as website projects and marketing plans, are more complex than others, the vast majority of agency services can be standardized by clearly defining the scope of what is to be done.

Sample Standardized Service

Standardized services, such as the following case-study example, commonly include description, features, benefits, and set price:

Provide prospects and customers with powerful examples of how your products or services deliver value and results. Case studies are ideal website content for your visitors, make great marketing and sales tools, and can be used as editorial submissions.

What Makes a Good Case Study?

- Satisfied, recent customer.
- Unique or high-profile application (company, product, event, etc.).
- Clearly defined challenge and solution.
- Impressive, quantifiable results.
- Innovative or customized solution.
- Hi-res photos available.
- Customer resources willing and able to be interviewed.
- Limited legal concerns with trade secrets/proprietary information disclosure.
- Story highlights key product/service benefits (speed, efficiency, productivity, profitability).

What's Included?

- Following a standard outline of challenge, solution, and results, PR 20/20's professional marketing copywriters will craft a case study for publishing on your corporate website, blog, or media room.
- Approximately 700 words.
- Optimized with priority keywords and written with buyer personas' key needs in mind.
- Additional fees apply for graphic design and strategic planning if you plan to use case studies in print or PDF form as sales support.
- Average turnaround: 15–20 business days.
- Price = $1,000.

The guiding principle was that set prices had to be value based, meaning they were to be determined based on perceived and actual value rather than the number of billable hours something takes to complete. So if a trifold brochure was priced at $2,500, then it did not matter if it took 15 or 35 hours to produce, the client would pay $2,500. The burden was on the agency to build systems and processes, and put the right talent in place, to profitably deliver at the set price.

In the traditional billable-hour model, the basic formula to determine cost is *hourly rate × billable hours*. It is simple, but as we have seen it is also inefficient and favors the agency's needs over the client's. On the other hand, the value-based pricing model takes seven primary variables into account:

1. Estimated hours.
2. Hourly revenue target (HRT).
3. Costs.
4. Perceived value.
5. Builder vs. driver.
6. Loss leader.
7. Service level.

In most cases, you will be able to determine prices by simply calculating *estimated hours × HRT*, but you want to take the other variables into account before finalizing the price.

Estimated Hours

At peak efficiency, how many hours will it take the agency to complete a project? Keep in mind *peak efficiency* is the key here, and one of the main differences from the traditional model. For services to be value-based, clients should not pay for agency inefficiencies. They should be charged for the estimated time in which the agency is capable of completing the service. The actual time invested will vary project to project, but if your estimates are accurate, and your team works efficiently, it should average out over time.

The best way to determine estimated hours is by referencing historical timesheets. Let's say you want to standardize blog post copywriting. Pull reports from the last 10 blog posts your agency has completed, and look at the average hours needed. If you do not have timesheets to reference, analyze the scope of the service, and forecast time to complete based on your experience and educated best guess.

I can tell you from more than six years experimenting with this model, value-based pricing is about testing and revising. You will get some pricing very wrong, and you will get burned a time or two, but as long as you have the right tracking and reporting systems in place, you can quickly adjust and move on.

It is important to note that the value-based model does not eliminate the need for timesheets. Accurate time tracking actually becomes more essential in order to monitor efficiency and productivity, evaluate employee performance, produce activity reports, and evolve pricing. We will talk more about time-tracking systems and software in Chapter 4.

Hourly Revenue Target (HRT)

How much revenue does the agency need to generate per hour of client work to achieve profit goals? For solo practitioners, the HRT will probably be similar to your hourly rate, but, for agencies with multiple employees, you will need to consider additional variables such as expenses, growth goals, payroll, and target profit margins.

In essence, the HRT is similar to a flat rate in the traditional billable-hour model, but now it is only one of seven factors taken into consideration when determining service prices. My best advice is to talk with your accountant or financial advisors to determine your agency's HRT, but following is a very simplified way to look at calculating it using the industry standard benchmark of revenue per employee.

We will assume an agency has five full-time professionals with varying client-service hour capacities. For example, the CEO may be forecasted for 50 hours per month, whereas the assistant account executive is targeted for 140 hours per month. The agency's annual revenue per employee goal is $120,000, which translates into $600,000.

CEO	= 600 client-service hours/year (50/month)
Vice president	= 960 client-service hours/year (80/month)
Senior account executive	= 1,200 client-service hours/year (100/month)
Account executive	= 1,440 client-service hours/year (120/month)
Assistant account executive	= 1,680 client-service hours/year (140/month)
Total client-service hours	= 5,880

So, if the agency delivers 5,880 client-service hours, it would need to earn $102 per hour in order to achieve its annual revenue goal of $600,000 ($600,000/5,880 = $102 per hour).

Again, this is not the only option to calculate HRT, but it provides a basic structure to determine a starting point.

Costs

Are there any costs associated with the production and delivery that will be built into the price? This may include fees from partner agencies for services such as graphic design, video production and editing, or licensing fees. I suggest considering these costs when determining your HRT.

For example, you may decide that, on average, it takes your agency eight hours to write a 1,000-word sales sheet, and your HRT is $105. Your price would be $840, but that does not take graphic design fees into account. So you contact your preferred designer and negotiate a fixed cost of $500 on design. Now you have a price of $1,340, which you can leave as is, or round up to $1,400 to account for markup or to give yourself a little flexibility on your time estimate.

Is a 1,000-word, professionally designed sales sheet worth $1,400? That question leads us to our next factor, perceived value.

Perceived Value

What is the fair market value? What are clients willing to pay for the service? In many cases, this is the most important factor to consider. By drawing on your own experience and researching what other agencies are charging, you can often settle on pricing that fits market demands.

Revisiting the example sales sheet, you may determine that $1,400 is too low. You have been charging clients $1,800 to $2,200 for the same job for the last two years and have had nothing but rave reviews. So put the price at $2,000 and move on to the next one. You have now created a value-based price that meets client needs, and gives you the chance to earn more than your HRT of $105. Use your time-tracking system to ensure that future jobs are actually getting completed on time and on budget, and adjust the set price as needed.

In some cases, clients will put tremendous value on project work that has no measurable impact on the bottom line. This may be because they simply do not have the resources or knowledge internally to deliver the services your agency is capable of providing, or because of basic supply and demand rules. If your agency has capabilities that are scarce and in high demand, then you are in a strong pricing position, and I suggest you take advantage of the fundamental economics working in your favor.

Builder vs. Driver

Is the service designed to set the foundation for future success (*builders*) or to produce short-term results (*drivers*)? This directly affects the perceived value and what clients are willing to pay.

For example, if a client comes to your agency for support to create and grow the company's social media presence, it is going to take time before your services have any real impact. You have a lot of building to do, and, therefore, the client may not consider the services as valuable. On the other hand, say a client comes to you with a sales database of 25,000 prospects, and your agency plans and conducts a webinar that generates 1,000 qualified leads. That is driving real business results that organizations highly value.

We will talk more about builders and drivers in Chapter 8.

Loss Leader

Is the service designed to entice first-time clients with attractive pricing? Is it proven to create cross-sell and up-sell opportunities?

In retail, loss leaders are products sold at lower prices in order to drive sales of more profitable items. For example, we originally used PR and marketing plans as loss leaders, assuming they would convert into ongoing campaigns. We would charge a few thousand dollars and invest 100 hours or more of our top talent's time building incredibly comprehensive and valuable plans. Project-based clients would thank us, use the plan to justify hiring more staff, and then take everything in-house.

We have learned that plans as loss leaders are a bad idea, so I do not suggest replicating that approach. I highly recommend requiring clients to commit to contracts of six months or more before providing detailed strategic plans.

This goes for the business development process as well. Do not give away the whys and how-tos just to win accounts. If prospects or clients want plans for free, they will never truly value your agency's services and knowledge. This is a primary reason that requests for proposals (RFPs) are often so detrimental to agencies, and such a flawed system. Agencies invest significant time and energy developing creative and strategic concepts for prospects, and the organization only compensates the firm that wins the bid. RFPs are an archaic process that devalues agency experience and expertise.

Service Level

Will basic-, intermediate-, or advanced-level talent produce and deliver the service? Even if you are no longer charging hourly rates, there is an hourly cost associated with every employee, so do the math.

A senior account executive making $75,000 per year in total compensation—salary, benefits, and bonuses—costs the agency approximately $32 per hour, while an assistant account executive earning $30,000 costs approximately $13 per hour. These hourly rates are based on 260 business days per year at nine hours per day, or a total of 2,340 hours.

$$\$75,000/2,340 = \$32.05/\text{hour}$$
$$\$30,000/2,340 = \$12.82/\text{hour}$$

Work that primarily requires basic-level service should cost less in the value-based model, and high-level services should cost more.

Consider the service-level factor in the example of an e-mail newsletter and a crisis-communications plan. Assuming both are completed in 10 hours, which is more valuable? I would argue that the crisis communications strategy, which requires advanced capabilities to devise, should be priced at two-to-three times the e-mail newsletter, which can be completed efficiently by an assistant account executive.

Remember, we are pricing on perceived value, and a strategic plan to mitigate risk and protect your client's brand is gold. When demand exists for advanced expertise, you have the opportunity to create and capture tremendous value. Always make your profits where they are justified.

Revenue-Efficiency Rate

Although estimated hours to complete a service are heavily weighted in the value-based pricing formula, prices are no longer based on how many hours it takes the agency to deliver services. Efficiency becomes the primary driver of success. So rather than relying on straight billable-hour reports to determine agency performance, we came to focus on revenue-efficiency rates (RER).

Simply stated, the RER measures how efficiently your agency turns one hour of service into X dollars in revenue, with X being the HRT.

The RER formula is relatively straightforward, once you know your target HRT. Let's say that your agency strives to generate $100 in revenue for every client service hour. The goal is to deliver the service as close to 100 percent efficiency as possible in order to achieve your desired profits. As we discussed in the previous section, you want to take costs into account as well. Here is how to calculate the RER of a completed project: RER = [(Price – Costs)/Hours]/HRT.

Sample 1: Website Project

Price = $20,000
Costs = $8,000 (graphic design and programming are outsourced)
Gross Profit = $12,000
Hours = 120
Hourly Revenue Target = $100
[($20,000 − $8,000)/120]/$100 = 100 percent

This is excellent. The agency's gross profit (or revenue after subtracting vendor fees) on the project was $12,000, and it invested 120 hours to complete the project. That means that it generated $100 for every hour of service for a 100 percent efficiency rating. Assuming that the services were provided by an account executive earning $45,000 per year, or approximately $19 per hour ($45,000/2,340 hours), the agency has plenty of room in there to cover operating costs, employee compensation, and a nice profit margin.

Now let's look at an example of how this can go wrong.

Sample 2: Marketing Plan

Price = $5,000
Costs = $0 (completed by internal staff)
Gross Profit = $5,000
Hours = 120
Hourly Revenue Target = $100
[($5,000 − $0)/120]/$100 = 42 percent

Marketing plans can be time intensive, and they often drain significant agency resources to execute. In this scenario, the HRT is $100, and, like the website project, it takes the team 120 hours to complete the project. At set price of $5,000, the revenue-efficiency rate is only 42 percent. In other words, the agency only generates $42 per service hour. To make matters worse, the marketing plan requires heavy senior-staff involvement, which costs the agency more to deliver the service.

The agency can absorb the inefficiencies as long as it is being delivered as part of a larger contract and campaign, otherwise it can be a major problem. But what is the alternative? Charge the client for all 120 hours at whatever the hourly rate is?

If we assume a billing rate of $150 per hour, then it would be $18,000 for a marketing plan that will be outdated by the time it is presented. Are there clients willing to pay that much for a plan? Even if there are, will you be comfortable with the value they will get from it, knowing how quickly plans change?

I would argue that with a 12-month contract in place, this is potentially a loss leader worth taking. Your goal is to build long-term client relationships, and this gives your team the chance to immerse itself in the industry and put a solid foundation for success in place. However, do not make a habit of taking on low-efficiency projects like this.

When Do Billable Hours Make Sense?

Even knowing all the challenges with billable hours, when variable scope is involved, they may be the only viable solution. This applies to services such as consulting time and media relations, which can be very difficult to forecast, given their dependence on variables such as ever-changing client needs and demand from third-party audiences.

For example, a PR firm may forecast 20 hours to make targeted pitches to 10 high-priority journalists, and coordinate any follow-up communications and interviews. If it takes 15 hours to research, craft, and distribute the 10 pitches, 5 hours are left for any additional work. However, when all 10 journalists respond and request supporting materials and onsite interviews, the agency realizes it dramatically underestimated hours.

My solution would be to define the known scope—research, craft, and distribute 10 highly targeted pitches—and commit to a value-based set fee for that first phase, regardless of how long it actually takes to complete. Then, have a contingency allotment of service hours available based on media demand. Although still integrating billable hours, this approach is preferred for a few reasons:

- Clients know exactly what it will cost to develop and send the pitches, and they agree to the value of that work, knowing it does not come with any guarantee of results. In other words, they see the value in the outputs provided by your firm, which they would prefer not to handle in-house.

- The up-front set fee forces your professionals to be focused and work as efficiently as possible, knowing that if it takes longer than forecasted, the agency, not the client, is losing time and money.

- The hourly-rate contingency will only be activated if the client will gain additional value from your services, because it only comes into play when the media responds and expresses interest.

FOCUS ON RECURRING REVENUE

There is an enormous, albeit unstable, market for project-based services. The success of solutions such as Logoworks, crowdSPRING, and the HubSpot Services Marketplace has demonstrated a rising wave of interest in affordable marketing support. As a result, agencies and professionals that figure out models to profitably meet growing demand for project work stand to prosper.

However, project-based work is less predictable, making it incredibly difficult to forecast workflow, expenses, staffing, and income. In other words, if you are planning to stay a solo practitioner or if you are building a distributed network of contractors, project-based opportunities may be exactly what you need. However, for those of you focused on building an agency, success depends on your ability to create recurring revenue from a diverse and stable client portfolio.

The goal should be to sign up the majority of your client base to long-term contracts, preferably 12 months or more, and to have 80 percent or more of your annual revenue coming from those contracts. This ensures a predictable and steady cash flow, assuming clients pay their bills on time, and it gives you the confidence to invest in growth and take the calculated risks needed to innovate and excel.

While building your contract base, your largest client should not account for more than 20 percent of your annual revenue. This rule is flexible if it is a long-time loyal client that has grown organically over time, but never for newer, high-risk accounts. You take on too much exposure, to borrow an insurance industry term, when you rely so heavily on one account.

No matter how good you are, there are too many variables out of your control that can lead to an account loss. We have had solid contract accounts disappear overnight due to bankruptcy, mergers and acquisitions, internal shakeups, and poor management decisions. On the other hand, we have also had to drop clients for a variety of reasons. You have to protect yourself and your employees. When accounts leave, you are stuck with the overhead, and you either need to quickly replace the business or make difficult decisions to cut back expenses, which may include staff reductions. You can mitigate your risk and give yourself the freedom to walk away from deadbeat accounts by having a well-balanced portfolio.

CHAPTER HIGHLIGHTS

- The traditional billable-hour system is tied exclusively to outputs, not outcomes, and assumes that all agency activities—account management, client communications, writing, planning, consulting, creative—are of equal value.

- The amount professionals are paid does not have a direct correlation to the quality or value of the services they provide, especially when you consider the impact of change velocity, selective consumption, and success factors.

- Distractions lead to higher costs and lower quality.

- Transparency in pricing builds trust, removes friction from the client-agency relationship, and makes it simpler to sell services to the mass market.

- If you can define the scope, you can standardize the service and assign a set price.

- The burden is on the agency to build systems and processes, and put the right talent in place, to profitably deliver services at set prices.

- The value-based pricing model takes seven primary variables into account: estimated hours, hourly revenue target (HRT), costs, perceived value, builder vs. driver, loss leader, and service level.

- Accurate time tracking in a value-based pricing model becomes more essential in order to monitor efficiency and productivity, evaluate employee performance, produce activity reports, and evolve pricing.

- If prospects or clients want plans for free, they will never value your agency's services and knowledge.

- Your goal should be to sign up the majority of your client base to long-term contracts, preferably 12 months or more.

- The largest contract client should not account for more than 20 percent of your annual revenue.

- Efficiency is the primary driver of success.

chapter **2**

Transform into a Hybrid

A real-time world demands real-time agencies.

EVERY FIRM IS A TECH FIRM

Hybrid agencies will come to rule the marketing world. These emerging leaders are tech savvy, offer integrated services, hire and retain versatile talent, and profit from diversified revenue streams. They thrive on change, and continually apply shifts and advances in technology to strengthen their businesses, evolve their services, and deliver greater value to clients.

As change velocity accelerates, traditional agencies unwilling or unable to adapt will quickly be left behind. Meanwhile, more nimble upstart firms are utilizing technology to construct efficient agency-management and client-services models. Whereas legacy systems slow down large, established agencies, hybrid firms can activate software and introduce processes that lower operating costs, increase productivity, and drive profitability. They are able to build more scalable models that largely operate in the cloud, capitalize on advances in online communications and mobility, and rely on their social graphs to create a more open and collaborative agency ecosystem.

The cloud, which metaphorically refers to the Internet, has given agencies access to affordable hosted solutions for time tracking, project management, customer-relationship management (CRM), lead nurturing, sales, accounting, data storage, campaign management, monitoring, analytics, website content-management systems (CMS), enterprise social networks, technology infrastructure, virtual meetings, and communications.

These cloud applications, which run on third-party servers rather than internal networks and local computers, become the backbone to more dynamic and innovative agencies. Systems and processes that used to take years to build on internal networks can now be activated and integrated in real time, often for small monthly fees.

Technology-Driven Services

As selective consumption—the principle that consumers choose when and where to interact with brands—continues to drive marketing strategies and budgets, agencies must seek opportunities to bundle their services through value-added reseller (VAR) and affiliate programs.

The HubSpot VAR Program is a perfect example of the opportunities that exist around technology-driven services. In February 2010, HubSpot cofounder and CEO Brian Halligan (@bhalligan) introduced their VAR program and began investing significant company resources in training and certifying marketing agencies on the use of its inbound marketing software.

Certified partners—more than 500 agencies in more than 15 countries—are given access to educational resources, selling tools, training programs, and private online communities that facilitate customer interactions and peer-to-peer communications. In addition, partners who resell the HubSpot software receive a 20 percent margin on each license for the life of the customer.

Agency partners are featured in the HubSpot Services Marketplace,[1] an online directory that connects providers with organizations seeking marketing support. HubSpot uses a Customer Happiness Index (CHI) score, which is automatically calculated by its software, to grade partners based on the marketing success of their clients. HubSpot and non-HubSpot customers can search the Marketplace for services including:

- Do inbound marketing for me
- Call to action button design
- Landing page design
- Lead nurturing
- Social media marketing
- Blog article writing
- On-page search engine optimization (SEO)
- Pay-per-click (PPC)
- Video production

- Premium content
- Website design

According to HubSpot's Jordyne Wu (@jordyne), director of business development, the Marketplace has referred more than 2,500 transactions to VAR partners totaling more than $4 million in service revenue for the agencies.

My firm was HubSpot's first partner agency as part of a beta program that began in spring 2008. We tapped into HubSpot's training and methodology to evolve our traditional PR and marketing services into the emerging areas of search marketing, social media, and content marketing. Our value-based pricing model made it possible to effectively bundle and promote service packages designed specifically for the needs and goals of HubSpot customers.

Without investing a single dollar or minute in the development of our own software, we were able to accelerate our growth and drive sales by expanding our digital services and marrying them with a third-party solution. It is partnerships like these that agencies can use to disrupt and thrive in the new marketing world.

Insight into the HubSpot VAR Program

I asked HubSpot's Peter Caputa (@pc4media), director, Value Added Reseller Program, to share his thoughts on the program and the growth opportunities that exist for agencies moving forward:

Recently, a prospective partner said to me, 'There's no one out there like HubSpot who is trying to help marketing agencies be better marketing agencies.' There are so many challenges that marketing agencies face that are externally imposed, such as the changing landscape of services they must learn and deliver, as well as internal challenges including client acquisition, profit margins, and account retention. From working with hundreds of agencies of all types and sizes, we've discovered ways to help agencies with these challenges and for several years have been packaging up training and support services on top of our core product to help them.

(continued)

(*continued*)

Most agencies and consultants lack the time to even do their own marketing, let alone do the research and development to know where the market is heading, what services they should offer, and how to offer them efficiently so that they can help clients maximize their return on investment. More than 170,000 people who are either self-employed as marketing consultants, or who work at a marketing agency, have downloaded the thought-leadership content that our marketing team has produced. With data from more than 5,000 customers using our integrated marketing platform to both execute and measure their online marketing activities, we have insight into what works and what doesn't.

When we publish guidelines, share tools, and provide best practices that are specific for agencies, thousands of agencies download the information and share it with their peers. Sharing this with our partners has made it possible for them to sell, measure, and deliver ROI to our mutual clients, making it a win-win-win. While many of our long-standing partners have seen a 200-plus percent growth in revenue, there is still a huge opportunity for agencies, as evidenced by the more than 30-plus new partners that come on board each month, and the thousands who report that they are still struggling with how to build their marketing agency. We're tripling down on our partner program this year based on our successes and the demand.

The Challenges of Becoming a Product Business

The most profitable and efficient opportunity for most agencies is in third-party software integration; however, there are a number of reasons marketing service firms may venture into proprietary product development, including: pursue perceived market opportunities, create recurring revenue streams, differentiate from competitors, improve internal processes, and increase valuation.

Although some marketing firms, such as SEOmoz, an SEO software company, have successfully transitioned from a predominantly service-based to product-driven business, it is a challenging proposition for most.

In an April 24, 2011 TechCrunch article, "What Should You Do With Your Crappy Little Service Business?"[2] Mark Suster (@msuster), a two-time entrepreneur and venture capitalist at GRP Partners, articulated why service businesses should not become product businesses. Although the post specifically addresses technology service providers, the same principles and reasoning apply to marketing agencies.

"This is where many service businesses make mistakes and go pear shaped. They get 'product business envy' because they read too much TechCrunch about their product brethren raising money at crazy valuations and getting sold at even crazier ones. So they set out to build a product business within a services company," said Suster.

He goes on to describe the three main problems that arise, which can negatively impact an agency's core service business.

1. Agencies do not realize how difficult product businesses are to build, and they falsely assume their successes selling services will translate into a competency selling products.

2. Increased costs associated with product development create larger exposure risks in down markets, thus destabilizing the business.

3. As resources are funneled into the product side, firms can lose sight of their core business—services.

The moral of the story: Be cautious when pursuing shiny objects. Do not let delusions of grandeur or product envy cloud your vision for building a strong service-based agency.

The Tech-Firm Transformation

Evolving into a technology-driven service firm, an essential component of every hybrid agency, requires two common elements: immersion and integration. Let's examine how each plays a role in an agency's transformation:

Immersion Agencies, particularly their leaders, must have an insatiable appetite for knowledge about the technology industry, and a desire to be early adopters of products and services. Agencies that understand technology trends and innovations are able to more readily adapt their own business models, continually increase efficiency and productivity, evolve client campaigns, and make strategic connections of seemingly unrelated information. This requires professionals to:

- Read the essential publications, such as *TechCrunch, Engadget, GigaOM, Gizmodo, Silicon Valley Insider, All Things Digital,* and *Wired.*
- Watch the technology trendsetters, such as Apple, Google, Facebook, Salesforce, and Twitter. Monitor for news that affects client campaigns and look for opportunities that apply to agency services and agency management.
- Follow and engage with influencers, including media, bloggers, venture capitalists, and entrepreneurs.
- Attend conferences and webinars in search of inspiration and ideas. Seek out events that deal with start-ups, mobility, and enterprise technology.

To understand the value of technology immersion, let's take a look at how changes to Google's algorithm—admittedly, pretty geeky stuff to follow—directly affect marketing agencies. Although SEO professionals and webmasters are commonly in tune with Google news, I would argue that the search giant's moves are equally important to PR, advertising, web, and content agencies.

In February 2011, Google began rolling out its Panda algorithm changes. The goal, as stated on the official Google blog, was simple: "To give people the most relevant answers to their queries as quickly as possible."[3] The first rollout impacted 12 percent of Google queries, and was designed to reduce rankings for low-quality sites in favor of sites that featured valuable original content, such as research, reports, and thoughtful analysis.

We will stop there for a minute. Google, which controls approximately 65 percent of the search market, was telling companies in very plain terms that duplicate, low-value content is bad, and original, high-value content is good. This was not anything new, but for years outlaw agencies have built their businesses preying on clients' needs for short-term results at any cost. They use unethical black-hat SEO tactics, and flood the Internet with low-quality content, in an effort to boost search-engine rankings and drive website traffic. These agencies are a black eye on the marketing-services industry. They sell shortcuts, not long-term solutions.

Agencies that had not taken note of Google's moves yet hopefully were on high alert at this point. However, just in case companies were not making the connections, Google, which usually is relatively tight-lipped about its algorithm changes, made another announcement in April 2011 on its Webmaster Central Blog.[4] This change, which affected all English-language Google users around the world, incorporated user feedback signals to help people find better search results. Google claimed it affected approximately 2 percent of U.S. queries.

Then, in May 2011, Google provided very pointed guidance on how to build high-quality sites, and explained how the Panda change was just "one of roughly 500 search improvements" they were expecting to rollout in 2011. Their advice to marketers in general, and spammers, scrappers, and content farms in particular, was this:

> *Search is a complicated and evolving art and science, so rather than focusing on specific algorithmic tweaks, we encourage you to focus on delivering the best possible experience for users.*[5]

Google went on to offer 23 questions that organizations can ask themselves in order to assess site and content quality.

Google's core message, which has not changed through the years, is to create lots of valuable content that people will want to link to and share. Therefore, in order to grow smarter and faster than the competition, organizations (your clients) must continually publish multimedia content online through blogs, podcasts, videos, optimized press releases, case studies, white papers, ebooks, and bylined articles. As a result, savvy agencies have been listening and building services around demand for high-quality content creation.

However, it does not stop there. Remember the lesson of selective consumption and the importance of recurring revenue in building a strong agency. Agencies have to construct campaigns that cater to consumers' evolving needs and demands. They have to help consumers find the information and products they are looking for when they are looking for them. Content creation is just the beginning. How will the content be spread (social media, e-mail, and PR), found (SEO), and consumed (web and mobile)?

In other words, this one example of Google's algorithm change, which professionals who were immersed in the technology world saw first, demonstrates the need to constantly adapt and integrate services across traditionally detached marketing disciplines. Digital and traditional services have to be aligned, and specialized agencies must begin working more closely together for the sake of clients and each other. It is the only way to create stable recurring revenue from campaigns, and achieve the success factors that matter to clients today.

Integration   Being immersed in the tech industry is the first step, but, as we saw in the Google Panda example, you must have the willingness and ability to change your agency's services, processes, and infrastructure to accommodate market shifts. This requires the consistent investment of time and money, often without an expectation of ROI. The key is to take calculated risks, and learn to trust your instinct.

My agency's relationship with HubSpot started this way. In fall 2007, when we first signed on as a customer, I had no idea how we were going to use their software, but, at the time, I felt the industry was rapidly moving toward search, social, and content. I had read about HubSpot in a tech article, and I saw them as a vehicle to train our team in new methodologies and to eventually differentiate us from other firms. It was only a matter of months before we began to recognize the true potential of bundling our services with their software and expanding our capabilities to provide more measurable impact on our clients' businesses.

I have had similar experiences with other software platforms after first reading about them in tech blogs, and learning about them at technology conferences. Applications such as Yammer, Basecamp and Highrise (both 37Signals products), GoToMeeting, Skype, TweetDeck, and Evernote have changed the way we do business. Although you will invest a lot of time and energy in testing platforms that are not a fit, you should always be experimenting and looking for ways to improve efficiency and increase the value delivered to clients. We will talk more about technology and core agency platforms in Chapter 4.

MEET THE DEMAND FOR DIGITAL SERVICES

The demand for digital services is immense, and growing. According to the *Ad Age* 2011 Agency Report, digital services accounted for an estimated $8.5 billion, or 28 percent, of U.S. agency revenue in 2010.[6] In addition, Forrester has reported that interactive marketing spending on mobile marketing, social media, e-mail marketing, display advertising, and search marketing will near $77 billion by 2016, representing 35 percent of all advertising dollars.[7]

However, it is becoming more difficult to differentiate these dollars. Every agency, or at least the ones that will still be relevant in the coming years, is a digital agency. Although the resources dedicated to social, search, mobile, web, e-mail, and other digital strategies will vary, interactive marketing should be fully integrated into every program and budget.

Having a digital division or group within an agency is not sufficient. Your agency's future depends on its ability to adapt, deliver measurable and meaningful results, and develop professionals who are capable of providing consulting and services across multiple disciplines. Although there are tremendous opportunities to build businesses focused on niche markets and services, the generalists who excel at blending interactive and traditional strategies, will control the power and budgets.

Resist the Dark Side of Digital

There are no shortcuts to success. Building your digital capabilities is a process that requires significant time, training, and experience. If you want to move into blogging, social media consulting, SEO, video, e-mail marketing, mobile, and other high-demand areas, prove you can make it work for your agency first.

Invest the resources now to launch a blog, engage in online communities, gain a following, experiment with new content-publishing channels, conduct webinars, boost search-engine rankings, and generate leads through custom-built landing pages. Focus on creating value, and use it to demonstrate your expertise and advance your agency.

The market is moving fast, with growth opportunities everywhere, but do not come into it unprepared and try to sell services you are not qualified to deliver. Agencies can quickly get themselves in trouble when they overpromise clients to win new business. Never lose sight of your ethics and reputable business practices in pursuit of a dollar. The cost to your agency, and the reputation you have spent your career building, is far too great.

Let's examine the case of JCPenney to see what happens when digital services go wrong, and explore four lessons agencies can learn from the debacle.

JCPenney Wears the Black Hat   In an exceptional piece of modern-day investigative journalism by David Segal, the *New York Times* uncovered an elaborate JCPenney link-building scam, orchestrated by its former black-hat SEO firm. Allegedly unbeknownst to JCPenney, the firm built thousands of spammy paid links to JCPenney.com for key search terms such as *area rugs, dresses,* and *furniture.*

The result was top rankings in Google for JCPenney products that most likely drove millions of organic site visits during the 2010 holiday season—a critical time for the retailer, which had seen sales sink to 2001 levels and was still reeling from the death of its catalog business. According to the *Times,* the number-one spot in Google for *dresses* alone could have generated as many as 3.8 million organic visits per month.

The *Times* had an SEO expert, Doug Pierce, head of research at Digital Due Diligence Advisors (formerly with Blue Fountain Media), analyze JCPenney's remarkable organic performance. Pierce described the program "as the most ambitious attempt to game Google's search results that he has ever seen." The *Times* turned over its findings to Google, which took "strong corrective action," according to Matt Cutts, head of Google's webspam team, resulting in significant drops in JCPenney's organic rankings.[8]

So what can agencies learn from the JCPenney fiasco when building their digital services? Here are four takeaways:

1. **Google will win:** Google's webspam team is on a mission to protect the quality of Google's search results. They are smarter than SEO professionals and far more powerful. So it is best to play by the rules. Like anything else in life and business, just because the other guys are getting away with it (for now), does not mean it is all right to cheat the system.

2. **Don't be desperate:** Decisions driven by desperation can be very dangerous to your agency's long-term health. Do not let client demands for short-term results, underperforming campaigns, or financial pressures force you to sacrifice your integrity.

3. **There are no shortcuts or guarantees:** Pleading ignorance when Google catches you will get you nowhere, so make sure your practices are ethical and that they pass the "icky" test—that feeling you get in business when something just does not feel legitimate and most likely is not.

   Authentic SEO requires time, and a combination of on-page optimization—page titles, URLs, page descriptions, ALT text, headers, copy—link building from credible sources, and regular content publishing on your clients' domains. Commit to doing it right over time, and you will reap the rewards.

4. **Focus on content and the long tail:** Content publishing is the most powerful strategy available to build inbound links, boost search-engine rankings, drive website traffic, and generate leads. Concentrate your services on attracting organic traffic from long-tail keyword phrases.

   The long tail applies to the collective strength of lower search volume, longer keyword phrases in the demand-curve tail, and their ability to outproduce a relatively small number of top traffic-driving keywords at the head of the curve (or header phrases). For example, *marketing agency* would be considered a header term, whereas *how to build a hybrid marketing agency* would be a long-tail phrase.

Great page for content

4

The Greatest Opportunity for Growth: Content

Although agencies have been clamoring for their share of digital budgets and influence in the areas of search, mobile, and social, content publishing has largely been overlooked. Agencies that provide strong, multimedia content services are a rare and valuable asset in the new ecosystem.

Powerful, action-oriented content has become an essential part of every marketing strategy, and it offers an enormous opportunity to differentiate and grow your agency and your clients' businesses. There are undisputed benefits to blogging—more indexed pages, inbound links, website visitors, and social media reach—and tremendous lead-generating potential in ebooks, case studies, webinars, white papers, and original reports. The general rule is, the greater the value of your content, the greater the return on your investment.

However, continually producing premium content worthy of links and leads is not easy. It requires significant time and resources, executive support, long-term vision, internal expertise, and often a willingness to share the knowledge businesses once held sacred. More than anything, it requires the ability to be effective business copywriters, generating content that engages audiences and motivates them to take action.

There are many talented writers and content services available, but few that possess the wide range of capabilities needed to satisfy the core elements of effective business copywriting. Public relations agencies, communications pros, freelancers, former journalists, and traditional publishers are all in the conversation as possible sources, but many have yet to step up and evolve their capabilities to meet the growing demand for results-driven online content.

Let's take a look at seven core elements of effective business copywriting, and some tips on what to look for when hiring writers:[9]

1. **Strategic:** Online content has to connect to business goals and brand messaging. Hire writers that understand marketing strategy, and how to deliver copy that integrates across web, search, social, and PR strategies.

2. **Brand centric:** A brand is the sum of experiences and perceptions. When someone hears a company name, or sees its logo, what comes to mind? It may be based on their last interaction with a customer-service representative, the referral of a friend, or a lifetime of personal experiences with its products or services.

    Words, images, and actions define your brand every day and, with selective consumption, websites and online content may often serve as the first—and possibly only—opportunity to make an impression. Business copywriting must convey core brand messages, tell an organization's story, and create positive perceptions that motivate action.

3. **Buyer-persona focused:** Great copywriting makes personal connections with readers. Copy needs to speak directly to buyer personas, address their pain points and bring value. Therefore, copywriters—whether internal or outsourced—must have a clear understanding of your client's target audiences, and know how to engage them.

4. **Optimized for search engines:** Online content must be crafted for visitors, but optimized for search engines. Ideally, business copywriters will have core SEO knowledge and capabilities.

5. **Technically sound:** Technically sound copy is concise and powerful. It uses proper grammar and is written at the appropriate reading level. It is also consistent in person, voice, tone, and format. Copywriters need strong technical writing skills and the ability to apply these skills whatever the task, medium, or subject matter.

6. **Creative:** Never underestimate the value of quality creative writing. Although many of the other elements we have discussed can be learned, business-savvy creative writers are in high demand and scarce supply, and can be an invaluable asset to your agency.

7. **Results driven:** Copywriting needs to be tied to organization objectives, and should play a key role in delivering results, such as generating leads, educating key audiences, and positioning as an industry leader.

   Copywriters should be invested in tracking the content's success through metrics such as pageviews, content downloads, social media reach, and leads. This enables future content to be strategized based on past performance, and can encourage the incorporation of new ideas and topics, to drive traffic and capture audiences.

UNDERSTAND YOUR ROLE IN THE ECOSYSTEM

The evolving marketing-services ecosystem consists of six agency classifications: disruptors, traditionalists, softservers, specialists, connectors, and soloists. Each plays an essential role in the development of a more open and collaborative community.

Let's first take a look at the marketing agency profiles, then visualize how the ecosystem functions.

Disruptors

Disruptors will be the dominant players in the new ecosystem. They are the most advanced of the hybrids in terms of technology integration, diversified services, and talent versatility. Disruptors are always pushing to evolve services and pricing, and they have the most aggressive growth goals. Unlike their traditional-agency brethren, disruptors are risk takers that fight to remain nimble, always thinking like startups and acting like underdogs.

Few firms have emerged to date that embody all the elements of these leading hybrid agencies. As a result, tremendous opportunities exist for the agencies with the will and drive to develop model firms.

- **Services:** Able to build fully integrated marketing campaigns that adhere to the principles of selective consumption. This includes content publishing, social media consulting, SEO, online advertising, mobile marketing, website development, e-mail marketing, lead nurturing and analytics, as well as evolved forms of PR and brand marketing. Core capabilities will center on digital services, with a mix of traditional activities as needed. Some services will be outsourced to partner agencies, including soloists and specialists, especially in the early years as they develop talent and advance internal capabilities.

- **Staff:** Versatile professionals with strong backgrounds in marketing, communications, and business. A high value will be placed on expert copywriters who are trained in authentic on-page and off-page SEO methodology and can function as Internet marketing consultants. All employees are heavily engaged in social media. We will further investigate staffing in Chapter 3.

- **Pricing:** Value based with wider appeal to the mass market of small businesses.

- **Results:** Leading marketing agencies consistently produce more measurable outcomes, including inbound links, website traffic, leads, and sales. Quickly shifting away from arbitrary metrics such as media impressions, reach, advertising equivalency, and PR value.

- **Technology:** Fully immersed in the technology industry. Will breed a new generation of tech-savvy, entrepreneurial-minded professionals. Cloud platforms play a key role in their growth and adaptability.

- **Infrastructure:** More agile and tolerant to risk than traditional marketing service firms. Built to be highly scalable in terms of number of clients and employees, geographic markets, and revenue streams.

- **Leadership:** Prototype founders have 5 to 10 years of agency experience, with exposure to a diverse collection of accounts and industries, and strong insight into agency management. They will be digital natives who understand what is broken within the current agency model, and have the drive and desire to do it differently. There is significant financial risk, so the ideal professional lives a modest lifestyle, has solid personal savings, and, ideally, has some level of bank- or angel-investor funding to provide a 12- to 18-month runway to figure things out. We will go further into funding and financials in Chapter 4.

- **Growth:** Dramatically more aggressive growth models due to mass-market appeal. A wave of mergers and acquisitions of complementary firms—PR, SEO, advertising, web developers, e-mail marketing, mobile marketing—is possible, although most will look to remain independent and grow within the collaborative ecosystem.

- **Market focus:** The industry leaders will have a mass-market focus and international appeal (the Internet has no borders), but, like any emerging industry, there will be plenty of room for smaller agencies to prosper by concentrating on niche market segments and/or services.

Traditionalists

The unfortunate truth is that traditionalists are the irrelevant aristocracy. They are still influential due to their large networks, established client rosters, and legacy brands, but they have minimal impact on the emerging disruptor class. Their archaic business models are difficult to evolve, and, therefore, they will struggle to compete as more companies seek innovative approaches to interactive marketing needs.

The advertising and PR industry conglomerates are not going anywhere soon, but in the meantime, disruptors will gladly chip away at the underserviced small-to-midsize business (SMB) markets, and begin infiltrating larger enterprises one division at a time, slowly undermining the traditionalists' influence and authority. Following are characteristics of traditionalist agencies:

- Current market leaders with solid reputations and brands, and respected leadership teams.
- Strong in traditional services, but struggling to profitably integrate digital services. In many cases, they may have divisions or groups internally that specialize in digital; however, digital services and thinking are not ingrained throughout the agency.
- Staffed with some of the industry's best and brightest young talent, but stand to lose A players to emerging firms that offer more innovative cultures. Top traditionalist professionals are also prime candidates to launch disruptor firms.
- Maintain top-heavy staffing models with high-paid executives and partners. This makes it difficult to evolve pricing models and build more efficient, value-based services.
- Stuck in legacy systems that inhibit their ability to make the drastic infrastructure changes needed.
- Some top traditionalists have the resources to acquire upstart disruptors in an effort to remain relevant, but many will look to merge or get acquired as competition intensifies.

Unless these firms make dramatic changes, they run the risk of becoming obsolete over time.

A subcategory of traditionalists will develop that successfully evolve into tech-savvy, hybrid agencies but lack the vision and growth goals of disruptors. They will be able to maintain strong, profitable businesses as long as they can retain their top young talent, but these professionals will be highly motivated to find more dynamic career paths with disruptors and softservers.

Softservers

Softservers are a relatively unknown yet quickly evolving breed. Technology companies, which concentrate on marketing software development, are building service divisions, either based on customer demand for advanced product expertise, or out of necessity to improve utilization and performance, thereby reducing churn rates—a key metric for software companies. Note these characteristics:

- Softservers is an emerging classification that includes marketing software companies, such as HubSpot and Radian6, which offer varying levels of services and consulting.

- Their presence creates an intriguing dynamic in the ecosystem given their intimate knowledge of client needs, financial resources, and their role in driving change velocity. In essence, they have significant leverage, and can always be one step ahead of the agencies that rely on them for referrals.
- Their services are directly tied to supporting adoption and success with their proprietary products.
- Softservers are unlikely to build full-blown, in-house agencies in the near term, since service-based businesses earn lower valuations. However, their presence can be a disrupting force for marketing agencies.
- Overall, the existence of softservers pushes marketing agencies to continually innovate. As a result, they present more opportunities than threats to the ecosystem.

Specialists

Specialists focus on niche markets and opportunities. The top specialists are in high demand, and thus, they can charge premiums for their services. Specialists also have opportunities to build strong brands as thought leaders by sharing their expertise on blogs and within their social networks. These agencies may have direct clients, but also commonly rely on full-service agencies and online marketplaces for business development. Specialists are:

- Narrowly focused on maintaining expertise in niche markets and services, such as SEO, PR, web development, content creation, video, mobile, or graphic design.
- Niche focused, which may still be lucrative, but limits motivation to evolve.
- Finding it increasingly difficult to remain specialized in service areas, as selective consumption principles are driving increased client demand for complete marketing solutions. For example, website effectiveness is commonly being measured by lead generation, which requires content strategies and social-media integration.
- Sometimes building strong partnerships with traditionalists and other specialists that they rely on for business development and revenue.
- Likely more project based, which makes it difficult to create reliable recurring revenue needed for growth and stability.

- Prime candidates for acquisitions by full-service hybrid agencies looking to pull resources in-house.
- Firms who, if they stay independent, can prosper through disruptor agency partnerships—as long as there is limited crossover in services.

Connectors

Connectors are often the thinkers and networkers, not the doers. They prefer to make connections and build provider networks that enable them to earn comfortable profit margins. This business model frees up their time to pursue multiple ventures, and affords them the opportunity to prosper off their reputations and profiles through activities such as consulting, speaking, and publishing. Common connector characteristics include:

- Their strongest capabilities lie in networking, promotion, sales, and/or project management.
- They rely on a distributed network of soloists and specialists to do the work, while they may remain involved in planning and consulting.
- They are likely more interested in building wealth and a balanced lifestyle than investing the time and energy required to create a full-service hybrid agency.
- They are often social media influencers who have built large followings that give them flexibility in their career paths.
- They could be a primary competitor to disruptors with the right partners and systems in place. However, they will struggle to compete at lower prices, due to tighter margins from the distributed workforce model.

Soloists

Soloists have modest growth goals. They are limited by their own time capacities, and, therefore, either have a small collection of larger accounts, or are taking advantage of emerging online service marketplaces, such as crowdSPRING, to find consistent project work. Soloist characteristics include:

- Not looking to build an agency, but to simply make a comfortable living as a part- or full-time freelancer and subcontractor.

- Possibly motivated more by lifestyle goals than monetary achievements.
- Most likely gained experience from prior agency or corporate marketing positions.
- Work directly for clients or as outside agency contractors.
- Expected to benefit from a more collaborative ecosystem, but capacity is always an issue—which makes them difficult to rely on for growing agencies.

According to the Deal Radar, crowdSPRING, which describes itself as, "the world's largest online marketing for buyers and sellers of crowdsourced creative services," has completed approximately 18,500 projects through its network of 83,000 creative professionals. The site has more than 25,000 registered buyers.[10]

Visualizing the Ecosystem

The ecosystem is client centric, meaning agencies must continually evolve to meet their needs and demands. Change velocity, selective consumption, and success factors are the *environmental factors* that dictate agency pricing, services, staffing, and infrastructure.

Disruptors and softservers, the most motivated to continually adapt, will come to control the workflow and budgets, whereas specialists, connectors, and soloists will increasingly rely on the leading agencies for opportunities and growth. Traditionalists gradually will fade from prominence and lose market share to disruptors and softservers.

The ecosystem diagram (Figure 2.1) is designed primarily to demonstrate workflow and relevance. Here is a breakdown of how it works:

- Clients are shown at the center of the ecosystem.
- Change velocity, selective consumption, and success factors are the catalysts that are fueling agency transformation and driving the evolution of client needs and demands.
- Solid lines represent direct workflow from client to agency and agency to agency. For example, clients may work directly with specialists or the work may flow from clients to traditionalists, who then outsource work to specialists.

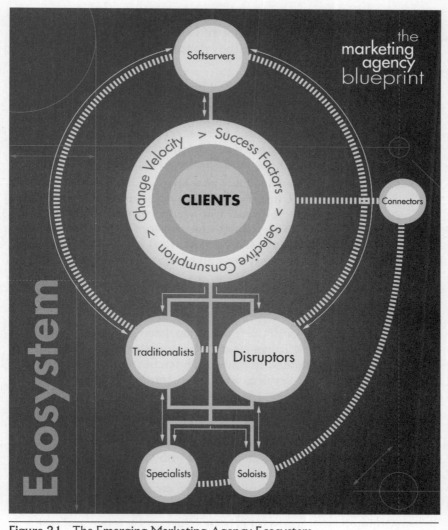

Figure 2.1   The Emerging Marketing Agency Ecosystem

- The arrows along the lines are multidirectional in many cases, because work may flow both ways. For example, an SEO specialist firm may bring in a disruptor to handle content marketing or a disruptor that does not have SEO capabilities in-house may outsource to a specialist.
- The dashed lines represent pass-through work and referrals. For example, softservers have a solid line from the client

demonstrating that they may do direct consulting, and they also have a dashed line that runs to the other side of the ecosystem, which shows how they commonly refer clients to other agencies.

- Varying sizes of the agency circles are meant to show relevance in the evolving ecosystem.
- Softservers and connectors are isolated from the other agencies because they are not pure service firms. Softservers are primarily marketing software companies, whereas connectors are mainly networkers, educators, and facilitators.
- Proximity to the core shows how strongly connected agencies are to clients. Disruptors, traditionalists, and softservers tend to have the most in-depth knowledge of the client, and the deepest relationships throughout the companies. These agencies often are the most heavily involved in strategic planning, and have access to analytics and business-intelligence data.

Are PR Firms the Perfect Hybrids?

As budgets continue to shift to content marketing, search marketing, and social media, PR firms have an opportunity to assume unparalleled levels of leadership and influence in the marketing mix, if they can expand their services and consistently deliver measurable value to their clients.

Consider the following:

- Social media participation is nothing more than relationships and communications through online channels. That is what PR pros do—build relationships and enhance communications with audiences—employees, media, customers, prospects, vendors, and partners.
- Although advanced SEO is both an art and science and reserved for brilliant minds like Rand Fishkin (@randfish) and Danny Sullivan (@dannysullivan), most core SEO concepts and methodologies can be easily learned and executed as part of a larger content strategy. Plus, platforms such as HubSpot and SEOmoz create a low barrier to entry for PR firms interested in integrating basic SEO services such as keyword analyses, link building, and on-page optimization.
- It seems to be universally accepted these days that "content is king" in the new marketing world. Content marketing requires strong technical and creative writing skills, business acumen,

marketing savvy, and strategic thinking. Again, a perfect fit for the capabilities of top PR professionals who tend to have strong copywriting skills.

- Content-management systems (CMS) have made web development and management far less complex. Websites have become communications and content-distribution vehicles. As a result, professionals who understand brand positioning and buyer personas, as well as the content and social media strategies, should guide website design and content. PR firms and web developers are a natural fit for future mergers, acquisitions, and partnerships.

Unfortunately, PR firms remain their own worst enemy. As a whole, they have been slow to seize the opportunities to evolve. In a 2009 study, we found that only 38 percent of *PRWeek*'s top PR firms published a blog.[11] Although the numbers improved in 2010 to 63 percent, it appears the industry at large is struggling to integrate social media, SEO, and other interactive strategies. For now, they are not the perfect hybrids, but the possibility is there for forward-thinking PR firms to emerge.

Are You Building a Disruptor?

Building a dynamic, full-service hybrid agency designed to grow beyond 10, 20, and even 50 employees, requires incredible drive, remarkable patience, and an undying belief that you are creating something of great significance. Money cannot be the primary motivator. It is the need to create change, to push boundaries, and to positively impact the lives of others. Professionals who choose to build disruptors believe they have a higher purpose. It is not the right career choice for everyone.

Some professionals will be better suited to make their mark as soloists, connectors, or specialists. Historically, many agencies have been built by professionals who, having excelled at their work, wanted the freedom and financial rewards that came from owning their own business. They were practitioners by trade, not businessmen and women. However, in order to construct a disruptor, the practitioner function must become secondary, and your passion has to be for building and running a business.

Like all entrepreneurs, agency principals have to make sacrifices in the early years, especially if you have a vision for growth. This includes working endless days followed by sleepless nights, taking smaller paychecks (if at all), investing profits back into the agency, fighting with increasingly conservative lenders to secure capital, dealing with mundane details such as health-care benefits and taxes, putting employee and client needs ahead of your own at all times, and learning to live with and embrace the unknown. In order to thrive in the new agency ecosystem, you have to start by being honest with yourself:

- What are you willing to sacrifice?
- What motivates you?
- How will you define success?
- What type of agency do you want to build?
- What are your greatest strengths?
- What are your greatest weaknesses?
- Are you a leader?
- Are you in the financial position to take the risks needed?
- Do you have the ability to recruit and retain top talent?
- Will you be happy running a business, rather than doing the work?

If you plan to build a disruptor, you will come to spend 90 percent or more of your time on three things: (1) recruiting and retaining talent, (2) setting and pursuing the vision, and (3) driving growth. If you do not have the desire or ability to excel in these areas, you either need to find a business partner who does to assume the role of CEO, or you should consider pursuing a different path in the ecosystem.

We will further explore these ideas in Chapters 9 and 10 where we focus on embracing failure and pursuing purpose.

THE ART OF OUTSOURCING AND COLLABORATION

Whether you are building a disruptor or planning to stay small and enjoy the freedom that comes from life as a soloist, outsourcing and collaboration are essential. Change velocity makes it nearly impossible to stay at the forefront of every trend, and selective consumption is driving demand for a vast array of services and expertise that most firms are not prepared to deliver.

Until you can make a strong business case for bringing new capabilities in-house, either through an acquisition or hire, it is best to focus on your agency's core competencies and find great partners for the rest. Start by determining the service mix needed to plan and execute client campaigns, and then go to work finding the right partners.

Based on digital-services demand and selective consumption, standard agency competencies will include: brand marketing, website development, SEO, online advertising, local search, e-mail marketing, social media marketing, copywriting, video production, PR, graphic design, and mobile marketing. Services that require very specialized capabilities, software, or equipment are logical competencies for full-service firms to outsource to specialists and soloists.

What Makes a Great Partner?

Like any relationship, trust and shared values are essential to building strong agency partnerships. Every time you choose to outsource, you are putting your brand, reputation, and financial success in another agency's hands. Here are some of the key factors to consider when evaluating and selecting partners:

- **Services:** Services must be complementary, with limited crossover between agencies. Crossover services can create confusion among clients and conflict among partners who have different styles.

- **Pricing:** There must be transparency and consistency in pricing for partnerships to work. Ideally both agencies use similar pricing models, and are in the same general cost range. For example, an agency focused on selling $1,500 to $3,000 per month retainers will not work well with a graphic design specialist firm that charges $400 per hour.

- **Process:** The most efficient and productive partnerships will share very similar project management and communications styles. As the ecosystem evolves, agencies will search for partners who use the same cloud-based management platforms, ensuring seamless integrations. For example, two firms that both use 37Signals' Basecamp project-management system will more quickly achieve economies of scale in the planning, production, and delivery of joint services.

- **Performance:** Partners have to deliver on budget and on time with the highest quality work. You must have complete confidence in your partners' ability to perform at the levels you demand from your internal team.

- **Financial strength:** Do not be afraid to ask the tough questions about your partners' financial health. Agencies that struggle financially often are under pressure to keep overhead costs down, which directly impacts the quality of their staff and their capacity to take on new projects. Be especially cautious with soloists and specialists who are more reliant on project work, and, therefore, generally less stable. You cannot rely on partners who are stretched too thin or are too dependent on you to stay afloat.

DIVERSIFY YOUR REVENUE STREAMS

Hybrid agencies will be immersed in technology, and they will deliver a results-driven blend of digital and traditional services, but the most important factor in their ability to surpass traditional financial performance benchmarks lies in diversified revenue streams.

For some, that will mean moving into software development, which can offer higher profit margins and lucrative licensing fees, but the more logical strategy for most agencies will be to explore channels as educators, publishers, value-added resellers (VARs), and affiliates.

Educator and Publisher

Once an agency positions itself as a thought leader, and establishes a proven performance track record, it opens up opportunities to create and capture value on a larger scale through speaking engagements, online courses, webinars, digital publications, book publishing, and teaching.

In order to monetize your knowledge and capabilities outside of services, you have to differentiate yourself and bring real value to audiences. Do not be afraid to start small, and remember to have patience. Creating recurring revenue through education and publishing requires that you build up significant reach and influence through online and offline channels.

Seven Steps for Building an Effective Speaking Strategy

A sound speaking strategy can have a dramatic effect on the growth of your agency, and it can position your professionals as thought leaders and innovators. Here is a step-by-step guide we often use to help clients looking to build speaking strategies that deliver results.

Step 1—Identify Topics

• Speaking topics establish the foundation for a sound speaking strategy. These topics, which will evolve over time, and support the identification and pursuit of opportunities.

Step 2—Select Audiences

• Define, segment, and prioritize target audiences.

Step 3—Define Objectives

• Establish quantifiable objectives to provide direction to the program and define success. These may include number of appearances, content downloads, SlideShare views, and leads generated.

Step 4—Research and Evaluate Opportunities

• Identify venues for potential speaking engagements, including colleges, trade shows, conferences, seminars/workshops, career fairs, and professional-organization events.

• Establish a valuation system to rate each opportunity based on defined criteria, such as event organizer, audience, topic, date, location, and objectives.

• Create an event calendar of opportunities at targeted venues.

• Contact venues to inquire about submission guidelines.

• Prequalify high-value engagements through media coverage, past speaker status and feedback, attendance history and projections, and first-hand experience with venues.

• Monitor and assess trends to identify timely opportunities with targeted venues.

Step 5—Positioning and Placement

• Create a speaker's packet, including biography, bylined articles, testimonials from past organizers and attendees, topic list, photos, contact information, A/V requirements, and rate card. Although it may not be required, a speaker's packet gets you organized and prepared.

• Research and evaluate membership in professional speaking organizations.

(*continued*)

(*continued*)

- Build the speaker's resume through preliminary appearances within an existing network of business and trade organizations, as well as academic institutions.

- Enhance credibility and value through PR and content marketing programs, including the submission of bylined articles and guest blog posts to targeted outlets.

- Use the event database built in step 4 to pursue high-priority speaking opportunities.

- Maintain communications and relationships with all targeted venues.

- Define protocol and prepare responses for declining unsolicited opportunities that do not meet defined criteria.

Step 6—Preparation

- Attend events at which you plan to speak in the future. For example, if you want to present at South by Southwest (SXSW) Interactive, attend it first to gain an understanding of the audience, content, and venues.

- Create presentations.

Step 7—Evaluation

- Establish a grading system to measure the return on investment (ROI) for speaking appearances.

- Assess and grade each appearance and venue.

VAR and Affiliate Programs

Value-added reseller (VAR) partnerships, such as the HubSpot VAR Partner Program, are an ideal way to generate referrals, differentiate your firm, and create recurring revenue through license fees. In VAR relationships, agencies provide services, consulting, training, customization, and integration around third-party products. VAR programs give agencies the ability to expand their services and reach, without investing resources in developing their own software.

Affiliate programs also offer opportunities to nurture recurring revenue through referred business. However, do not get distracted from your core business pursuing too many affiliate relationships. Focus on the software products you know and trust, and if you think your clients, prospects, or peers would gain value from utilizing them as well, then consider affiliate opportunities.

Following is a sample listing of organizations that offer partnership programs for marketing agencies:

- ConstantContact—www.ConstantContact.com
- Eloqua—www.Eloqua.com
- ExactTarget—www.ExactTarget.com
- HubSpot—www.HubSpot.com
- iContact—www.iContact.com
- MailChimp—www.MailChimp.com
- Marketo—www.Marketo.com
- Salesforce—www.Force.com
- SEOmoz—www.SEOmoz.org
- VerticalResponse—www.VerticalResponse.com

CHAPTER HIGHLIGHTS

- Hybrid agencies and professionals will come to rule the marketing world.
- Evolving into a tech-savvy hybrid firm requires two common elements: immersion and integration.
- Agencies, in particular their leaders, must have an insatiable hunger for knowledge about the technology industry, and a desire to be early adopters of products and services.
- Digital and traditional services have to be aligned, and specialized agencies must begin working more closely together for the sake of clients, and each other.
- Becoming a hybrid firm requires the consistent investment of time and money in technology, often without an expectation of ROI. The key is to take calculated risks, and learn to trust your instinct.
- Every agency, or at least the ones that will still be relevant in the coming years, is a digital agency.
- Building your digital capabilities is a process that requires significant time, training, and experience. If you want to move into blogging, social media consulting,

(continued)

(*continued*)
SEO, video, e-mail marketing, mobile, and other high-demand areas, prove you can make it work for your agency first.

- Agencies that provide strong, multimedia content services are a rare and valuable asset in the new ecosystem.

- The evolving marketing-services ecosystem consists of six agency classifications: disruptors, traditionalists, soft-servers, specialists, connectors, and soloists.

- Whether you are building a disruptor or planning to stay small and enjoy the freedom that comes from life as a soloist, outsourcing and collaboration are essential.

- Every time you choose to outsource, you are putting your brand, reputation, and financial success in another agency's hands.

- Once an agency positions itself as a thought leader and establishes a proven performance track record, it opens up opportunities to create and capture value on a larger scale through speaking engagements, online courses, webinars, digital publications, book publishing, referrals, and teaching.

chapter 3

Think Talent and Team

Talent cannot be replicated.

GREAT TEAMS FINISH FIRST

Intrinsically motivated professionals who are driven to be great will redefine marketing agencies and the industry. They derive fulfillment from being a part of something greater than themselves. Their success is not defined by money, fame, or power, but rather by the pursuit of purpose. They challenge authority and quickly tire of tradition, seek autonomy and flexibility, desire balance, and value the freedom to pursue their passions outside their careers.

These professionals excel in agency cultures that reward collective success over individual achievements. They care less about why, and more often ask, "Why not?" Theirs is a world of endless possibility, and they are the future. Your agency will be defined by its ability to recruit and retain the best.

When all else is equal—processes, services, pricing, and infrastructure—it is talent that cannot be replicated.

The Model Agency

Model agencies are constructed one employee at a time. They do not allow market demand or outside expectations to dictate their growth, and they do not sacrifice the quality of their hires to satisfy short-term needs. They take a controlled, almost methodical, approach to expansion. They develop talent from within, and construct teams based on shared values, innate abilities, and complementary character traits.

These agencies are built on a culture of we, succeeding and failing as one. There is no room for egos, selfish behavior, or a sense of entitlement. They are led with an air of openness in which professionals at all levels are involved in agency strategy and decisions, and heavily engaged in its growth and success. As a result, professionals are passionately loyal to the agency and to each other. They believe that their work truly matters to the agency and its clients, and they feel their time and energy in being invested in the achievement of a higher goal.

Although the founders may be the highest profile members of the team, they go to tremendous lengths not to overshadow the agency brand or its employees. Unlike many traditional firms that were named after their founders, hybrid agencies look to alternate naming conventions in order to focus attention more on the team, vision, processes, and culture. They know that in order to scale a transformational agency, client acquisition and retention must be driven by the collective strength, reputation, and capabilities of the firm. Leaders assume full responsibility when things go wrong, and turn the spotlight on the team when things go right. They take greater pride in the success and development of their employees, than in their own achievements.

System-wide efficiency and productivity are essential. Any weaknesses or flaws within the agency's processes or people are quickly exposed. Professionals who are unmotivated or failing to live up to their potential can negatively impact the team's performance, but, more important, they can drag down the morale and momentum of peers and leadership. Model agencies have to commit to consistently recruiting the best. This fosters a competitive, yet supportive and collaborative, environment. At the same time, to protect the agency's strength and stability, managers have to be able to effectively transition consistently underperforming professionals into alternate career paths.

Hiring standards are high, and expectations for employees are even higher. Professionals are given unparalleled opportunities for career advancement and encouraged to build strong personal brands. From day one, they are immersed in comprehensive training and education programs designed to accelerate their learning and capabilities. They are brought up in the agency's well-defined systems and processes, and immediately thrust into key account roles.

Young professionals quickly gain invaluable knowledge and experience, and, in return, they continuously infuse energy, curiosity, and fresh perspective into the agency and its account teams. All employees have a confidence born from preparation and understanding, and nurtured through the firm's persistent adherence to the highest standards. Professionals expect excellence from themselves and demand it from each other.

A PLAYERS, THE DRAFT, AND FREE AGENCY

Constructing an agency filled with top talent establishes a distinct and formidable competitive advantage. According to Bradford D. Smart, PhD, "High performers—the A players—contribute more, innovate more, work smarter, earn more trust, display more resourcefulness, take more initiative, develop better business strategies, articulate their vision more passionately, implement change more effectively, deliver higher-quality work, demonstrate greater teamwork, and find ways to get the job done in less time with less cost."[1]

Model agencies are constantly in search of professionals who have the desire and drive to be great. Social media has made it more efficient to identify and passively engage with these candidates over time. Their activity on Twitter, Facebook, LinkedIn, and blogs provides windows into their personal brands, including communication styles, interests, and motivation.

At the same time, A players are able to more easily analyze agencies through blogs and social networks. These high-potential producers are very selective, and they usually have options, so firms must separate themselves in the recruiting process.

A Player Competencies and Traits

How do you recognize an A player? What are the common competencies and traits they possess that make them more qualified than their peers?

Although intelligence and experience are key, their character, internal drive, personalities, and innate abilities are the intangibles that truly differentiate great candidates from good ones. Let's take a look at some of the most desirable competencies and traits of marketing agency A players:

- **Analytical:** They make quick decisions based on logic and reason. They love data, and use it to educate, build consensus, and drive action. They are measurement geeks, and look to apply critical analysis to agency activities, and they integrate it into every phase of client campaigns.
- **Balanced:** They maintain a strong work-life balance. They have personal interests and hobbies that regularly present opportunities to unwind and recharge. This keeps stress levels

controlled and energy high. Balance becomes more critical as professionals move up into management levels, and their responsibilities and stress levels grow.

- **Confident:** They put in the extra time and energy needed to gain knowledge and experience, which translates into confidence and composure. Confidence is not to be confused with arrogance and entitlement, which are two of the most undesirable traits of an agency professional.

- **Creative:** They bring innovative approaches and thinking to projects. They have an innate ability to work within standard systems while efficiently integrating original ideas and strategies that strengthen the agency and client campaigns.

- **Detail-oriented:** They are incredibly organized and thorough in all communications and activities, which instills tremendous confidence in their clients, peers, and managers. They rarely make careless mistakes. Their attention to detail enables them to excel at time management and project management.

- **Focused:** They avoid multitasking in favor of concentrated effort. They know priorities at all times and work efficiently to deliver. They have the ability to shut off distractions, and are often the most productive and efficient workers.

- **Intrinsically motivated:** As defined in Daniel Pink's classic book, *Drive*, intrinsically motivated people seek: *autonomy*, the desire to direct their own lives; *mastery*, the urge to get better and better at something that matters; and *purpose*, the yearning to contribute to something greater than themselves.[2]

- **The "it" factor:** They maintain a strong presence and positive aura. They command attention when they walk into a room and exude confidence without an air of arrogance. They have an intangible element that cannot be defined, but it makes them uniquely capable of succeeding in an agency. They are born leaders.

- **Listener:** They excel at listening and understanding the needs of others. They are adept at making others the focus of conversations.

- **Positive:** They bring a positive energy to the agency that is uplifting and encouraging to the entire team. They make favorable first impressions. People want to be around them and work with them.

- **Relationship-builder:** They know that strong relationships are the key to success in business, and proactively build connections with peers, clients, media, partners, and vendors. They are strong communicators who do the little things that matter, such as sending personal notes to recognize achievements and milestones.

- **Risk-taker:** They take calculated risks. They do not let fear of failure hold them back, and, as a result, they tend to be more aggressive and proactive professionals on behalf of the agency and its clients.

- **Social web savvy:** They monitor and participate in forums and social networks relevant to their interests and the industry. They engage with peers and influencers, and they maintain a professional presence on all social networks that positively represents themselves and their agencies.

- **Strategic:** They are capable of fully assessing situations, and considering short- and long-term outcomes. They know how decisions and activities affect different audiences, and how they work to achieve business goals. They make seemingly unrelated connections others commonly miss.

- **Team player:** They function extremely well within a team environment, but they also excel when working independently. They always seek opportunities to support team members and encourage collaborative learning.

- **Tech-savvy:** They stay immersed in technology news and trends. They continually evaluate emerging products and solutions for opportunities to improve efficiency and performance.

- **Writer:** They possess exceptional writing skills and the capability to clearly and concisely articulate their thoughts. They use creative and technically sound writing to produce powerful and effective communications. Copywriting is one of the most valuable competencies in a marketing-agency professional.

Building through the Draft

The top firms, which will lead industry transformation and deliver the most value, are built from within. Like professional sports teams that build through the draft, these model agencies excel at identifying and nurturing high-potential young talent, ideally straight out of school. These professionals are groomed within defined systems and trained to adhere to agency standards for performance.

Top performing young professionals are the most important foundation for hybrid agencies, specifically disruptors. In order to excel and continually differentiate, agencies must have a solid strategy to recruit, advance, and retain emerging talent. Standard processes enable agencies to quickly get professionals onboard and transition them into revenue-producing roles. Meanwhile, the shift to predominantly digital marketing services transitions the balance of work to basic and intermediate levels, keeping labor costs low, pricing affordable, and profit margins high.

However, agencies cannot push growth beyond their capability to service it. One of the most challenging aspects of building through the draft is what I call the *patience of potential*. Although your recruits may have A-player potential, not all top picks are ready for primetime right away. Any number of factors can influence how quickly they adapt from college life to the real world and embrace the opportunities ahead of them. These are a few of the more common factors agencies face:

- **Commitment:** It is common for professionals in their early-to-mid-20s to struggle and even question their career choices as they adapt and seek balance in their lives. Those who resist fully committing to their careers in the early years risk falling significantly behind their peers' development, and stalling the agency's growth.

  This is why it is imperative to recruit internally driven professionals who have an insatiable desire to improve, advance, and succeed. They will put in the extra time and energy needed to build a solid foundation of knowledge that will rapidly propel them into leadership positions. Intelligence becomes secondary to effort in the agency world.

- **Perspective:** Some young professionals lack the perspective to appreciate opportunities presented to them. They may feel underpaid or undervalued because they do not understand the economics of agencies. Or they may have a skewed sense of entitlement and not want to put in the work necessary to advance. A lack of perspective can be poisonous to agency cultures, and it may lead to high turnover rates, so agencies must be transparent and open with young professionals.

- **Speed:** You often hear National Football League quarterbacks talk about how fast the game moves when they transition from college to the pros. The game plans are more complex, the competition is stronger and quicker, and they can no longer get by on athleticism and instincts alone.

  Marketing agency professionals experience the same phenomenon. Expectations are high, and things move so quickly in the first year. In addition, mistakes are common, which can negatively affect a young professional's confidence. Eventually, everything slows down as their knowledge and experience grow, and they are able to gradually improve their performance.

Some professionals are born ready, and others need help to realize and embrace their capacity for greatness. Agency leaders must be able to identify high-potential talent and have the patience to develop and nurture these emerging leaders.

Bringing in Free Agents

In professional sports, teams sign free agents with proven track records of success in order to strengthen their organizations. When the time is right, agencies have to do the same and make the move to bring in seasoned talent. Their experience and capabilities enhance the team's capacity for growth, and they add much-needed leadership to help develop and advance young professionals.

However, be cautious when bringing in free agents. Professionals shifting from larger, more established agencies, or those coming from less demanding corporate and nonprofit jobs may struggle in the early going to adjust to the speed of agency life. This can directly impact the agency's efficiency and productivity, and if they do not quickly adjust, their higher salaries can have an undesirable affect on profitability. Additionally, each hire adds a new dynamic to the agency culture, which is delicate during early growth phases.

To avoid making costly hiring mistakes, it is important to have very clear and open dialogue about opportunities and expectations. Make sure candidates understand the systems they will be asked to work within, and buy into the agency's vision. There cannot be any doubt on either end, or else it will never work in the long run.

View free agents as the final pieces to the puzzle, rather than the building blocks of your agency. Use the infusion of experienced talent and fresh perspective to push the agency to the next level.

HIRE, RETAIN, AND ADVANCE HYBRID PROFESSIONALS

Although recruiting talent is a primary responsibility of the agency CEO, prospecting for the next great hire should be top of mind for every team member. Whether you are acquiring young professionals through the draft, or enhancing your mid- and upper-level staff with free agents, the two best sources for prospects are *inbound candidates*—those who complete an online form or submit un-solicited resumes—and *social candidates*—students and professionals who separate themselves through their use of social media.

Let's examine nine steps agencies can take to build strong pipelines of both inbound and social candidates:

1. **Start with brand and culture:** You must define and differentiate your brand in the market and create a dynamic culture that attracts young professionals and free agents. Top talent is drawn to innovative organizations with strong reputations.

2. **Define the career path:** Highly motivated professionals will always be looking ahead and striving to advance. Although organizational charts evolve and new positions develop, there needs to be clearly defined career paths in place. Do not get too caught up in titles but focus on creating logical career milestones, and understand how important it is for professionals to feel that they are developing and advancing.

3. **Maintain a strong online presence:** Social media participation is essential to build reach and engage with professionals, and a strong agency website is the hub for educating and capturing candidates. Model agencies connect with professionals through the agency brand, and extend their networks through the personal brands of their employees. A strong online presence includes the essential elements of website, blog, Facebook, Twitter, and LinkedIn, as well as any secondary accounts and sites that are proven recruiting channels.

4. **Capture inbound candidates:** Build a careers page on your website with calls to action that enable you to capture candidates, gather intelligence, and grade their interest, just as you would with new business leads. Encourage professionals to connect on your social networks as well, and watch for candidates who differentiate themselves by engaging with the agency brand and its employees.

   Also, consider adding a brief online survey on your careers page that professionals can complete to further qualify themselves. We use SurveyMonkey for this purpose, and it has been very effective at filling the pipeline with candidates.

5. **Invest in informational interviews:** Even when you are not hiring, take the time to conduct 30-minute interviews with qualified candidates at all levels. This enables you to build goodwill, extend your network, and identify top talent, should hiring needs change.

6. **Be selective:** Model agencies never settle for less qualified talent. Commit to excelling at recruiting and retaining the best. As a starting point, refer to the competencies and traits of A players featured earlier in this chapter.

7. **Monitor and engage with social candidates:** Use social media channels to monitor and stay connected to top candidates. Private Twitter lists are a great way to keep close tabs on prospective hires that have demonstrated A-player potential. Also, look for professionals who continually differentiate themselves through their actions, activity level, and interest in your agency.

   Candidates can also disqualify themselves from consideration by being overly aggressive and persistent in their use of social media.

8. **Go offline:** Do not forget to make time for traditional networking. Get out to marketing club events, industry association gatherings, conferences, and professional happy hours. Nothing replaces the value of a good face-to-face conversation.

   Support employees who demonstrate a desire to be active in the industry and business community. Consider covering their membership fees and event costs, and providing flexible schedules that enable them to get involved in committees. These are great ways to meet candidates.

9. **Activate a standard candidate grading system:** Talent evaluation requires systems that can be taught and implemented agency wide. Consider the traits and competencies most important to your agency, and build a simple grading chart to assess and compare candidates based on their interviews.

Following are sample factors to consider. I suggest a 1- to 5-point scale for each factor, with 1 being poor and 5 being excellent. This will give you a basic overall rating for each interviewee:

- First impression.
- Social media savvy.
- Tech savvy.
- Experience.
- Confidence.
- Listening skills.
- Verbal communication.
- Goal focused.
- Preparation.

Most importantly, include a yes/no field for "it" factor. If you are not sure, the answer is no. Not all A players have the "it" factor, but you will know it when they do. It is usually obvious within the first minute of the interview.

When Is It Time to Hire?

Agencies are most productive and efficient when functioning near capacity. The heavy, yet manageable, workloads keep professionals focused and in rhythm. Hiring too early and overstaffing in small and early-stage growth agencies are dangerous propositions that can lead to cash-flow crunches and productivity losses.

If there is not enough revenue-generating work to go around, it is only human nature to relax and not push as hard. Temporary lulls can be beneficial to recharge professionals, but challenges arise and bad habits form when they start to extend beyond a few days. There is no perfect formula to tell you when it is time to hire, but, with the right system, agencies have far greater intelligence to make educated decisions.

Let's examine the key elements of a reliable system.

Know Your Capacity   Start with a breakdown of your client-hour capacity across the agency. If we revisit the example five-person agency from Chapter 1, the monthly capacity looks like this:

CEO	= 50 hours
Vice president	= 80 hours
Senior account executive	= 100 hours
Account executive	= 120 hours
Assistant account executive	= 140 hours
Total	= 490 client hours per month

So we know the agency has the capability to deliver just less than 500 hours in a month at a 100 percent productivity rate. In theory, the team is performing at its peak, and the agency is very profitable at this threshold. However, this is what I consider a *soft capacity*, meaning that there is room to flex above if needed to meet short-term demands for major projects and campaign fluctuations.

These one-time spikes can create false hiring signals, so it is recommended to take a quarterly approach to forecasts when nearing soft capacity. Exceeding soft capacity for one or two months is not the right trigger point to hire. Although there are exceptions, you should be able to predict sustained growth for at least three months before you commit to a new hire.

It is important when forecasting and determining when to hire to leave room for a 20 percent spike above the soft capacity, or what I call the *absolute capacity*. In other words, if soft capacity is 490, and next month's forecasts call for 540 client hours (approximately 10 percent above soft capacity), you should be able to deliver up to standards with the current staff. You will notice in the example agency that the CEO, vice president, and senior account executive all have some room to pitch in during heavy months if they temporarily shift priorities.

However, if forecasts exceed 588, or 20 percent above, then you are in the danger zone. Your team will be spread too thin, deadlines will be missed, and quality will suffer if you do not take action. This means either making an immediate hire, outsourcing to a trusted partner in the ecosystem, or, as a last resort, delaying project deliverables.

Build a Strong Forecasting and Reporting Model Hiring decisions must be data driven, otherwise you are putting your agency's financial stability at risk. Monthly forecasts give you predictive data—what you anticipate will happen—and time-tracking software provides the historical data—what has happened to date. Both are essential.

For predictive data, managers should be able to view and edit monthly forecasts by client and employee. Unfortunately, I have yet to find a reliable software product to perform this task, so we have built an Agency Manager dashboard in Microsoft Excel (Figure 3.1). It requires manual updates, so it is not ideal, but it works well for PR 20/20. If you figure out ways to improve on the template, I would love to hear about it.

For historical data, I have always relied on TimeFox by FunctionFox (www.FunctionFox.com). As I mentioned in Chapter 1, accurate time tracking is essential to build an efficient and profitable hybrid agency. TimeFox gives agency professionals the ability to run real-time reports on hours by project, client, and employee. This information is vital to keep campaigns and budgets on track, produce monthly activity reports and invoices, and also incredibly valuable when conducting professional performance reviews.

Shift to Campaigns Concentrate on shifting 80 percent or more of your client base to long-term contracts, which creates predictable recurring revenue and workflow. For agencies that are predominantly project based, forecasting is nothing more than futile guesswork. If you plan to grow a stable and scalable agency, you must build a campaign-based agency.

MONTH AND YEAR

CLIENT CENTER					FORECASTED MONTHLY HOURS BY EMPLOYEE							
Client	Type	Group Manager	Account Manager	Account Team	Pro 1	Pro 2	Pro 3	Pro 4	Pro 5	TOTAL	Notes (Active projects, pipeline projects, proposals, account status)	Forecasted Monthly Income
Client A	Campaign											
Client B	Campaign											
Client C	Campaign											
Client D	Campaign											
Client E	Project											
Client F	Project											
Client G	Project											
					0	0	0	0	0	0		$0

Figure 3.1   Basic Version of the PR 20/20 Agency Manager Template

Define Ahead-of-Need Triggers Sometimes you have to throw out all logic and data, take a leap of faith, and hire ahead of need. The triggers will be different for each agency, but common ones include:

- Launching a major growth initiative.
- Anticipation of significant demand from a new partnership.
- Deep new-business pipeline with potential for a number of short-term conversions.
- Preparation for the transitioning of underperforming employees.
- Understaffed core campaign accounts.
- Opportunity to land a high-potential A player.

The Retention Issue

Identifying and recruiting A players is challenging, but retaining them long term can prove to be even more difficult, especially given the industry's employee retention issue. According to the Transforming Talent Management report from the American Association of Advertising Agencies (4A) and Havas' Arnold Worldwide, 30 percent of the collective agency workforce will be gone in 12 months, and 70 percent of employees would call a recruiter back if one reached out to them.[3]

Model agencies recruit to retain. They seek to hire career professionals who view the agency as a destination rather than a stepping-stone. Although some top employees will move on to lead or found other agencies, the goal is to maintain stability through retention. As professionals advance and compensation packages increase, this becomes more difficult, so agencies must grow and continually evolve to offer competitive pay and rewarding environments.

Keep in mind that A players are in high demand. Just like free agency in professional sports, there is always another organization willing and able to pay more. This is why culture and the pursuit of purpose, which we investigate in Chapter 10, are so essential to your agency's success.

Retention starts by hiring intrinsically motivated talent. Although everyone has baseline financial needs that must be met through salary, bonuses, and benefits, money is not the primary motivating factor for these professionals. Compensation certainly must be fair and competitive, but once they reach certain financial thresholds, and all their basic needs are met, more money has minimal impact on their motivation or happiness.

Assuming that an agency maintains competitive compensation packages, if someone leaves on their own free will, and it is a solely money-motivated decision, then they were not a fit for the firm from the start or they lost their connection to the culture and purpose somewhere along the way. In either case, as hard as it is to replace top talent, it is probably for the best that they leave.

Model agencies are built around loyal professionals who passionately believe in the mission, vision, and values. They are your greatest asset, and the only means by which you will create a significant and lasting brand.

Training Hybrid Pros

The most valued talent in the emerging marketing agency ecosystem will themselves be hybrids. Although specialists, connectors, and soloists can still excel with focused competencies and service offerings, disruptors are built on the versatility of social media and tech-savvy professionals. They possess exceptional copywriting skills, along with dynamic personalities that enable them to build strong personal brands.

Hybrid professionals are trained to deliver services across search, mobile, social, content, analytics, web, PR, and e-mail marketing. They provide integrated solutions that used to require multiple agencies and consultants. However, because there are not any college programs that I am aware of producing graduates with these diverse skill sets, the onus falls on agencies to develop customized training programs.

Agencies can mold young professionals into valuable consultants and practitioners by mixing internal curriculum and exercises with the wealth of education and resources available on the web. Agency training programs should be structured like internal academies, with standard curriculum and milestones. Let's take a look at key components of a powerful agency program.

Webinars   Content-savvy organizations are using webinars as lead-generating and thought-leadership tools. These are commonly free, and often available on demand, which makes them incredibly efficient training resources. Agency leaders should identify priority webinars on an ongoing basis, and make them required viewing for professionals.

Books   Never underestimate the value of a great book. Create a recommended reading list, share outlines, and even consider starting an agency book club. Although there certainly are some great titles available that deal with specific services and disciplines, here is a list of some of my favorite general business, marketing, and management books to get you started:

- Anderson, Chris. *The Long Tail: Why the Future of Business Is Selling Less of More.* New York: Hyperion, 2006.
- Bedbury, Scott, and Stephen Fenichell. *A New Brand World: Eight Principles for Achieving Brand Leadership in the Twenty-First Century.* New York: Penguin, 2003.
- Christensen, Clayton M. *The Innovator's Dilemma: The Revolutionary Book that Will Change the Way You Do Business.* New York: HarperCollins, 2003.
- Collins, Jim. *Good to Great: Why Some Companies Make the Leap . . . and Others Don't.* New York: HarperCollins, 2001.
- Fried, Jason, and David H. Hansson. *Rework.* New York: Crown Publishing Group, 2010.
- Halligan, Brian, and Dharmesh Shah. *Inbound Marketing: Get Found Using Google, Social Media, and Blogs.* Hoboken, NJ: John Wiley & Sons, Inc., 2010.
- Harnish, Verne. *Mastering the Rockefeller Habits.* New York: SelectBooks, 2002.
- Maister, David H. *Managing the Professional Service Firm.* New York: Simon & Schuster, 1993.
- Medina, John. *Brain Rules: 12 Principles for Surviving and Thriving at Work, Home, and School.* Seattle: Pear Press, 2009.
- Murray, Alan. *The Wall Street Journal Essential Guide to Management: Lasting Lessons from the Best Leadership Minds of Our Time.* New York: HarperCollins, 2010.
- Pink, Daniel H. *Drive: The Surprising Truth About What Motivates Us.* New York: Penguin, 2009.
- Scott, David M. *New Rules of Marketing & PR: How to Use Social Media, Blogs, News Releases, Online Video, and Viral Marketing to Reach Buyers Directly, 3rd ed.* Hoboken, NJ: John Wiley & Sons, Inc., 2011.
- Smart, Bradford D. *Topgrading: How Leading Companies Win by Hiring, Coaching, and Keeping the Best People.* New York: Penguin, 2005.
- Tellis, Gerard J., and Peter N. Golder. *Will and Vision: How Latecomers Grow to Dominate Markets.* New York: McGraw-Hill, 2002.
- Zyman, Sergio. *The End of Marketing as We Know It.* New York: HarperCollins, 1999.

Real-Time Sharing   Find reliable solutions for the sharing of communications, experiences, and ideas with employees as they happen. It is so easy, especially for senior personnel, to go about their days conducting meetings, communicating with clients, and making key strategic decisions about the agency without thinking to share what they are doing and why they are doing it. However, these types of activities are some of the most practical learning experiences for young professionals. Furthermore, it keeps all employees engaged in the agency and encourages a more collaborative culture.

We rely on two platforms—Yammer, and Highrise by 37Signals— for the majority of our real-time, agency-wide sharing.

We use Yammer as our private, internal social network, which enables threaded and searchable conversations. If you are not familiar with Yammer, or competing solutions, it is basically like Facebook for the enterprise. Here are some of the ways agencies can take advantage of a solution like Yammer:

- Post timely links and resources.
- Share good news and positive client results.
- Ask questions of peers.
- Publish account management tips.
- Get real-time feedback on client campaign strategies.
- Provide account and group updates.
- Suggest upcoming webinars.
- Recommend books and blogs to read, and influencers to follow, as they are discovered.

Meanwhile, Highrise is a customer relationship management (CRM) cloud-based solution that enables agencies to track conversations, calls, e-mails, and meetings. Professionals can log in at any time and view the latest activities on the dashboard, and then click through to any items that are relevant. This is an effective way for the entire team to stay informed of what's happening within the agency. Also, from an educational perspective, it gives young professionals insight into standard communications styles and habits.

Knowledge Transfer   Use management videos, presentation recordings, case studies, and handbooks to document policies, procedures, and best practices. Consider the most effective ways to capture and store your agency's collective knowledge, so that it can be passed on to the next generation of employees as the organization grows.

Role Playing   Practicing in front of peers and managers can be intimidating at first for many, but it is a great way to gain experience and build confidence. Look for opportunities, such as calls, meetings, and presentations, to integrate regular role-playing sessions into your training program.

Conferences   Attending conferences can get expensive with fees and travel costs, but they definitely provide valuable content and networking opportunities, as well as unique experiences for your team.

There is a seemingly endless list of marketing industry events to consider, but for agencies serious about transforming into a tech-savvy hybrid, SXSW Interactive is the one cannot-miss conference. The conference, which happens every March in Austin, Texas, brings together the brightest, most innovative minds in marketing and technology for five days of learning. If you have never attended, it is worth the investment.

Online Courses   There are some amazing online resources available to train agency professionals. For example, Google offers free courses that provide comprehensive training in Google Analytics and Google AdWords, and HubSpot certifies professionals through its Inbound Marketing University. Consider the areas your agency needs to strengthen, and look for third-party courses to enhance internal materials.

Blog-Post Writing   Turn learning exercises, such as book reading, conference attendance, and webinar participation, into agency blog posts. This is a perfect way to share valuable content on your blog, and gives professionals the chance to hone their writing skills.

Group Exercises   Assign challenges to the entire agency or select teams, and then meet to review, share, and learn together. For example, in 2009, we created a book project designed to educate employees on how an agency operates, and get them more engaged in the direction of the firm. We bought everyone a copy of *Managing the Professional Service Firm* by David H. Maister.[4] We wanted them to be able to critically analyze themselves and the agency as a means to improve efficiency and productivity. The book gave them much needed perspective.

They had one month to read the book and respond to a series of questions. We then got together the next month to discuss everyone's thoughts and responses. Here are sample questions that we actually used in the exercise:

- How can we make the agency more profitable?
- What can be done to improve client relations?
- What can you do personally to improve your performance and value to the agency?
- How can account groups run more efficiently?
- How would you strengthen employee training and education provided by the agency?
- If you were in charge of the agency, what three actions would you make the top priorities to improve efficiency, value delivered to clients, and profitability?

Group exercises like this are difficult to keep up with when client workflow is heavy, but model agencies recognize their importance and make them a priority.

TALENT EVALUATION AND PROFESSIONAL REVIEWS

Formal professional reviews are an essential element to training and advancement. They ensure that employees are staying on track with their development, and identify opportunities to address concerns and challenges. Although annual reviews should be standard for all professionals, more regular sessions throughout the year are a great way to keep managers in tune with the team's energy and motivation.

For most small agencies, the human resource duties often fall to the management team, which, most likely, does not have any advanced human-resource training. My best advice in these cases is to seek out reputable online sources for guidance, take a few classes at a local university, consider hiring a consultant if you can afford the investment, find trusted advisors to support your programs, and read *Topgrading* by Bradford D. Smart, PhD.[5]

Topgrading provides a wealth of detailed and practical advice on "how leading companies win by hiring, coaching and keeping the best people." It is one of the most influential books I read while building PR 20/20's talent evaluation and advancement programs.

The Basics

Professional reviews should analyze competencies and traits, motivation, and performance. We use a process that encourages self-analysis as a means to discovery and understanding.

Professionals are presented with approximately 140 statements, which they answer with a 1–5 rating: 1 (strongly disagree), 2 (disagree), 3 (neutral), 4 (agree), and 5 (strongly agree). Each statement also has a notes column, which responders may use to further explain any ratings. There are no right or wrong answers, and we do not consider the cumulative total of the ratings.

Our goals are to:

- Create a snapshot of mindset and motivation, individually and as an agency.
- Clearly define expectations.
- Strengthen the team.
- Provide all the feedback, guidance, and support needed for success.
- Improve performance, and prepare for opportunities and growth.

The review is not meant as a burden or a test. Instead, it is an opportunity for professionals to gain a strong grasp on where they stand in their professional development, and identify opportunities to enhance their value and careers, while helping to grow the agency.

Once professionals complete their self-analysis, managers review responses and develop qualitative follow-up questions based on personal ratings, performance history, and supervisor feedback. Individual review meetings are then conducted with professionals and managers. Based on discussions, professionals develop and submit action-oriented, results-driven advancement plans. These serve as the basis for future evaluations.

Establishing Systems with a Personal Touch

Do not commoditize your talent. Although it is important to establish evaluation and advancement programs, take the time to personalize your approach based on the unique needs and personalities of each professional. Understand what is important to them, and treat them with respect and honesty at all levels.

Following are core components of an agency talent-evaluation system.

Define the Career Path   Where are they going? What are the opportunities ahead? How can they build a successful career at your agency? These are the types of questions you need to answer with a career path. It lays out the roles, responsibilities, expectations, and opportunities at different levels of the agency.

Start with Metrics   Give professionals a clear understanding of how they will be evaluated. Determine the metrics that matter to your agency and to the professional's advancement, and integrate them into evaluations. Model agencies focus on client retention and growth, as well as productivity, efficiency, and profitability.

Assess Competencies and Traits   Challenge professionals to critically analyze their strengths and weaknesses. Focus on the competencies and traits that are essential to their development. Here are sample statements you may present, and then have them rate their level of agreement with each, using the 1–5 rating system: 1 (strongly disagree), 2 (disagree), 3 (neutral), 4 (agree), and 5 (strongly agree).

- I am quick to make decisions based on logic and reason. I am decisive in my actions.
- I believe risk and failure are essential paths to success.
- I have difficulty focusing on a single project or task for extended periods of time without being distracted.
- I am adept at managing and controlling my stress levels, even when under tight deadlines.
- I tend to get defensive when peers challenge my work or opinions.

Evaluate Drive   Professionals must maintain high motivation levels. Although drive is readily apparent to perceptive managers, it is important to gauge how individuals feel they are performing. You can use statements such as:

- I focus the majority of my time and energy in business and life on the things I can control. I don't get distracted and overwhelmed by things I cannot influence.
- I find myself constantly setting goals (personally and professionally) that require me to test my own capabilities, commitment, and limits.
- No one will ever question my effort and desire to improve and succeed.
- I create more value than I capture.

Connect to Performance   The most effective evaluations are directly tied to performance. Professionals should understand, and be able to prove, their value to the agency. For example, have

professionals assess how their contributions have led to key outcomes for the agency, such as account retention and growth, and for
its clients.

Create Advancement Plans   Use advancement plans to concentrate time and energy in the right areas moving forward based on
training and education priorities. Advancement plans are personalized to address weaknesses identified in the evaluation process, and
include detailed activities and timelines.

LEADERS MUST LEAD: THE LEBRON JAMES PARABLE

Cleveland is my hometown. I was born and raised in the city, and
when I started PR 20/20 in 2005, I opened our office in a historic
downtown building overlooking Progressive Field, home of the
Cleveland Indians, and a block away from Quicken Loans Arena,
home of the Cleveland Cavaliers.

I have been a die-hard Cleveland sports fan since I was eight
years old. I remember when it started because that was 1986—the
year of what simply became known as *The Drive*. John Elway, the
quarterback of the Denver Broncos, broke our hearts that season
with a 98-yard drive in the closing minutes of the AFC Championship game. It cost our beloved Cleveland Browns what would have
been their first Super Bowl appearance.

We have dealt with countless collapses and close calls since that
time, but when Cleveland's own LeBron James, the self-proclaimed
King, was selected with the number-one overall pick in the 2003 NBA
draft, that was all supposed to change. It would be only a matter of
time until Clevelanders basked in the glory of our first professional
sports championship in more than four decades, but it was not to be.

The Leader Who Refused to Lead

Shortly before NBA superstar LeBron James infamously took his tal-
ents to South Beach in 2010 to join Dwayne Wade's team, the Miami
Heat, he played against the Boston Celtics in one of the most pivotal
games in Cleveland Cavaliers franchise history.

The stage was set. Following back-to-back MVP seasons, James
was poised to solidify his place as the greatest basketball player—
and probably athlete—on Earth, laying the foundation for his legacy
as the greatest of all time.

After a lackluster game two in the 2010 NBA conference semifi-
nals against the Boston Celtics, which can best be described as out of

character, James returned to MVP form in game three with a scintillating performance, scoring 21 of his 38 points in the first quarter.

He seemed to be the man on a mission that Cleveland fans and national media expected, but then something inexplicable happened—he quit.

For the first time in his illustrious career, James' uninspired performances in games five and six left analysts and fans questioning the King's heart and will to win, and speculating on what happened. All the rumors and injuries aside, the best player in the game did not show up for his team when they needed him most. The most amazing part was that he did not seem to care. Although it might have been destroying him inside, perception is reality.

The competitive fire that burned inside him, after seven years of hearing that he did not have Kobe Byrant's killer instinct or Michael Jordan's drive, just appeared to go out. Instead of moving onto the NBA finals, and securing his first ring, James quietly planned for his exit through free agency.

Great Teams Need Great Leaders

As a fan and someone who deeply cares for Cleveland, I was disappointed when James left, but only because I believed he had the ability to be so much more, and do such amazing things for the city. As an entrepreneur, I took a more objective approach and tried to find some relevant meaning in the situation.

At the end of the day, it is irrelevant how many MVPs and titles James wins in Miami, or if he continues to disappear on the Heat as he did in the 2011 NBA finals. He had the potential to be the greatest of all time, and bring his hometown of Cleveland its first professional championship since 1964. However, when things got hard, he chose to walk away. He was not the leader we all wanted him to be.

James has the ability to dominate every game, and win every scoring title. Instead, he does what leaders often do, he delegates and builds his team's confidence and morale by involving them and giving them opportunities to excel and achieve.

However, there comes a time when leaders must lead in a different way. They are obligated to take their game to a whole new level, and pull everyone along with them. Their passion, drive, and refusal to lose must shine through. Think James in game five of the 2007 conference finals against the Detroit Pistons—48 points, including 29 of his team's last 30. That is the James the Cavs needed against the Celtics in 2010 and the leader every organization needs when it is all on the line.

What It Means to Your Agency

Throughout this chapter, we have talked about the importance of building teams of hybrid professionals who are driven to be great. We covered how to attract and retain young professionals whom you can mold in your system, and then complementing them with the right mix of seasoned professionals when it is time to go to the next level.

However, the final and most essential piece of every great team is a great leader. There will be difficult times ahead. Your agency will face endless obstacles in its pursuit of success, and true leaders step up when they are needed most.

Sometimes success and victory come down to the sheer will of a leader's refusal to lose.

CHAPTER HIGHLIGHTS

- When all else is equal—processes, services, pricing, and infrastructure—it is talent that cannot be replicated.

- Model agencies take a controlled, almost methodical, approach to expansion. They develop talent from within, and construct teams based on shared values, innate abilities, and complementary character traits.

- The most desirable A-player competencies and traits include the following: analytical, balanced, confident, detail-oriented, focused, intrinsically motivated, "it" factor, listener, positive, relationship-builder, risk-taker, social-web savvy, strategic, team player, tech-savvy, and writer.

- The top firms, which will lead industry transformation and deliver the most value, are built from within, meaning they hire and develop young professionals.

- Agencies cannot push growth beyond their capability to service it.

- Commitment, perspective, and speed are three factors that can affect how quickly A players realize their potential.

- Intelligence becomes secondary to effort in the agency world.

- View free agents as the final pieces to the puzzle, rather than the building blocks of your agency. Use the infusion

(*continued*)

(*continued*)

of experienced talent and fresh perspective to push the agency to the next level.

- The two best sources for prospects are *inbound candidates*—those who complete an online form or submit unsolicited resumes—and *social candidates*—students and professionals who separate themselves through their use of social media.

- Agencies are most productive and efficient when functioning near capacity.

- Hiring decisions must be data driven otherwise you are putting your agency's financial stability at risk.

- Model agencies recruit to retain. They seek to hire career professionals who view the agency as a destination rather than a steppingstone.

- Agencies can mold young professionals into valuable consultants and practitioners by mixing internal curriculum and exercises with the wealth of education and resources available on the web.

- Professional reviews should analyze competencies and traits, motivation, and performance.

- There comes a time when leaders must take their game to a whole new level and pull everyone along with them. Their passion, drive, and refusal to lose must shine through.

Build a Scalable Infrastructure

The best plan is to prepare for perpetual change.

MAKE DECISIONS THAT FIT YOUR GROWTH GOALS

In my experience as an entrepreneur, and through our work with hundreds of clients, I have learned that opportunity is everywhere for unique and innovative companies that bring real value to customers. However, opportunity can be overwhelming if you do not adapt to changing markets and increasing demand, and build a scalable infrastructure capable of effectively accommodating growth.

Intro to Infrastructure

Infrastructure refers to structures and systems that facilitate the production and delivery of agency services. Basically, it includes any physical or organizational element required to run and grow your agency. Core components include financial systems, information technology, management systems, and human resources.

Growth for growth's sake, without a profitable business model, results in little more than an entrepreneurial ego boost. Expansion in prototype agencies is driven primarily by the desire to attract and retain talent. They opt for controlled growth, often resisting the urge

to accelerate business development initiatives. They focus on building a stable operational foundation with nimble management
systems that enable them to execute and adapt faster than the competition. They make calculated investments in hardware, software,
staffing, partnerships, advisors, and office space designed to support
their foreseeable future needs, while maintaining the highest levels
of service quality, efficiency, and productivity today.

Making decisions too far ahead of the growth curve can cost you
valuable resources now, but not planning for the contingencies of
growth can be detrimental to your ability to profitably build your
business in the future.

Goals, Trends, and Timing

There is no standard formula to guide infrastructure investments.
You have to consider your unique business goals and growth trends.
For some, that means modest growth of 5 to 10 percent per year,
whereas others may have aggressive growth prospects of 50 to
100 percent or more per year. The more aggressive agencies must
be incredibly smart about their infrastructure choices. It is easy to
spend thousands of dollars on a phone system, server, or project-
management platform that becomes obsolete as you expand.

You also have to consider your timetable when planning infrastructure. I tend to look at business decisions as current (next 12
months), short term (1–3 years), midterm (3–5 years) and long term
(more than 5 years). Infrastructure planning should account for current and short-term needs, with contingencies for midterm possibilities. Change velocity principles dictate that trying to plan for
anything beyond three years is an exercise in futility. Have a vision
for the long term, but make infrastructure decisions based on current and short-term realities.

For example, when PR 20/20 reached five employees in 2008, I
began working on a 2x–3x scale. This meant that for every decision I
made, I would consider whether or not the solution would be viable
at 10–15 employees. At that time, we built out an office space capable
of accommodating up to 15 employees in 2–3 years, but we also included an option on the adjacent space that would fit up to 25
employees in 3–5 years. We installed a sophisticated phone system,
upgraded our Internet bandwidth, and set up a new server and internal computer network.

All told, we invested more than $50,000 to build out an infra-
structure that was capable of handling up to 15 employees, but
extendable to dozens of employees if needed. We accommodated
our current needs without overextending ourselves, and put a

contingency in place for future expansion. Does that mean it was a perfect solution? Absolutely not, but we had the funding to comfortably make the investments and buy ourselves a few years until we had to revisit these core pieces.

Keep in mind this was all happening within 12 months of Apple unveiling the iPhone, and more than two years before they released the iPad, so we did not have a mobile workforce accessing files, information, and applications from multiple devices. Plus, the metaphorical cloud was still in its infancy as a mainstream business concept. In other words, just three years later, the decisions I would make today regarding our infrastructure are dramatically different than those I originally made in 2008.

Lessons from the Inside

I started PR 20/20 in November 2005 after 21 months of intense planning. It was the most exhilarating and exhausting time of my life. Fueled by a powerful cocktail of youthful exuberance, adrenaline, and caffeine, I spent what seemed like every waking minute outside of my day job (VP at a traditional PR agency) building a dream.

I loved the agency I came from, but I had become convinced there was a better way. I feared that if I stayed where I was and continued to follow traditional marketing agency methods, then I would always regret not taking a chance on something in which I so passionately believed. Besides, what did I have to lose? I was young, and my wife and I were happy living a modest lifestyle. At the time, I was making just enough money to pay our bills, put away a few dollars in a retirement account, and have a little left over for travel. The worst-case scenario if the agency did not flourish was that we would struggle financially for a while, but at least I would have given myself the chance to fail.

So, at the tender age of 27, I left the comfort and security of my career to turn my own vision into reality. I set out to make marketing services accessible and affordable to the mass market of small businesses.

In retrospect, although the business model was sound, and we still function on the basic principles of the plan, my financial forecasts were overly ambitious, if not absurd. Forecasts called for $19 million in revenue and 140 employees by year five. I showed my business plan to a number of advisors before launch, and even submitted it to a local start-up challenge. Response was always positive, but I never got the feeling that anyone saw the potential I did in building a technology-driven hybrid agency, and no one really seemed to fully understand what I was trying to do.

With limited guidance, I set out to build an entirely new marketing agency model focused on the small business market. The first few months were easy when my infrastructure consisted of a home office, a single phone line, a MacBook, and a Palm Treo, but it was not long before things began to change.

Let's take a look at five of the critical agency infrastructure lessons we have learned through the years.

Lesson 1. Prepare for Perpetual Change   I launched PR 20/20 with $25,000 in loans from the friends-and-family network. I did not have any personal savings to fall back on, so this gave me a six-month runway to cover basic start-up expenses, health-care benefits, and a paycheck. I worked out of local cafes, and developed a particular liking for Panera, which offered free Wi-Fi and coffee refills, both of which were vital in the early days.

Although I had lofty aspirations for growth, the agency began with just three nonpaying clients—a barter deal, my wife's art business, and my parents' cookie franchises. The first few months were spent finalizing the service and pricing guide, which had more than 100 standardized services when we published it online in January 2006.

The 20/20 Standard

The 20/20 Standard service and pricing guide was the original core concept behind PR 20/20. In essence, it was built as an online marketplace for a la carte, project-based services. There were 19 categories with 102 services when it was first introduced in 2006. In most cases, the standard services, such as press releases, brochures, logo designs, print ads, and websites, featured set prices.

Soon thereafter, we started getting calls from larger enterprises. Though the model was designed for small businesses, friends and business associates at these corporations immediately viewed us as an alternative to the traditional agencies they were used to engaging. They loved the transparency in pricing, the simplicity of the services, and our focus on producing measurable results. So, as they would say in the technology world, I pivoted the agency. I set the small business plan aside and immediately began adapting the model to meet larger enterprise needs.

In March 2006, we hired our first employee, signed our first lease, and began the baptism by fire of building a scalable infrastructure.

We made a lot of mistakes, burned through funding reserves on numerous occasions, got screwed by countless vendors, and battled some deadbeat clients as we fine-tuned our financial systems. However, we never got discouraged or stopped believing in what we set out to achieve.

I knew from day one it would be an iterative process, and it still is today. The velocity of change, especially in technology, is relentless. You must construct an agile infrastructure that positions you to continually evolve.

Lesson 2. Build through Trusted Solution Providers Whereas large traditional agencies are often bogged down by legacy systems, emerging firms have the flexibility to experiment with product innovations and hot new start-ups when building their technology infrastructure.

Change velocity in essence dictates that something better and more efficient is bound to come along sooner than later. Often, the breadth of options can be overwhelming and confusing for agencies. There are endless providers to evaluate, with seemingly redundant feature sets. Some claim to do everything in one platform, and others are narrowly focused on single pain points. Researching, evaluating, and selecting the right solutions for your agency can be a mind-numbing and frustrating experience. This also makes it difficult to pull the trigger on major technology infrastructure decisions.

A service that is here one minute can be gone the next. For example, in 2010 we discovered an amazing file-sharing platform. It was feature rich, yet intuitive, and exactly what we needed to transfer large files over the Internet and collaborate with clients on projects. We began integrating it into account-management systems, and clients seemed to really like and value the service. Then Facebook bought the company to acquire its talent, and within a month the company and its service were gone.

The lesson here is always test innovative solutions from emerging technology companies, but turn to proven organizations when it comes time to make major infrastructure decisions. Look for organizations with track records of performance, transparency, stability, continuous innovation, and exceptional customer/community support. There will always be risks when you rely on third parties for key pieces of your infrastructure, so do your due diligence and find partners that give you confidence and peace of mind.

Although there certainly are viable competitors you should consider in each area, here are some of the providers that we have come to rely on for our technology infrastructure. (Pricing shown is accurate as of July 2011.)

Time Tracking

Company: FunctionFox (www.FunctionFox.com).

Product: Timefox.

Pricing: $20/month and up.

Notes: A number of other solutions we use offer time tracking features as part of their products, but we have always preferred Timefox. It is intuitive and reliable, and easily scales as new employees and contractors are added to the system. Even though it is designed to accommodate billable hours, we were able to customize it to fit our model of service packages and set pricing.

As discussed in Chapter 1, it is important to note that the value-based pricing model does not eliminate the need for time-sheets. Accurate time tracking actually becomes more essential in order to monitor efficiency and productivity, evaluate employee performance, produce activity reports, and evolve pricing.

Project and Campaign Management

Company: 37Signals (www.37signals.com).

Product: Basecamp.

Pricing: $24/month and up.

Notes: Basecamp is one of the most essential components of our agency management system. Every project, task, and milestone is maintained in the system, and all campaign-based clients are given dedicated client centers.

These online group hubs are designed to foster communication and collaboration between the agency and its clients. They let businesses track campaign milestones, monitor agency tasks and progress, share files, view communications, and submit and read messages. There is also a great iPhone mobile app called Insight available for $9.99.

Customer Relations Management (CRM)

Company: 37Signals (www.37Signals.com).

Product: Highrise.

Pricing: $24/month and up.

Notes: Another product in the 37Signals suite, Highrise is our CRM solution used to manage all agency contacts, including clients, prospects, media, and employees. It is billed as "simple CRM," and though it definitely lacks some of the features in more robust CRM platforms, we have always found it be effective.

We use Highrise to track all important notes, calls, meetings, and e-mails, which gives managers and account teams 24/7 access to everything happening throughout the agency. Plus, mobile apps make it easy to stay connected and informed while traveling and working from remote locations.

Internet Marketing

Company: HubSpot (www.Hubspot.com).

Product: HubSpot.

Pricing: $3,000/year and up.

Notes: HubSpot is an all-in-one marketing platform. It includes tools to help companies get found online, convert visitors into leads, and continually analyze marketing investments. HubSpot also offers a wealth of education and training resources, an active online customer community, and a team dedicated to working closely with VAR partner agencies.

Accounting

Company: Intuit (www.quickbooksonline.intuit.com).

Product: Quickbooks Online.

Pricing: $12.95/month and up.

Notes: In 2010, we made the switch from Quickbooks for Mac to Quickbooks Online. It was one of the best decisions we have made. Moving from the desktop version to the cloud simplified our accounting systems, improved our accounts receivable and accounts payable processes, gave us real-time insight into our financial health, and made it possible to integrate financial data into our account management systems.

Internal Social Network

Company: Yammer (www.Yammer.com).

Product: Yammer.

Pricing: $5/user and up.

Notes: After a one-month beta test with a small group of PR 20/20 employees, we rolled out Yammer as our internal social network in December 2010. As our staff grew, we needed a better solution to encourage collaboration, continuously transfer knowledge, and perpetuate our culture. Yammer provided all of that and more. There are higher-end solutions in this space, such as Jive Software, but based on our experience, Yammer is an ideal solution for small-to-midsize agencies. Here are some of the ways we use it on a daily basis:

- Post timely links and resources.
- Share good news and positive campaign results throughout the day.
- Ask questions of our peers.
- Offer tips and share observations.
- Add topics and daily notes for discussion during the next morning's group meeting.
- Get real-time feedback on campaign strategies.
- Publish account and group updates.
- Take polls and announce agency events.

Online Meetings and Webinars
Company: GoToMeeting (www.GoToMeeting.com).
Product: GoToMeeting and GoToWebinar.
Pricing: $49/month and up.
Notes: GoToMeeting gives agencies an affordable solution to conduct online meetings and webinars. We use it for new business presentations and monthly client campaign reviews, as well as education and training. An online meeting platform, such as GoToMeeting, is essential for every agency.

In addition to the solutions just outlined, here is a collection of additional elements that agencies need to consider when building a scalable technology infrastructure:

- Agency management.
- Calendar/scheduling.
- Communications.
- Computer network.
- Data storage.
- E-mail.
- Hardware: computers, printers, cameras, mobile devices, servers, phones.
- Marketing automation.
- Online surveys.
- Website analytics.

Lesson 3. Understand Your Limits Marketing agencies are bound by the limitations of human resources. One new employee is needed for every 120 to 140 hours of additional client service work per month. This not only affects payroll, but it impacts every piece of the agency's infrastructure. Therefore, as your agency is forecasting its growth plans, it is important to take a macro-level view of how increases in revenue and staffing will impact your organization.

At the end of the day, great people define great agency brands. If you push growth too hard, you run the risk of burning out your most valued assets. If you hold back too much, you may not create enough opportunities to retain them. You can only grow to the rate permissible by your infrastructure. This not only applies to information technology, such as phones, servers, computers, and software, but to your talent.

If you are considering an aggressive growth model, ask yourself questions such as:

- Do we have the right leadership team in place?
- Are we expecting practitioners to naturally evolve into managers or are we providing the resources needed to prepare them for the challenges ahead?
- How will our agency management systems perform if we increase monthly client hours by 25 percent? 50 percent? 100 percent?
- Is our current staff overworked?
- How will the increases in staff affect payroll and productivity?
- Is our training and education program maximized to quickly onboard new professionals?
- Is our career path defined?
- Do we have a solid recruiting program in place to fuel our need for entry-level A players?

Lesson 4. Find Reliable Advisors and Mentors Make it a priority to connect with and engage an advisory board for your agency. When I was building PR 20/20's original business plan, I identified my weaknesses and tried to find advisors who could bring complementary knowledge and skills to the table. Specifically, consider core business areas such as finance, technology, human resources, legal, and accounting. If you are going to scale an agency, you need insight and guidance from professionals you can trust.

Also, look for mentors who have built and/or transformed businesses of their own. Entrepreneurs tend to welcome opportunities to help other entrepreneurs, and share what they have learned along the way. Their experiences can be invaluable to your development as an agency.

Lesson 5. Create a Funding Runway   High-growth agencies take more risks than their peers. Risk is necessary to expand, but it comes at a price. In an ideal world, your agency has the profits and cash flow to fuel growth, but, more likely than not, you are going to need access to capital in order to excel and continuously innovate. Cash-flow crunches are debilitating to agencies. If you do not have the proper capital reserves in place, making payroll and covering accounts payable can cause the best of agencies to stall.

THE REALITIES OF COSTS, FUNDING, AND CASH FLOW

Although top-line revenue goals are important benchmarks for many agencies, rapid increases in sales and staffing can quickly lead to costs rising out of control. If these are not carefully planned and managed, then revenue growth becomes a zero-sum game. This is a difficult, and sometimes painful, reality for agencies. Despite tremendous demand for services, and seemingly endless project pipelines, systems become strained, processes falter, staff performance suffers, and cash reserves run dry.

Agencies must have strategic approaches to their accounting and finance systems. We will cover some basics here, but model agencies will take the initiative to continuously expand their knowledge and competencies in these core areas. It helps to have trusted outside accountants and financial advisors, but it is also important that agency leaders maintain a keen interest in the agency's finances.

Investing in Growth

There was a time when I was considering a significant expansion strategy that would have required approximately $250,000 in new financing. I spent a year or more meeting with advisors, talking to banks, and discussing options with potential investors. At the end of the day, I opted for a more conservative approach, but in the process learned some valuable lessons about funding growth.

Here are six of the most important takeaways from my experiences.

1. Build a Stable, Profitable Business   You are a service business. Although the goal is to build a hybrid agency with multiple revenue streams, no marketing agency is cashing in on the preprofit valuations enjoyed by upstart tech companies we read about in TechCrunch. In order to secure debt and/or equity funding, you must prove you can run a profitable business that is capable of servicing its debt and providing a return on investment to its shareholders.

2. Understand Your Value   Determining your agency's valuation can be very difficult, since everyone seems to have a different formula. According to HubSpot CEO, Brian Halligan, "When marketing services firms get acquired or merge with another firm, they are typically valued at a low multiple of EBITDA (Earnings Before Interest, Taxes, Depreciation, and Amortization) or a low multiple of revenue because services revenue streams are relatively low margin and inherently lumpy."[1]

For this reason, it is challenging to go after investments from angel investors and venture capitalists, and somewhat of a crapshoot if you decide to start selling shares of your agency. The reality is that most agency leaders think their firms are worth more than they really are. However, disruptive agencies, with innovative models and diversified recurring revenue streams, are likely to stand the greatest chance of receiving strong valuations should they choose to pursue equity funding.

3. Explore Your Options   Having been through years of investigating and pursuing a variety of funding options, and reading endless books and blogs on the topic, I would advise that you focus your energy on the friends-and-family network. This will likely be the primary source of debt and equity funding for most small-to-midsize agencies that require additional capital to grow their businesses. Whether the financing is structured as a loan, line of credit, or convertible note, friends and family usually are the most captive audiences for entrepreneurs, and most flexible on terms.

During early growth phases, and once your agency matures, bank lending can be a viable option as well. However, if the agency has weak financial statements, banks will require that you or your business partners put up significant collateral in order to secure loans and lines of credit. This makes it difficult for start-ups to turn to traditional lenders for help.

4. Ensure You Can Service the Debt   It is easy to drown in debt if you are not careful. Be realistic about your recurring revenue and your ability to service additional debt. For example, say your agency is forecasted to generate $600,000 in revenue, with a respectable

10 percent net profit margin. So on average, your agency earns a $5,000 net profit per month. Let's assume you make $3,500 per month in loan payments to service your existing debt, which leaves $1,500 in cash each month.

$$\begin{array}{r} \$5,000 \text{ net profit} \\ -\$3,500 \text{ loan payments} \\ \hline \$1,500 \text{ cash} \end{array}$$

Now, expansion plans call for more staff and technology infrastructure upgrades. You do not have the cash reserves to fund the growth, so you consider another loan. The terms would require an additional $2,500 per month loan payment, which would put you at a monthly deficit since you only have $1,500 in cash at your current size. Banks will not touch this, and you should not put friends and family in the position to make a tough call. It is time to scale back your plans.

This is a very simplistic example, but it is meant to demonstrate the importance of seeing the big financial picture when planning growth and scaling your agency.

5. Never Lose Sight of Cash Flow   Cash is absolutely king when scaling your agency. As we discussed in the previous section, revenue and profits can be deceiving signs of financial health. At the end of the day, agencies must be cash flow positive in order to maintain stability.

For example, consider the following scenario:

- Your total average monthly operating costs are $70,000, but you forecast an additional $7,000 in expenses this month due to travel and conference costs. Plus, you make $5,000 per month in payments on a term loan. So your total money out for the month will be $82,000.

- Invoices for the month total $84,000 and are distributed on the first of the month with standard net-30 terms.

As long as all your clients pay on time, you will be cash flow positive for the month—in other words there will be more money coming in than going out. However, what happens if one or two of your clients are late on their payments? On top of that, you have to call for IT support midmonth to fix critical issues with the server and internal network. The IT costs run another $3,000, and their standard terms are due on receipt.

All of a sudden, a month that looks solid from a revenue perspective turns into a financial mess. You have to draw on cash reserves to pay your bills on time and make the end of month payroll.

So, do not assume a strong month of invoices and receivables translates into positive cash flow. Keep a pulse on money coming in and going out at all times.

6. Know Your Exit Strategy What are you building for? Succession? Acquisition? If so, what is your price? Agency leaders should know their end game. How is it possible to define your agency's purpose, and build a culture of passionately loyal employees, if no one knows where you are going? Plus, the answer to this question dictates the decisions you make regarding funding and growth.

AGILITY, MOBILITY, AND THE CLOUD

According to Forrester, the global cloud computing market is estimated to increase from $41 billion in 2011 to $241 billion in 2020.[2] Cloud computing, which consists of Software as a Service (SaaS), Infrastructure as a Service (IaaS), and Platform as a Service (PaaS), is revolutionizing business-technology infrastructures.

I will focus on cloud application services, or SaaS, in this chapter, but for rapidly growing agencies, I would advise consulting an IT professional about implications and opportunities in all three areas of cloud computing.

Moving to the Cloud

Cloud applications offer rapid deployment, often without professional IT support. They enable agencies to build more agile systems that are capable of adapting quickly to changing business environments. SaaS solutions tend to be more cost effective upfront and long term, and can play an important role in improving productivity and efficiency. They are designed to scale as the agency grows, while facilitating a more mobile workforce, which is imperative as the utilization of smartphones and tablet computers explodes.

Here are four key points to keep in mind as your agency evaluates opportunities to integrate cloud applications.

1. Solve Real Business Problems Look for software that brings real value to the agency and its clients. It is easy to get seduced by trendy new technologies, but do not force solutions into the agency that are not needed. You should be able to make a clear business use case for cloud applications, just as you would any investment. Consider the following questions when evaluating solutions:

- What problem will it solve?
- Will it enable us to improve efficiency, productivity, or profitability?
- Will it increase the value and results we deliver to clients?
- Will it reduce information technology costs?
- Will it create a more secure, stable, and reliable technology infrastructure? This may include server uptime, Internet speed, and data security and backup.

2. Reduce Redundancies and Avoid Feature Overload   There are solutions, such as NetSuite, which offer all-in-one software. NetSuite OpenAir, for example, is a cloud-based professional services automation software that includes project management, invoicing, project accounting, expense management, timesheets, resource management, and professional services dashboards.

These types of robust solutions may be ideal for some agencies. However, be careful to limit the redundancies across your agency's platforms, and avoid adding unnecessary expenses for features that you will never use. For example, if your agency already uses 37Signals' Basecamp for project management, TimeFox for time tracking, and Quickbooks Online for accounting and invoicing, then you are probably not in the market for a feature-rich platform that does it all.

I tend to look for solutions that excel in specialized areas. This means that our infrastructure consists of a collection of disconnected cloud platforms, which certainly presents management challenges, but the benefits we gain outweigh the inconveniences.

3. Have an Integration Plan   New cloud applications require sound integration plans to bring the desired benefits to your agency. Consider how the software will integrate with existing solutions, how you will encourage adoption by targeted users, and how you will monitor usage. You also want to know from the start how you will determine if the solution was a successful investment.

4. Know the Risks and Challenges   Cloud applications are not perfect. There are a number of inherent risks and challenges, whether you build your infrastructure through a few more robust solutions, or rely on a diverse collection of specialized providers. Let's consider some of the more common issues:

- **No central dashboard:** Although there may be ways to customize program integrations, most solutions do not talk to each other. In other words, the data and activities in each platform are isolated, which creates inefficiencies in tracking and reporting information. In some cases, this may even create the need for the manual entry of duplicate content. For example, TimeFox does not integrate with Quickbooks Online, which means we have to manually enter timesheet data into a separate program in order to create invoices.

- **Inefficient user management:** Without a single management portal, managers must develop their own systems for controlling user permissions and access across all platforms. For example, if a new employee joins the agency, a manager may have to update access across more than a half-dozen applications.

- **Outgrowing solutions:** As your agency continues to expand, there may come a time when you outgrow the cloud solutions on which you have built your business. This is why it is so important to evaluate your growth trends and timeline when building your infrastructure. If there is a chance you will require a larger solution down the road, consider issues, such as data portability, now.

- **Changes out of your control:** There is risk associated with every cloud company, no matter how stable they are. Factors such as service outages, mergers and acquisitions, and product updates can all directly affect your agency. The key is to mitigate your risk as much as possible by doing your homework and selecting trusted providers. Read the service level agreements closely, and ensure you have the ability to access and extract your data should you choose to change providers.

- **Monitoring and security:** With the proliferation of mobile devices in the workplace, unauthorized access, and lost and stolen devices, can be a cause for concern. Again, the key here is to take precautions and educate your employees.

Chapter Highlights

- Model agencies make calculated investments in hardware, software, staffing, partnerships, advisors, and office space designed to support their foreseeable future needs, while maintaining the highest levels of service quality, efficiency, and productivity today.

(continued)

(continued)

- Infrastructure planning should account for current and short-term needs, with contingencies for midterm possibilities.

- Always test innovative solutions from emerging technology companies, but turn to proven organizations when it comes time to make major infrastructure decisions.

- Look for technology partners with track records of performance, transparency, stability, continuous innovation, and exceptional customer/community support.

- Marketing agencies are bound by the limitations of human resources.

- Make it a priority to connect with and engage an advisory board for your agency.

- In order to secure debt and/or equity funding, you must prove you can run a profitable business that is capable of servicing its debt and providing a return on investment to its shareholders.

- Whether the financing is structured as a loan, a line of credit, or a convertible note, friends and family are usually the most captive audience for entrepreneurs, and they are often most flexible on terms.

- Cloud applications enable agencies to build more agile systems that are capable of adapting quickly to changing business environments.

- Make a clear business use case for cloud applications, just as you would any investment.

- New cloud applications require sound integration plans to bring the desired benefits to your agency.

chapter 5

Devise an Inbound Marketing GamePlan

Doing is the key to differentiation.

THE SHIFT TO INBOUND MARKETING

Inbound marketing focuses on getting found by customers. People are tuning out traditional, interruption-based marketing methods, and choosing when and where to interact with brands. This basic evolution of consumer behavior, which we have come to call selective consumption, impacts agencies in the same ways it affects your clients.

Model agencies are expanding their capabilities to meet growing demand for inbound marketing services, as well as using inbound marketing strategies to build their own brands.

Inbound marketing has given agencies the power to differentiate by doing. Agencies are using blogs, social networks, online video, e-mail marketing, webinars, podcasts, and ebooks to connect with prospects and clients in more meaningful and effective ways. They are creating value, while demonstrating their expertise and growing their businesses.

The marketing world is full of thinkers, talkers, and self-proclaimed gurus, but after awhile they all start to sound the same. What we need are more doers—agencies and professionals that drive change by practicing what they preach. The market is moving fast, and growth opportunities are everywhere.

This chapter is about using inbound marketing to define and differentiate your agency and brand. We walk through practical steps to generate more leads and build greater loyalty. Then, in Chapter 6, we focus on how to control your sales funnel, and turn leads and loyalty into revenue.

The Universal Goals: Leads and Loyalty

Inbound marketing gives agencies the ability to boost search engine rankings, generate inbound links, and drive website traffic, which are proven lead generators. In addition, inbound marketing strengthens your brand and enhances your thought-leadership positioning, which can have a much greater impact on your long-term growth, stability, and success.

The most powerful and profitable inbound marketing campaigns will use content and community to build loyalty, resulting in:

- **Higher retention rates:** Less churn in your client portfolio means a more stable and reliable recurring revenue base.
- **Greater profit margins:** Long-term client relationships lead to improved efficiency, which translates into higher profits.
- **Goodwill benefits:** Strong relationships lead to more opportunities and greater creative freedom.

ORIGINS OF THE INBOUND MARKETING GAMEPLAN

I originally developed the Inbound Marketing GamePlan in early 2008 as a service chart used in PR 20/20 business-development proposals. The goal was to offer prospects an easy-to-understand visual that outlined proposed services for a 12-month campaign, broken out by quarters. However, over time, we realized the concept was too tactical in nature, and our approach was much too focused on lead generation. It was a step in the right direction, but we needed to evolve our thinking.

In late 2009, we set out to better align our core services with current and future market demand. Based on lessons learned and data gathered supporting dozens of client inbound marketing campaigns, we were able to see trends emerging, both in terms of needs and goals, and the strategies and activities that were most effective in generating leads and building loyalty.

We saw an opportunity to redefine the Inbound Marketing GamePlan as a strategic process. Today, the GamePlan follows a standard eight-step approach that concentrates on shifting budgets and resources to more effective and measurable inbound marketing strategies.

- **Step 1:** Clearly define and differentiate your brand.
- **Step 2:** Design and deploy a content-driven website.
- **Step 3:** Go beyond prospects, and consider the impact of your agency's marketing efforts on all audiences.
- **Step 4:** Establish measurable and meaningful campaign objectives designed to achieve the primary goals of leads and loyalty.
- **Step 5:** Build an integrated campaign fueled by the four core inbound marketing strategies: search marketing, social media, content marketing, and PR. The success of each strategy creates momentum that drives your agency forward.
- **Step 6:** Establish dynamic budgets that can be easily shifted based on campaign performance and analytics.
- **Step 7:** Define campaign timelines with milestones, tasks, and responsibilities.
- **Step 8:** Measure everything, and be willing to adapt and evolve.

Why a Football Field?

More than anything, we needed a simple visual (see Figure 5.1) that represented all facets of an inbound marketing program. There were too many elements for a Venn diagram, and football is the perfect metaphor for an inbound marketing campaign:

- **The stadium and the field:** The stadium is your website and online communities—the places that you will draw audiences to—and the field is your brand, upon which your agency and marketing campaigns are built.
- **Quarters:** The game—technologies, strategies, and innovations—is changing so rapidly that your campaigns should be planned and updated in real time, with in-depth quarterly reviews. Agencies with static strategies struggle to compete with more agile firms.
- **Personnel:** Consider the impact of the draft and free agency on a professional football team. Because so much of inbound marketing is driven by content and relationships, the selection and retention of top personnel—A players—has never been more essential.

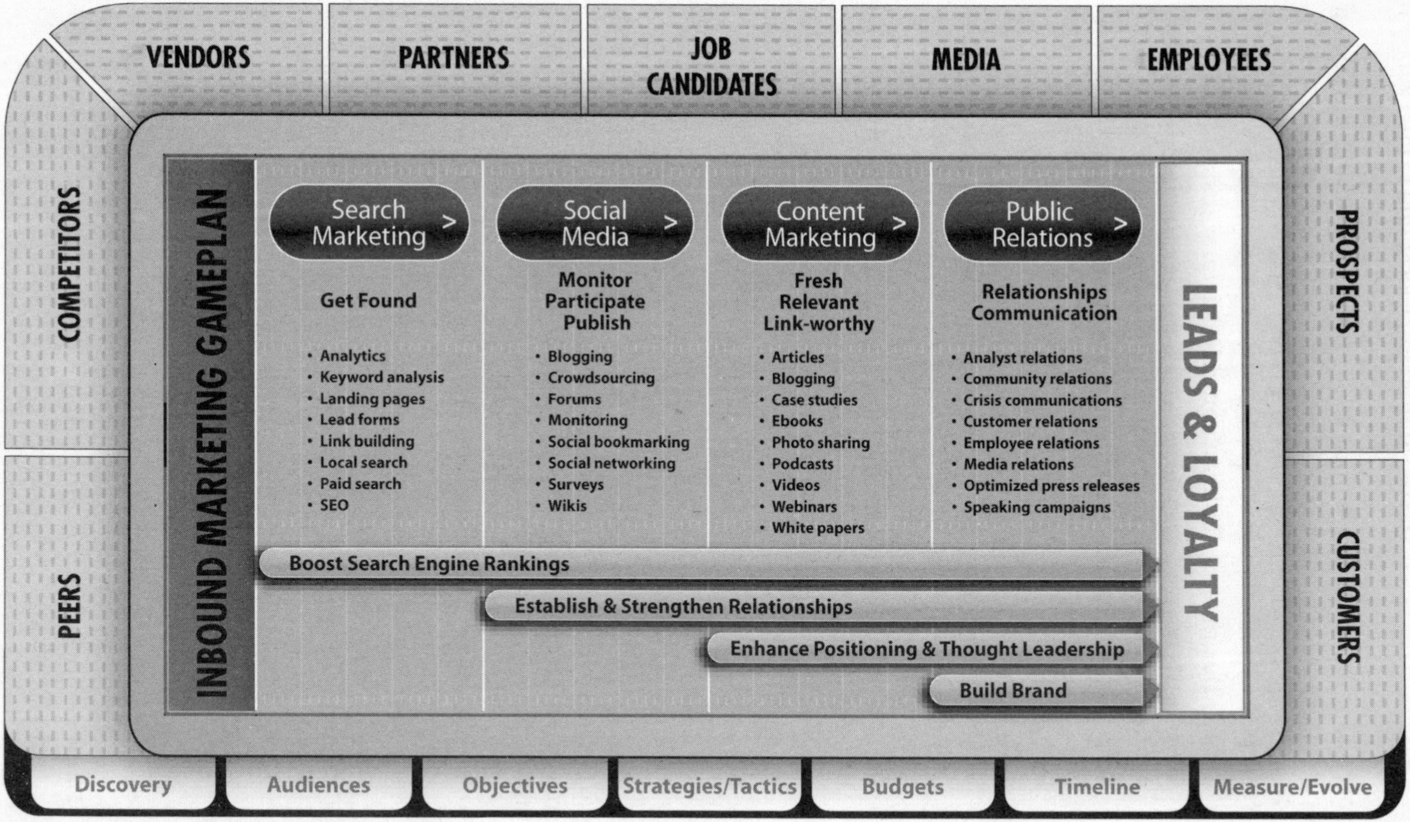

Figure 5.1 The Inbound Marketing GamePlan

- **Teamwork:** Inbound marketing requires a highly coordinated effort and calls on a diverse skill set, including: strategy, copywriting, design, data analysis, programming, messaging, promotion, and relationship building.

- **Commitment:** Inbound marketing success does not happen overnight. It requires practice and patience. You need to build reach and strong relationships through social networking and by consistently publishing valuable content.

- **Passion:** You have to want it more than the other team. It is that simple. If you do not, it will show in your services and communications.

- **Goals:** The end zone was the most obvious reason for the field. Every organization must generate leads and build loyalty to thrive. So, we started in the left end zone with the GamePlan, and then built the objectives and strategies from left to right, driving toward these goals.

- **Objectives:** You must measure progress, and adapt based on performance and market changes.

- **Strategy:** In football, you have offense, defense, and special teams. None of them on their own win the game. The same is true for inbound marketing: Brand, web, search, content, social media, and PR must work in sync to be successful.

THE FOUNDATION: BRAND AND WEBSITE

Every Inbound Marketing GamePlan begins with brand and website. These are the two critical building blocks for marketing agencies, and their clients.

Brand Marketing: Define and Differentiate

Every agency must define and differentiate itself. Share your story through your website, content, social media activity, and PR, but remember that your brand is defined by experiences and perceptions. Start by answering these questions to define your brand:

- Who are we, in 160 characters or less, and without meaningless jargon?
- What are the three greatest strengths/weaknesses of our brand?
- What are our greatest opportunities for growth?

- What keywords would people search to find our agency/services?
- Who are our buyer personas?
- What makes us different?
- How do we express that differentiation in words, images, and actions?
- What is our sustainable competitive advantage?
- What value—expertise, resources, guidance, and tools—can we bring to our audiences?
- What are we doing to innovate and move the industry forward?
- What problems and pain points do we solve?
- What makes clients buy from us the first time (acquisition)? What keeps them coming back (retention)?

When an agency begins, it inherently takes on the persona of its founder. However, as the agency grows, it becomes essential to take a more strategic approach to how you present your agency online and offline.

The key is to give your agency brand personality. You want clients, prospects, and other audiences to connect with your organization on a more meaningful level. You want to build trust and create positive perceptions about the agency and its people.

Here are some of the ways you can convey the unique attributes of your agency brand:

- Be consistent in how you define the agency across social networks, your website, internal documents, and new business proposals. Also, consider how your employees define the agency on their social profiles and when asked in person.
- Use your agency Facebook page to share photos and unique content. For example, PR 20/20 has a public quote board on the discussions tab of our page (www.Facebook.com/PR2020). This is where we post some of the quirky things our team says, giving us the chance to show a lighter side to which people can relate.
- Integrate video of your team into your agency website. Consider whiteboard sessions, interviews, case studies, and weekly podcasts as ways to demonstrate your expertise. Feature your team's personalities and better engage audiences.
- Hire professionals with shared values, and give them the freedom to build personal brands that complement and augment the agency brand.

The Power of Personal Brands As we have discussed, great agencies are built on the strength of great talent. Now, more than ever, the individuals within an agency have the opportunity to build powerful personas that drive agency growth.

Every agency professional has a story. We are all defined by our actions, beliefs, experiences, perceptions, and choices. We each maintain a unique personal brand that is defined by the sum of people's experiences with us and perceptions about us. However, we are our own gatekeepers. Thus, our brand varies from person-to-person based on how much of our story we choose to share.

We live in an online world dominated by content and community. And whether we like it or not, social media has made personal branding a 24/7 experience for many of us. The mass-market adoption of social networking has forever changed the way that our stories are told and shared. We publish pictures, articles, opinions, and updates that each tells a small piece of our story:

- What is important to us.
- What we value.
- Where we are going.
- What we are doing.
- Who we are with.
- What we buy.
- What we think.
- What we are passionate about.

Though many of us may not realize it, everything we do and say is crafting our personal brands, and either helping or hurting the agency brand. So, whereas taking the approach of not caring what other people think works for some personalities and career paths, most agency professionals will need to take a more thoughtful approach to their personal brand.

What is your story? What defines you? Would your definition of your personal brand closely match others? Here are 10 personal-branding questions to ask yourself and to consider when assessing and developing your personal brand and helping your employees to define theirs:

1. What three adjectives would people use to describe you?
2. What makes you unique?
3. What life experiences have altered your views and actions?

4. What motivates and inspires you?

5. What are you passionate about?

6. How do you balance your personal and professional lives?

7. Do your friends and family have different perceptions about you than your professional peers?

8. Do you see challenges in life as obstacles or opportunities?

9. Are you stubborn and closed-minded? Or, do you view each experience as a chance to grow and expand your knowledge?

10. Do you take responsibility for your own success or failure?

Answers to these questions help to define who you are. How much of your story you choose to share and the manner in which you share it, play large roles in defining your personal brand.

Personal Branding Snapshot—The Case of Matt Cutts Google is valued at more than $150 billion dollars. It controls approximately 65 percent of the U.S. search market,[1] and its tightly guarded algorithm determines the fate of millions of businesses online.

But Google has a complex and nagging problem—webspam—that challenges the integrity of its search results, and is creating reputation concerns for a brand that once could do no wrong.

In the middle of the battle for search supremacy is a man who strikes fear into the hearts of black-hat SEO pros, web spammers, and content farmers around the globe—Matt Cutts (@mattcutts).

He is leading the engineering charge to fix search-quality issues caused by webspam. However, equally important is his expanding role in elevating the public perception of Google and its search results through his personal brand.

By all accounts, Cutts is a brilliant engineer and one of the most respected minds in the search industry. However, his personal brand is becoming one of Google's most valued assets. Consider the following:

- Cutts has more than 131,000 Twitter followers, and is actively engaged with the community.

- He regularly appears at industry events on behalf of Google.

- His Gadgets, Google & SEO blog (www.MattCutts.com/blog) has an Alexa rank of approximately 4,100.

- The Google Webmaster Help YouTube Channel, which features Cutts answering user questions, has 34,000-plus subscribers and more than 3.9 million channel views.

- He is frequently featured in mainstream and online media channels. Run a Google News search for *Matt Cutts* and you will find hundreds of articles and blog posts quoting Cutts on the issues most important to Google, such as competition, search quality, content farms, and link spamming.

Here is a snapshot of what marketing agency professionals can learn from how Cutts manages and builds his personal brand:

- Maintains a strong personal brand that aligns with the corporate brand and gives it an authentic human voice.
- Creates tremendous value online through multimedia content, including blog posts and videos, and presents information with a high degree of transparency. This positions him as a thought leader and industry expert.
- Uses social media to reach, influence, and engage with key audiences.
- Serves as a trusted resource to journalists and bloggers, and builds relationships with influentials online and offline.

A hybrid agency is defined by the collective strength of its employees' personal brands. Your job as an agency leader is to clearly establish the agency brand, and then give your team the freedom and support to build and evolve theirs.

Website Development: Design, Connect, and Grow

Your website is a lead-generation and multimedia content publishing tool. It gives your agency the ability to build a strong brand online, create value, connect with audiences, and generate leads.

When developing or re-designing your website, do not overlook the importance of strong website copywriting that is optimized for search engine rankings and visitors. Effective copywriting conveys key brand messages, stresses features and benefits, and drives visitors to a desired action, such as a call, contact form, or content download.

Once your website design and copywriting are complete, there are significant opportunities to build a more powerful site through SEO, blogging, social media participation, content marketing, PR, calls to action, and landing pages.

Treat your agency website with the same care and attention that you do your clients' websites. Continually analyze, track, and monitor its success through inbound links, traffic, referrers, and website visits by keywords, among other metrics.

AUDIENCES: SEGMENT AND PRIORITIZE

Inbound marketing is primarily talked about for its lead-generating potential, but it can do so much more for your agency. For example, consider its brand loyalty and retention attributes with existing clients. Or, how about its ability to help recruit and retain employees, connect with mainstream and social media, influence competitors, and engage with peers?

When building your strategy, be sure to think beyond prospects, and design a GamePlan to reach and influence all audiences relevant to your business. Let's take a look at how inbound marketing can influence your agency's key audiences:

- **Peers:** The social web has made it common practice to connect and share with your professional peers like never before. In many cases, your peers, often from competing agencies, are the ones sharing and linking to the content you publish.

    Agencies and professionals that focus on collaboration over competition will have greater opportunities to thrive in the emerging marketing agency ecosystem. Seek opportunities to engage with and support your industry peers through Twitter, Facebook, Google+, and LinkedIn.

- **Competitors:** The race for search-engine rankings and influence has made professionals more open, and online tools have given marketers greater access to competitive intelligence. As a result, it is far easier for competitors to research and evaluate one another's strategies, strengths, and weaknesses.

    At the same time, savvy agencies can use inbound marketing tools—blogs, videos, social networks—to influence their competition's thoughts and actions. Think of it in terms of marketing warfare. Although it is good to support your peers, remember that your competition is reading and watching. Be strategic in your thoughts and actions.

- **Vendors:** Your vendor network is essential to your organization's success. Build more valuable vendor relationships by engaging them in your inbound marketing campaign. Share guest blog posts, exchange links, and help to promote their capabilities and expertise.

- **Partners:** Business partners share risk, and rely on one another to deliver results and achieve a common goal. Partners are essential to success in the more open and collaborative agency ecosystem.

Inbound marketing has made identifying and evaluating potential partners more efficient. However, remember that the actions of your partners directly affect your brand, so have a system in place to continually evaluate the strength and profitability of each relationship. Be sure to subscribe to your partners' blogs and connect with their leaders in social networks. In addition, look for opportunities to create content that features your partners.

- **Job candidates:** Use content publishing and involvement in online communities to tell your brand's story and attract social-media-savvy professionals.

    Understand how job candidates communicate online, where they congregate, and what keywords they search, and then use that information to adapt your recruiting strategy. Also, screen job candidates through their public profiles and online activities before you even grant an interview. Start with name searches on Google, Facebook, LinkedIn, and Twitter.

- **Media:** Use inbound marketing to connect with reporters online, learn their interests, understand their writing styles, and note their preferred means of communication. PR firms regularly do this to build more effective media relations programs, but every agency should consider ways to proactively build deeper connections with media contacts.

- **Employees:** Every employee maintains a personal brand that can directly affect the strength of your organization's brand. Use inbound marketing to increase employee retention and loyalty by supporting your employees' social media activities, and encouraging them to contribute to the development and management of your agency's content and brand online.

    Employees, especially younger generations, are active in social media with or without your agency's support. View social media as an opportunity, not an obstacle. Establish social media policies, encourage professional behavior, and embrace their involvement.

Establishing Your Agency Social Media Policy

When defining your agency's social media policy, start by stating the goal of the policy, and how it integrates with human-resources policies that already exist.

(continued)

(*continued*)

Then, lay out 10 to 15 guidelines for employees to follow in their online behavior. A best practice is to keep the tone positive by focusing on what is appropriate rather than what is not. Specific topics to cover may include:

- Authentic representation of brand and self: The importance of using real names and the lack of true anonymity on the web.

- Disclosure, confidentiality, and privacy issues, such as guidelines for sharing company information with the public; who has the authority to comment on behalf of the company; and when it is necessary to disclose affiliations with the company and/or clients.

- The purpose for online communications and how you will bring value to the community.

- Usage and productivity during business hours.

- Taking ownership of your words and actions, and respecting copyrights.

- How to address potential challenges before they occur, such as friending colleagues, clients, superiors, and subordinates.

Also, address plans for monitoring and enforcement, such as who is responsible for monitoring employees' online behavior and what this entails. Clearly state the ramifications of misuse and how policies will be upheld.

- **Prospects:** The most obvious and talked about inbound marketing audience, prospects, are actively seeking services and information online. Get found by prospects and keep your pipeline full by regularly publishing relevant content, and actively participating in social media to extend your reach and influence.

- **Clients:** Existing clients are your most profitable and important relationships. Building loyalty among this audience should be a primary goal of every inbound marketing campaign.

    Loyalty is driven by results, relationships, and communications. Inbound marketing gives you the power to dramatically increase the strength of all three. Connect with your clients in more personal and meaningful ways through social networks, and publish free content designed to expand their knowledge and strengthen your position as a thought leader and partner.

OBJECTIVES: SET YOUR SUCCESS FACTORS

Lead generation and loyalty building are the two primary goals of every marketing campaign, for both clients and agencies. We have consistently found that campaigns that focus inbound marketing strategies on achieving the GamePlan's four core objectives have the greatest potential to generate leads and build loyalty.

Let's take a look at each objective and introduce sample success factors that you may consider benchmarking and measuring to continually evaluate and evolve your campaign.

1. Boost Search Engine Rankings

Search engine results are rapidly evolving to be more personalized based on factors such as geography, browsing history, and social graphs. Although top-10 rankings are still relevant, it is far more important to monitor actual organic (nonpaid) traffic. Focus on:

- Lead-producing keywords.
- Sale-converting keywords.
- Traffic-producing keywords.

SEO Tip

Although your entire keyword universe may include thousands of phrases, most agencies should concentrate marketing efforts on the 30 to 50 most relevant keyword phrases.

---

2. Establish and Strengthen Relationships

Relationships can be difficult to measure, but the following metrics can be used to show that you are expanding your reach and building deeper connections online and offline:

- Blog comments.
- Engagement.

- Followers, friends, and likes.
- Referrals and recommendations.

Measurement Tip

Do not confuse reach with influence. Building followers and friends is meaningless without engagement and action. Benchmark and measure the metrics that will have the greatest impact on your agency's ability to generate leads and build loyalty.

---

3. *Enhance Positioning as a Thought Leader, Innovator, and Industry Expert*

Thought leadership is the result of doing. Get active, and create value through content and social participation. You can gauge your progress and success using the following:

- Blog subscribers.
- Content downloads.
- Guest-blogging opportunities.
- Inbound links.
- Inbound media inquiries.
- LinkedIn recommendations.
- Social bookmarks.
- Speaking opportunities.
- Webinar registrants.

Influencer Tip

Blogging and authentic social media participation are essential to build and enhance thought leadership, and position yourself and your agency as innovators and experts.

---

4. *Build Brand Awareness, Comprehension, and Preference*

Brand awareness means your audience recognizes the agency name, comprehension indicates that they understand who you are and what you do, and preference shows they would pick or refer your agency over the competition. Your agency needs to achieve all three to succeed. Measure your success with:

- Employee and client retention rates.
- Inbound job candidates.
- Lead volume.
- Media placements.
- Recurring revenue.
- Referrals.
- Website traffic.

Branding Tip

Third-party endorsements of your brand are more important than ever. Focus your content marketing and PR strategies on reputation, relationships, and brand building.

STRATEGIES AND TACTICS: TAKE AN INTEGRATED APPROACH

Each objective is supported by its corresponding inbound marketing strategy, as shown in the GamePlan (Figure 5.1). The GamePlan is intended to move from left to right, building strength and momentum as your agency activates each phase.

Once you have defined and differentiated your brand, and built a powerful, content-driven website, the next step is to strategize and manage an integrated campaign fueled by the four core inbound marketing strategies of search marketing, social media, content marketing, and PR.

Search Marketing: Get Found

Search marketing refers to the paid and organic activities, including SEO, that help boost your website's search-engine ranking, drive visitors, and generate leads. In short, it helps your agency get found online when people are searching for related services and information.

Agencies have the ability to reach and influence audiences directly at the exact moment they are searching online. In essence, they are granting you permission to market to them, but you have to be there and provide value.

There are no shortcuts in search marketing. Although traditional SEO tactics, such as on-page optimization, are still essential, concentrate your efforts on generating inbound links, traffic, and leads through remarkable content and social media participation.

Social Media: Monitor, Participate, and Publish

Social media is about listening, learning, building relationships, and bringing value to the communities relevant to your agency. It is a channel for engagement and sharing, not selling. You must make a commitment to connect with your audiences—clients, prospects, peers, media, bloggers, and partners—in more authentic and personal ways.

When defining your social media strategy, consider the agency brand and your team's personal brands. You want them to complement each other, without becoming redundant.

For example, if you have a 10-person agency, and every time a new agency blog post is published all 10 employees share the same tweet at the same time, then you are missing an opportunity to effectively spread your content. It would be more effective to mix up the tweets with varying messages, and publish them at different times throughout the day.

Your social media strategy should take all major social networks into account—Twitter, Facebook, LinkedIn, Google+, and YouTube— as well as niche communities that are relevant to your agency.

Thought Leadership through LinkedIn

A great way to establish your agency's experts as thought leaders is to create and manage a LinkedIn Group that enables you to share helpful information and engage members in discussions on topics of interest. Here are a few pointers to get started.

1. **Understand group dynamics:** Prior to diving in and creating a group, join a few groups that interest you, and actively participate in the conversations. Through this experience you will gain insight into how people interact within a group that can be drawn on later to stimulate conversations and manage users in your own.

2. **Do your homework:** The key to creating a LinkedIn Group is to find a unique position that is not already

dominated by one or more powerful groups. To do this, you must first have a full understanding of existing groups in your industry and topics discussed.

3. **Select a topic:** Combine your research of existing groups with your buyer personas' interests and needs to determine the most effective topic for your group. Remember, it is essential that the group be centered on community and education, and not be used to blatantly promote your services or employees.

4. **Create your group:** Following are best practices for building your group:

   ○ Select a title and description that clearly explains what the group is about and is attractive to target audiences.

   ○ Use a logo or image that is visually appealing to garner attention and so that members will add the badge to their profile page, thus exposing the group to their networks.

   ○ Choose your level of access based on the group's objectives.

5. **Prepopulate with content:** Set up a welcome message within your group to help new members understand what they have joined and how they can contribute. In addition, add some interesting questions and discussion topics into the forums to drive initial participation.

   Before actively promoting the group, encourage those within your network to join and participate in these conversations. This will guarantee that new users do not land on an inactive discussion.

Content Marketing: Fresh, Relevant, and Linkworthy

Content marketing enables you to differentiate your agency, while driving acquisition (leads) and retention (loyalty). It requires that you understand your audiences and continuously publish compelling, multimedia content.

Ask yourself: Who are my buyer personas? What are their needs and pain points? What value can my agency bring to the community? What problems can I solve? What can I publish that is relevant and linkworthy? Your core brand messages, vision, and values should be reflected in everything you publish, so start by looking in the mirror.

Content marketing is one element of an integrated marketing strategy. It feeds off the strength of your brand, website, search marketing, and social media strategies. Your success depends on the strength of your content team. You need business-savvy writers and an editor to guide planning and production and keep the team on track.

The Agency Blog Editor

Keeping your agency blog regularly updated with quality, buyer-persona-driven content can be a major factor in your blog's success. However, this can be challenging with busy schedules and client responsibilities.

Having multiple contributing bloggers is one solution; however, this comes with a downside of watered-down responsibility. With multiple authors, each individual blogger can more easily become complacent and expect others to take more responsibility for regularly writing and publishing new posts.

You can combat this apathy by appointing an agency blog editor. Much like the editor of a traditional media outlet, a blog editor is simply the person in charge of a blog's content. It is his or her job to ensure that blog articles are posted on a regular basis, consistent with company messaging, and that all authors are pulling their weight with regular contributions.

Here are a few of the blog editor's most important responsibilities:

- Maintain the editorial calendar.
- Keep the team on track.
- Proof all content prior to publishing.
- Ensure consistency of style, format, tone, and messaging.

Producing great business content requires a unique blend of capabilities. Your team (whether internal or outsourced) must be able to deliver content that is strategic, brand centric, buyer-persona focused, optimized for search engines, technically sound, creative, and results driven.

When building your content marketing strategy, it is important to know what your prospects and clients want to achieve, and then generate content that meets their goals. You can help them:

- Gain knowledge.
- Build confidence in their buying decisions.
- Achieve peace of mind that they are choosing the right agency.
- Increase efficiency and productivity.
- Differentiate their businesses.
- Drive growth.

Understand how your audiences consume information, and then choose the tools that speak to them. Blog posts, e-mail newsletters, and video seem to be the obvious choices for many agencies, but consider the potential of press releases, original reports, case studies, white papers, ebooks, content curation, webinars, streaming video, photos, social-network status updates, and podcasts.

Create quarterly editorial calendars that outline what content you plan to publish, including topics, authors, and deadlines. Also, consider developing abstracts to ensure each content piece is on message, relevant to your buyer personas, and connected to business goals.

Sample Blog Post Abstract

- **Topic:** How to handle negative comments about your brand online.
- **Audience/Buyer Persona:** Executives and brand managers who are nervous about social networking because of the loss of brand control.
- **Goal:** Education.
- **Abstract:** This blog post will provide actionable tips for brand managers on how to react to negative comments online—whether on review sites, personal blogs, social networks, or in response to company postings.

Public Relations: Relationships and Communications

Relationships and communications remain the foundation of PR, but they are being fostered through social networks, websites, self-published content—blogs, status updates, videos, case studies, ebooks—mobile apps, and the media (mainstream and social).

Public relations reaches and influences every audience that is relevant to your agency, and goes far beyond traditional media relations and publicity.

Public relations is the final, and essential piece to a comprehensive inbound marketing strategy. It is not about making your agency seem more remarkable than it truly is, counting clips, and generating impressions. Rather, it is about listening to your audiences, sharing your unique story, creating connections, gaining influence, and building loyalty in measurable and meaningful ways.

Use your content marketing to propel PR efforts. For example, consider the following:

- **Pitch original content to reporters and bloggers:** Include content in personalized pitches to reporters and bloggers. Use it as means to showcase thought leadership and experience in a particular subject.

  Sync your internal content editorial calendars with those of your target publications, many of which are published online. Plan ahead and write a blog post, ebook, or other related content piece on an upcoming topic, and then use that information to fuel your pitch.

- **Pursue guest articles and posts:** Many publications and blogs welcome contributions from outside writers. Using your content for article submissions and guest blogging can help expand its reach to new audiences outside of your existing network.

- **Support speaking submissions:** Securing speaking engagements is another area in which content can help. When building your speaking strategy and submitting applications, use content to showcase your credibility and value.

- **Create news:** During times when your agency does not have anything interesting or exciting going on, use content to create news. Send surveys, take polls, or review analytics data and other valuable information to create self-published research reports, ebooks, or whitepapers.

Budgets: Time and Money Investment

Inbound marketing pays for production and participation, and gives underdogs and innovators the ability to grow faster and smarter by outthinking, not outspending, the competition. The beauty for agencies when budgeting and building strategy is that much of the work can be done in-house or potentially bartered through agency partners. Thus, the greatest investment is often time, rather than money.

Agencies that understand inbound marketing will be able to prioritize activities with the greatest ROI potential. Assess the competencies of your staff in the core areas of brand marketing, website development, search marketing, social media, content marketing, and PR. Then, determine time availability of internal resources to contribute to an inbound marketing campaign.

Consider licensing fees and subscription costs for inbound marketing software and tools, such as press-release wire services, CRM, e-mail marketing, SEO, lead nurturing, and monitoring, and then define realistic investments of the time and money your agency is able to commit.

You will also want to consider the following budget factors when prioritizing activities and allocating resources:

- Strength of your current agency website and the need for design and optimization.
- Outsourcing of content creation, including copywriting and design of case studies, ebooks, blog posts, and white papers.
- Reliance on paid advertising for short-term lead generation and sales.
- Brand awareness in target markets.
- Aggressiveness of growth goals.
- Stage of business lifecycle.
- Inbound marketing competency levels and time availability of your team to contribute.
- Strength of competition.
- Commitment to vision and innovation.

Track Activities and Milestones

Although inbound marketing is all about the new rules of marketing, traditional project-management principles still apply. However, software innovations and mobile applications have made it more efficient than ever to manage to-do lists and track milestones.

Although your agency's campaign timeline will vary based on objectives, strategies, personnel, and budgets, it is essential to have a solid project-management system to keep your team on target. As highlighted in Chapter 4, we use 37Signals' Basecamp for agency and client project management.

Consider an online project-management solution that enables you to edit and review campaign activities and timelines anywhere with an Internet connection, including mobile phones.

Measure and Evolve: Use Analytics to Adapt

Focus on meaningful metrics, monitored and evaluated in real time, that enable your agency to constantly adapt and evolve. As a result, you will experience increased efficiency, improved ROI, more leads, and higher levels of loyalty.

Start with the basics to ensure you have access to the data that will drive your decision-making and strategies:

- Install website analytics to enable real-time tracking of traffic, referrers, pageviews, and keywords.
- Build unique landing pages that enable you to track views and conversion rates for content downloads, event registrations, contact requests, and other calls to action. Adjust your campaign strategies based on conversion rates.
- Track marketing events and milestones, and monitor how they correlate to spikes in website traffic, inbound links, leads, and sales.
- Assign a team member to monitor website analytics and social-media activity daily. Review and update your campaign strategy monthly.

DOES INBOUND MARKETING REALLY WORK FOR AGENCIES?

I had my first conversation with Dan Tyre (@dantyre) of HubSpot in September 2007, shortly after Brian Halligan and Dharmesh Shah founded the upstart software company. Tyre talked to me at length about search rankings, blogging, lead intelligence, website grades, inbound links, and content.

I have to admit that most of it was new to a marketing guy who had spent his career focused on PR, strategy, branding, and communications. However, despite my uncertainty, I saw a tremendous opportunity to evolve our agency, and our industry.

It took two more calls with Tyre before we signed on with HubSpot, plus another 10 months, and countless conversations with Halligan,

Shah, Tyre, and Peter Caputa (@pc4media), before we fully committed and began our transformation into an inbound marketing agency.

The Results

We have worked with dozens of clients to build inbound marketing campaigns. Regardless of the industry—financial, insurance, technology, retail, professional services, software, sports, consumer products, and real estate—we have seen consistent success for organizations committed to inbound marketing.

Although we cannot share their analytics, I believe so strongly in the value of inbound marketing, and its importance to marketing agencies, that I figured what better way to prove it than to share our own results.

So, starting in April 2008, when we fully activated inbound marketing for our own agency development, here is what has happened:

- Our website grade (via www.WebsiteGrader.com) has gone from 57 to 98. A website grade of 98/100 means that, of the more than 3.5 million websites previously evaluated, its algorithm calculated that our site scores higher than 98 percent of them in terms of its marketing effectiveness. The algorithm uses a proprietary blend of more than 50 variables, including search-engine data, website structure, approximate traffic, and site performance.

- We have seen dramatic increases in website traffic, driven almost exclusively by content marketing, search marketing, and social media participation. Our average visits have gone from less than 1,000 to more than 8,000 per month.

- Our blog has seen an increase in subscribers of more than 1,400 percent.

- Inbound links have gone from less than 100 to more than 12,000, whereas indexed pages improved from less than 100 to more than 900.

More importantly, our revenue growth has consistently outpaced industry norms, with the vast majority of our growth coming from inbound leads originating from our website, social networks, and referrals. In short, inbound marketing works.

The social web and inbound marketing have leveled the playing field. Do not be afraid to completely evolve what you have spent years building. Listen to the markets, adapt to demand, and move where others are not willing or able to go.

Chapter Highlights

- Inbound marketing has given agencies the power to differentiate by doing. They are creating value, while demonstrating their expertise and growing their businesses.

- We need more doers—agencies and professionals that drive change by practicing what they preach.

- An effective Inbound Marketing GamePlan can lead to higher retention rates, greater profit margins, and goodwill.

- A hybrid agency is defined by the collective strength of its employees' personal brands. Your job as an agency leader is to clearly establish the agency brand, and then give your team the freedom and support to build and evolve theirs.

- When building your marketing strategy, be sure to think beyond prospects, and design a GamePlan to reach and influence all audiences relevant to your business.

- Differentiate your brand and build a powerful, lead-generating website.

- Agencies and professionals that focus on collaboration over competition will have greater opportunities to thrive in the emerging marketing agency ecosystem.

- Lead generation and loyalty building are the two primary goals of every marketing campaign, for both clients and agencies.

- Strategize and manage integrated campaigns fueled by the four core inbound marketing strategies of search marketing, social media, content marketing, and PR.

- Use search marketing to get found when audiences are searching for knowledge and services.

- Social media is about listening, learning, building relationships, and bringing value to the communities relevant to your agency.

- Your core brand messages, vision, and values should be reflected in everything you publish.

- The blog editor ensures that articles are posted on a regular basis, consistent with company messaging, and that all authors are pulling their weight with regular contributions.

- When budgeting for an agency inbound marketing campaign, the greatest investment is often time, rather than money.
- Look beyond traditional wisdom and conventional solutions.

chapter 6

Control the Sales Funnel

Everything is sales.

AGENCY SALES SYSTEM ESSENTIALS

In its most basic form, a sales funnel consists of leads, prospects, and customers. Agencies need to fill the funnel at the top, nurture in the middle, and convert at the end. (See Figure 6.1.)

Every agency, no matter its size, can benefit from having a formal system in place to manage its new business development efforts. However, as we discussed in earlier chapters, growth in model agencies is driven by the need to attract and retain top talent. So it is important that agencies work to find balance when building their sales systems and plans.

If you grow too quickly, without the proper infrastructure and personnel in place, you run the risk of failing to deliver on promises to clients, stretching account teams too thin, and inflicting irreparable damage to your brand. Meanwhile, if you struggle to maintain a strong pipeline of qualified leads, you may face difficult challenges that can lead to cash flow crunches, cutbacks, and talent turnover.

The key is to concentrate on creating a sales system that meets your current needs for lead generation, and is scalable with your long-term growth goals. Let's start by considering some basic questions relevant to assessing and building your agency sales system. We further explore the following topics in this chapter:

- **What are our top lead sources?** Where are your leads coming from now? This may include referrals, service marketplaces, website contact forms, downloadable content, social media,

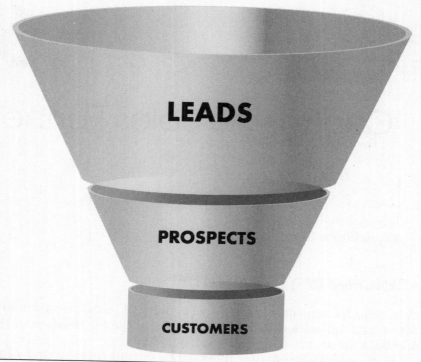

Figure 6.1 The Basic Sales Funnel Consisting of Leads, Prospects, and Customers

organic search, networking events, paid advertising, and more. Your agency's Inbound Marketing GamePlan should be focused on activities proven to generate the highest quality leads.

- **How many leads do we generate per month?** Know your current lead flow. Based on your conversion rate, are you generating enough leads to sustain growth? Agency leaders, even if they are not responsible for business development, should have 24/7 access to lead volume and opportunities in order to effectively forecast workflow, staffing needs, and revenue.

- **What percentage of those are quality leads?** Qualified leads, also known as prospects, have appropriate budgets, authority to make purchasing decisions, and the desire to work with your agency. Unqualified leads, sometimes referred to as suspects, are nothing more than a distraction, pulling valuable agency resources away from more productive activities. If the majority of your leads are low quality, then you may need to revisit your lead sources and how your agency is positioning itself.

- **How do we rank and prioritize leads?** As your lead flow increases, it becomes important to have standard methods to rank or grade your leads. These methods ensure prompt follow-up with high-priority individuals and reduce time spent on less desirable ones. If you use sophisticated sales software, lead scoring may be a built-in feature. Otherwise you can develop your own formula based on factors such as referring sources, industry, size, and service needs.

- **How do we track their progress through the funnel?** CRM systems have made it efficient to track and report on leads as they advance through the funnel. Larger agencies with significant lead flow (and revenue) may rely on higher-end platforms such as Salesforce and SugarCRM, whereas others are able to customize simpler solutions such as Highrise, which was featured in Chapter 4. The key is to have a reliable platform in which you can post activities, track opportunities/deals, and segment leads based on their position in the funnel.

- **How do we gain intelligence into our leads?** If you have the right marketing software, such as HubSpot, Marketo, Pardot, or Eloqua, once your leads have completed an online form, you have the ability to determine key data such as pages viewed, number of visits, forms completed, content downloaded, and events they have registered for on your site. You can even have e-mail alerts sent to your team to notify them when a lead returns to the agency site. All this lead intelligence can be connected to client conversions to give greater insight into the true ROI of your marketing and sales activities.

- **Who is responsible for lead generation, nurturing, and sales?** Whether you designate official titles or take a more informal approach, someone needs to own each element of the funnel. It is common for the onus to fall on the founder or leadership team in the early growth phases of an agency, but that can become an undue burden as the agency expands and other priorities creep into their daily routines.

- **Are our sales people receiving the proper training and education?** There is a rare breed of rainmakers who are seemingly born with the innate ability to sell, but most agency personnel will need formal training to excel in this area. Selling is both an art and a science that requires experience, education, and an intimate knowledge of the agency. In order to create a scalable sales system, agencies need to find and groom the right people for the job. We will review core competencies of top salespeople later in this chapter.

- **What are we doing to nurture leads?** Adding prospective clients to your agency's monthly e-mail newsletter is not lead nurturing. Instead, use original content such as blog posts, ebooks, videos, and webinars to deliver value to leads and pull them along through the funnel. Also, evaluate marketing automation solutions, which make it efficient to stay top of mind with prospects.

- **How efficient and effective are your sales efforts?** Do you know how much time it takes to convert a company from lead to client? Or how much new revenue is generated each year from your leads?

You can gain incredible insight into your business development efforts by applying the same time-tracking principles we discussed in Chapter 1. Enter every lead into your time-tracking platform, and track activities just as you do for clients. This creates a wealth of information that you can use to assess lead quality, nurturing processes, and the efficiency and performance of your sales team. It also enables you to adapt your Inbound Marketing GamePlan and make more educated marketing investments.

PEOPLE, TOOLS, AND PROCESSES

The three core elements to an effective agency sales system are people, tools, and processes. Let's examine each of these areas.

People

During my sophomore year at Ohio University, my Marketing 101 professor challenged the class to name a profession that was not sales. The room went silent for a few moments, then people started chiming in with careers such as doctor, lawyer, homebuilder, librarian, and professional athlete. He proceeded to demonstrate how, in fact, every one of them was in sales. He explained how their livelihoods depended on their ability to engage audiences and keep them coming back for more. His point was that *everything* is sales.

The same holds true in a marketing agency. You are always selling. You are selling an idea, vision, service, agency brand, personal brand, and belief that your firm is more capable and qualified than the next one.

However, in a professional service firm, sales happen at every level of the company. It is often the account executives that have the most direct client contact, and therefore, whether they are charged with it or not, they function as the agency's primary salespeople. They are the ones whose performance, behavior, and ability to build strong client relationships determine if an account stays or goes, and whether clients provide referrals and testimonials.

Plus, as we discussed in Chapter 5, model agencies are built on the strength of personal brands. The presence and engagement levels of your team in social media are an enormous driver of awareness and leads. Their blog posts are the greatest source of inbound links and organic traffic, and their networking at industry events creates valuable connections, which can lead to referrals and new business opportunities.

In short, when building your sales system, your most valued asset is your team. No one individual sales or business-development manager can possibly deliver the value and lead volume that you can create through a collective and strategic effort.

However, that does not eliminate the importance of having point people whose value and performance are measured in part based on their impact in growing the agency, specifically their ability to convert leads into clients.

Traits of Successful Salespeople   Steve W. Martin, who teaches sales strategy at the University of Southern California Marshall School of Business and is author of the critically acclaimed *Heavy Hitter* book series about enterprise sales strategies, has interviewed thousands of top business-to-business salespeople. He has also administered personality tests to more than 1,000 of them, primarily in high technology and business services.

His findings indicate that key personality traits directly influence top performers' selling style and ultimately their success. In a June 2011 Harvard Business Review blog post, "Seven Personality Traits of Top Salespeople," Martin detailed the key attributes:[1]

1. *Modesty.*
2. *Conscientiousness.*
3. *Achievement orientation.*
4. *Curiosity.*
5. *Lack of gregariousness.*
6. *Lack of discouragement.*
7. *Lack of self-consciousness.*

One of Martin's most interesting notes was that there seems to be a correlation between athletics and success as a salesperson.

Top performers with sports backgrounds "are able to handle emotional disappointments, bounce back from losses, and mentally prepare themselves for the next opportunity to compete."

Evaluating and Training Agency Salespeople   Kurlan & Associates was founded in 1985 by Dave Kurlan, a renowned expert in sales-force assessments, training, and strategic growth strategies, and author of *Baseline Selling—How to Become a Sales Superstar by Using What You Already Know about the Game of Baseball*.[2] The firm has helped companies of all sizes achieve growth, improve margins, recruit stronger salespeople, and develop high-performing sales professionals.

For the last several years, Rick Roberge (@RainMakerMaker) and Frank Belzer of Kurlan & Associates have focused on evaluating and training marketing agencies to grow their sales. Using a proprietary assessment process, Kurlan & Associates compares the skills and strengths of agency personnel to those of more than 500,000 salespeople who have previously been evaluated in the Objective Management Group Salesperson's Self Assessment system (www.Objective Management.com).

Roberge and Belzer shared some of their key findings, based on the evaluations of more than 100 marketing-agency professionals:

- None of the professionals could conduct a consultative sales process or close sales consistently.
- Less than 3 percent could adequately qualify a prospective customer.
- Thirty-nine percent were not trainable. Trainable means that a salesperson has the incentive to change. If there is no incentive to change, any training that is offered will result in a less than optimum ROI.
- Sixty-nine percent were uncomfortable dealing with competition.
- Eighty-nine percent were uncomfortable working in a straight commission environment.
- Ninety-two percent could not be counted on to hunt up new opportunities.
- One hundred percent were uncomfortable dealing with prospects that did not need their services nor want their services.
- One hundred percent did not follow a sales process. Salespeople that do not follow a process encounter and wind up accepting lots of put-offs, stalls, and excuses. A well-designed process

will raise and handle common stalls and objections before they become a barrier to closing a deal.

All in all, Kurlan & Associates' evaluations showed that, on average, agency professionals had 5 of the 23 skills that are required to sell, and on average they can expect to experience 17 of the 28 problems that may be encountered when selling.

Roberge states that there are two primary reasons that an agency salesperson does not do what needs to be done to get the business. The first is that they may not know what to do. For example, they may not know how to ask good questions or that they need to qualify prospects based on their budgets and abilities to make buying decisions. They may never have learned how to conduct a consultative sales call.

The second reason is that, although they may have taken some training or read sales books, there is something in them that is keeping them from executing as they were taught. These are the self-limiting beliefs, the hidden weaknesses, that undermine all the training and best intentions.

However, Roberge says that all these challenges can be identified with the right kind of assessment, and once identified can be understood. Then, with the proper training and guidance, you can prepare salespeople to excel and help your agency grow.

Objective Management Group assessments were developed by founder and CEO Dave Kurlan and are used by more than 8,500 companies. The assessments evaluate a potential sales candidate's strengths, skills, weaknesses, and challenges as they relate to 21 core competencies found in successful salespeople, which OMG defines as:

1. Has written goals.
2. Follows a plan to reach written goals.
3. Has positive attitude.
4. Takes responsibility.
5. Strong self-confidence.
6. Supporting record collection.
7. Controls emotions.

(continued)

(*continued*)

8. Doesn't need approval.
9. Recovers from rejection.
10. Comfortable talking about money.
11. Supportive buy cycle.
12. Consistent effective prospecting.
13. Reaches decision makers.
14. Effective listening and questioning.
15. Early bonding and rapport.
16. Uncovering actual budgets.
17. Discovering why prospects buy.
18. Qualifies proposals and quotes.
19. Gets commitments and decisions.
20. Strong desire for success.
21. Strong commitment for success.

Tools

Tech-savvy agencies that are integrating marketing and sales tools have a distinct advantage over the competition. They are able to gather and leverage lead intelligence at every stage of the funnel, and they use that information to enhance their nurturing efforts and dramatically improve conversion rates.

Following is a snapshot of essential sales system tools. You may be able to integrate multiple platforms together, or find a single solution that does it all. However, as we discussed in Chapter 4, be careful to limit the redundancies across your agency's platforms, and avoid adding unnecessary expenses for features that you will never use.

Customer-Relationship Management (CRM)   A CRM solution, such as Salesforce, SugarCRM, or Highrise, is the foundation of a solid sales system. You input leads into the platform as they enter the funnel, and you track and report activities as they progress. Ideally, agencies use a single CRM solution for all contacts, including leads and clients. This creates a more efficient and scalable system.

Content-Management System (CMS)   Agency websites need to be built on intuitive content-management systems. A CMS gives agency personnel the ability to easily add, edit, and move web pages as needed, without the support of an outside web developer. From a sales perspective, the CMS should include the ability to create landing pages and lead forms on the fly, which can be valuable components of lead-generation efforts.

Analytics   Salespeople require advanced intelligence into their leads' online behavior. Free solutions, such as Google Analytics, are excellent for providing base-level information on site performance, but in most cases agencies should consider additional third-party solutions for in-depth lead intelligence. Again, HubSpot, Marketo, Pardot, and Eloqua are platforms that provide more granular lead details.

Lead Nurturing   Depending on your lead-nurturing needs, there is an array of SaaS solutions worth considering, from comprehensive marketing automation software, to basic e-mail marketing platforms. Look for a solution that integrates with your existing software platforms and gives you the ability to automate essential marketing and sales activities.

Processes

Prototype hybrid agencies require standard processes to achieve success. The same rules of efficiency and productivity that govern agency and account management apply to the sales system. Regardless of your size, sales processes help define responsibilities, set performance expectations, give professionals the knowledge and resources to excel, and connect actions to business goals.

Let's look at the five core areas of the sales process: lead qualification, lead management, discovery, proposal, and presentation.

Lead Qualification   Whether you use software with built-in lead scoring, or develop your own internal formula, it is important to have a standard process for ranking and prioritizing leads.

Buyer personas are the foundation of any lead scoring system. Defining and building marketing and sales strategies around buyer personas enable agencies to better target communications and content while improving lead generation and conversion.

Start by profiling your personas so that you know strong leads when you see them. Some of the key factors to consider when creating your personas and determining lead quality include the following:

- Are they project or campaign based?
- What are their budgets?
- What metrics matter most? How will they define success?
- What is the contact's title and responsibilities? Is that person the decision maker?
- What are the problems, pain points, and obstacles to success?
- What are the priority needs?
- What is the account's growth potential?
- Does the agency have experience in their industry?
- At what stage in the business lifecycle are they?
- Are they seeking primarily tactical or strategic support?
- What are their internal marketing resources and capabilities?
- Do they have realistic expectation levels?
- What are their experiences with professional service firms?
- What is the risk level associated with the account?
- What is their decision-making process?
- What is their timeline to get started?
- How strong is the lead/referral source?

Using these questions as a basis, agencies can construct clear profiles of the prototypical client, and evolve their sales strategies to meet their needs and goals.

Sample Agency Buyer Persona: Long-Term Locke

Long-Term Locke is a campaign-based client that has strong profit potential, tends to be highly stable and predictable, has needs in line with the agency's expertise, maintains realistic expectations, greatly values the agency's services, and is interested in an ongoing relationship.

Long-Term Locke tends to sign 12-month service contracts for fully integrated campaigns; however, most Locke accounts have high-growth potential beyond the approved annual budget. There are strong possibilities for add-on services in the areas of content marketing, brand marketing, sales support, and strategic planning.

A solid portfolio of Locke accounts enables the agency to more accurately predict revenue and staffing needs. In addition, entry-level professionals can usually complete 30 percent or more of the workload, which is key to agency development and profitability. The target portfolio allocation is 60–75 percent Locke accounts. Retention is essential. Locke accounts have the following attributes:

- Budget: $5,000 or more per month.
- Needs: Advanced strategic planning and consulting with a strong mix of basic/moderate-level tactical services.
- Response: Responds to educational material and practical guides. Aware of solutions offered by marketing agencies, and seeks information to aid in the decision-making process.
- Authority: Yes, the primary contact is the decision maker.
- Services: Looking for fully integrated approach to search, social, content, and PR. Shifting budgets and resources from traditional to inbound marketing.
- Industry: Commonly comes from finance, health-care, and technology industries.
- Title: Tends to be a marketing executive—CMO, marketing director/manager, communications director/manager.
- Service Level: 30/60/10 (basic/moderate/advanced)
- Internal Resources: Usually has marketing staff, but lacks internal expertise in needed areas.
- Growth Potential: Moderate.
- Expectation Levels: High.
- Success Factors: Primarily interested in media coverage, website traffic, inbound links, and leads.
- Business Stage: High-growth and mature.
- Social Technographics: Joiners and creators, although probably at the individual vs. organizational level.
- Risk Level: Low.
- Profitability: Moderate-to-high.

Lead Management   Lead management is made possible by the sales tools you have put in place, and defining systems and standards for moving leads efficiently through the funnel. Consider the following when defining your lead-management process:

- Determine the procedure for entering and updating leads in the CRM throughout the funnel, and for assigning ownership of a new lead to the appropriate sales representative.
- Integrate the lead into the agency's time-tracking solution. This makes it possible to assess the efficiency of your business development efforts.
- Apply lead scoring to prioritize opportunities.
- Define follow-up procedures, including how quickly and in what manner sales representatives must respond.
- Establish call scripts and template e-mails for efficient communications.
- Create rules for list segmentation and lead nurturing.

Discovery   Agencies have a variety of ways to gather information about leads. In addition to Internet research, savvy firms utilize technology such as online surveys and website contact forms to develop a deep understanding of their leads' needs and goals before they even conduct the first meeting.

A strategic discovery process can differentiate agencies early on if companies are assessing multiple providers. The agency that comes to the table more prepared and confident, and demonstrates a greater understanding of the lead's business, has an immediate advantage over the competition.

If your agency has access to lead-intelligence analytics, the discovery process begins as soon as a website contact form is submitted. You can immediately assess the lead's level of interest in your agency based on their online behavior, and depending on the custom fields in your lead forms, you may already know answers to key questions such as budgets, title, timeline, needs, and goals.

Also, look at services such as SurveyMonkey to conduct prospective client audits. We have had tremendous success using an online survey that has a mixture of multiple-choice and open-ended questions. It takes approximately 15 to 20 minutes to complete, but there are no required answers, so companies can skip any questions that do not seem relevant or that they are not prepared to respond to at that time.

The survey is designed to address five key areas, which are the primary factors we use to qualify leads:

1. **Foundation:** What is the strength of their existing website, brand, infrastructure, and internal marketing capabilities and capacity?
2. **Platform:** How extensive is their reach and influence among target audiences, specifically as it relates to online marketing?
3. **Expectations:** What are their priority needs and goals, and how do they align with agency services?
4. **Potential:** What is the potential for the agency to have an immediate and sustained impact on their business?
5. **GamePlan strategy:** What strategies and tactics are we going to propose based on the other four factors—foundation, platform, expectations, and potential?

Sample Lead Survey Questions

Following are example qualifying questions we use in the PR 20/20 lead survey:

- In one or two sentences, define what makes your company unique/remarkable?
- How would you rate your brand positioning in primary target markets? In essence, do audiences clearly understand your organization's products/services and value proposition?
- How would you define your growth goals for the next 12 months? Basic, moderate, or aggressive?
- How would you rate support from your leadership team for digital marketing strategies, such as social media, search marketing, and content marketing?
- What do you see as your organization's top-priority needs as they relate to engaging an agency partner? For example: ranking higher on Google, creating original content, getting buy-in from leadership for social media, generating more leads now, raising our profile, improving the website, or launching a blog.
- Approximately how much is your monthly budget for agency services?

(continued)

(continued)

- Please provide estimated numbers for the following elements: employees, active customers, average monthly lead volume, blog subscribers, Facebook page likes, Twitter followers, YouTube channel subscribers, and LinkedIn company followers.

- What are your top sources for new leads?

- Briefly describe your current lead nurturing activities. This may include automated e-mails, phone calls, free trials, online demos, and more.

- How many hours per week does your organization spend monitoring and participating in social media? This includes activity on Twitter, LinkedIn, Facebook, forums, blog reading, and commenting.

- Do you provide training and education to employees on how to effectively participate in social media?

- Do you have content creators/copywriters on staff who are responsible for, or have the ability to create online content, including: blog posts, ebooks, white papers, case studies, press releases, webinars, and e-newsletters? Provide any details to help us understand your organization's copywriting capabilities and capacity.

- What are your primary success factors to measure the effectiveness of your agency partner? In other words, how will you determine the agency's value to your business?

Proposal We will cover the proposal more in-depth later in this chapter, but strong proposals are essential to increasing conversion rates. It is best to have a standard template, which is then customized to each company's needs and goals. Every proposal should feel completely personalized to the prospect, but each should be completed as efficiently as possible by your team. The key is to give just enough details to convince them you are the right firm, without providing a wealth of free consultation they can turnaround and give to another agency to implement. It is a tricky balance.

Presentation Like proposals, presentations should be standardized, but then continually adapted based on your prospect's preferences. Some contacts want to read the proposal first, whereas others prefer to see a condensed version in PowerPoint form through Skype or GoToMeeting.

If you have gotten this far in the process, go into the meeting with the intent to close. If you did not want the business, you should not have invested the time it took to get this far. Have the mindset that you are going to leave with an agreement. Consider the following questions, and come prepared:

- Is there an agenda?
- Is it in person or virtual?
- How many people from the client's side will be in attendance?
- Are the decision makers in the room?
- Are you ready to field questions, and effectively address objections?
- Who will be in the meeting from your team? Who will be the lead presenter?
- Have you done an internal practice run?
- Have you tested all the audio and visual elements?
- What next steps are you proposing?
- How will you hook them in the open, and close them in the end?

UNDERSTANDING THE BUYING CYCLE

In order to maximize the lead-generation and nurturing process, and increase the probability of conversion, it is important to understand how organizations make marketing-services buying decisions. Let's take a look at the five standard stages of a buying cycle, and consider how agencies can tailor their marketing and sales activities based on each phase (see Figure 6.2).

Stage 1 — Awareness: The organization recognizes they have an unsatisfied need, unresolved pain point, or new marketing challenge. This realization may be due to internal stimuli, such as the CEO pointing out they are nowhere to be found on the first page of Google results; or external stimuli, such as a savvy marketing agency identifying risks and gaps in their social media presence.

Stage 2 — Search: Research begins for information that will help further define their needs, identify prospective agency partners, and make an educated buying decision. Agencies with strong

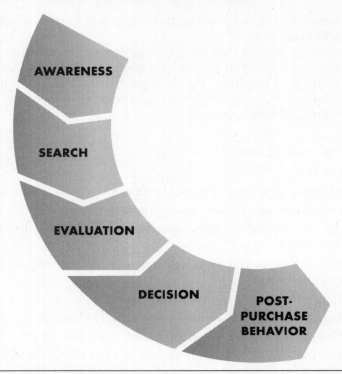

Figure 6.2 Five Stages of the Buying Cycle: Awareness, Search, Evaluation, Decision, and Postbuying Behavior

Inbound Marketing GamePlans have a distinct advantage at this stage, because prospective clients commonly turn to Internet searches and social networks to support their research efforts.

Stage 3—Evaluation: They are now entering the decision-making stage. Potential partner agencies have been selected, and are being evaluated based on criteria such as pricing, capabilities, experience, staff, proof of performance, and reputation. Agencies that have gathered the greatest intelligence on the lead, and done the best job of customizing the business development experience, rise to the top of the list.

Stage 4—Decision: The prospect has entered the final decision phase. This is commonly the time when they will ask for referrals, finalize scope, and negotiate the terms of engagement. There are still a number of factors that can cause the deal to fall through at this point, so it is important to prepare for objections and continue to instill confidence in the buyer. In some cases, this stage can drag on for months, depending on the prospect's internal processes.

Stage 5 — Postpurchase Behavior: Once the purchasing decision has been made, it is time for performance to meet expectations. There is a natural honeymoon period in which the client and agency get along great, but, as weeks and months go by, you better be delivering on your promises or relationships can quickly sour.

Anticipate postpurchase challenges and concerns as part of your process, and work to reduce the likelihood of them occurring after the sale. Continually seek opportunities to add value to your client, and never forget the importance of building strong personal relationships. Satisfied clients who feel appreciated are far more likely to stay and provide strong referrals to their friends and peers.

LEAD GENERATION

Developing a solid Inbound Marketing GamePlan is essential to lead generation, but for this chapter we will drill into some more specific strategies and tactics. Keep in mind that the most effective lead-generation campaigns are focused on creating value, not selling.

Before you initiate aggressive lead-generation efforts, it is important to address some points presented at the beginning of the chapter:

- Where are your best leads coming from now? Are there opportunities to generate more leads through these channels?
- Based on your historical (or forecasted) conversion rates and average revenue per client, how many leads do you need to generate per month to sustain and grow your agency?
- How do you identify and prioritize quality leads?

Now, let's take a look at ways your agency can fill the top of the funnel with qualified leads.

- **Pricing strategy:** Make the price value based, simple, and transparent. Turn your pricing into an asset in your sales efforts.
- **Brand positioning:** What comes to mind when someone hears your agency's name? Is your brand unique and memorable? Does it stand for something more than just marketing services? Do people feel an emotional attachment to it? These are

the types of questions you need to ask yourself when defining your brand.

Your messaging and actions should separate your agency from the competition. Create unique experiences online and offline that help you to stand out among the masses.

- **Referrals:** There is nothing quite like a great referral, especially if the referring source—peers, vendors, clients, and industry contacts—understands your brand and knows what a good lead looks like for you.

    Although it is acceptable to ask for referrals at times, the most valued leads come from contacts that believe so strongly in you and your agency that they go out of their way to send you opportunities. You can consistently earn referrals by keeping your agency in the minds of current clients and building a reputation based on proven performance, loyalty, honesty, and innovation.

- **Content marketing:** I led off Chapter 5 with the sentence, "Doing is the key to differentiation." Nowhere in marketing is it truer than in content creation. Model agencies use blog posts, ebooks, videos, podcasts, original reports, and more to continually create value for their audiences and differentiate their brands. Content marketing is the premier lead-generation strategy available to agencies today.

- **SEO:** Take the necessary steps to optimize your agency website—page titles, URLs, headers, copywriting, ALT image tags and meta descriptions—but concentrate your SEO efforts on generating inbound links and ranking for long-tail keywords, which you target through original content.

- **Personal brands:** Give your team the freedom and support to build powerful personal brands. Help them to effectively engage online, expand their connections, and bring value to their networks.

- **Service marketplaces:** Emerging online service marketplaces can be ideal sources for project work, specifically for soloists and specialists.

- **Ecosystem partners:** Develop relationships with agencies throughout the marketing services ecosystem. Look for opportunities to collaborate with prospective partners who share your philosophies and values and offer complementary services.

- **Niche markets:** There are endless niche markets for agencies that choose to focus their energy on building capabilities and expertise in specific industries and geographic territories. Consider what unique knowledge and experience your agency has that could translate into a leadership position in targeted markets.

- **Publicity:** The PR industry was built on the power of third-party endorsements. There has always been something magical about media coverage. Earning placements for your agency in online and traditional media outlets can have a tremendous effect on brand awareness, comprehension, and preference. Use your content marketing efforts and social media involvement to position yourself as a thought leader and create publicity opportunities for your agency.

- **Networking (the traditional kind):** Go meet people. Attend events for local organizations and niche industries. Look for unique venues that are not populated by competing firms. For example, if you are targeting small businesses, find opportunities to get involved with a chamber of commerce.

    Another great networking approach is to volunteer for committees of nonprofits that inspire you. You can make strong connections while contributing to causes you care about.

PROSPECTS AND LEAD NURTURING

As I mentioned earlier, there are endless variations on the sales funnel. In the Blueprint model, leads turn into prospects as they move through the funnel and are qualified as true sales opportunities. These prospects fit the agency's target buyer personas, including the classic marketing MAD-R characteristics:

- Money (M) to afford your services.
- Authority (A) to make buying decisions.
- Desire (D) for your services, and to work with your agency.
- Response (R) to your agency's marketing efforts.

Prospects are most likely in the evaluation stage of the buying cycle, and preparing to move into the decision phase. They are fully aware of their needs, have researched agency options, and are now looking for the best match. Your job is to convince them you are the right fit by alleviating concerns, anticipating objections, building their confidence in your agency, and creating as much value as possible. So how do you accomplish this?

- Connect and engage on social networks.
- Take a personal interest in their success by getting to know what motivates them in their lives and careers.
- Use automated e-mail drip campaigns to share relevant blog posts, case studies, ebooks, webinars, and other original content.
- Invite them to attend webinars and events that fit their interests and needs.
- Offer them free insight into their current marketing efforts.
- Build customized proposals that demonstrate your knowledge of them and your ability to take their marketing to the next level.

How to Handle Client-Reference Requests

It is common at this stage of the buying cycle for prospects to request client references. Although connecting prospects with satisfied clients can be a great way to give them confidence and put your agency over the top, it can become an inconvenience for your best clients. This is especially true for smaller firms, which have a limited number of clients to offer as references.

There is not a standard solution that works for every agency, so consider the perspectives of both audiences—prospect and client—when crafting your policy for references. Start by taking proactive steps to reduce the need for prospects to seek them in the first place:

- Encourage satisfied clients to share online reviews and recommendations.
- Compose client case studies that demonstrate results.
- Share your online portfolio of approved client work.
- Enhance your website with content that shares insights into your processes and methodologies, expertise, thought leadership, and in-depth profiles of the people behind your agency team.

If a prospect insists on speaking with references, I recommend only providing them if: (1) you are 100 percent convinced you want them as a client, and (2) you have confirmed they have reached the decision-making stage, and this is the final step before moving forward with the engagement.

In this scenario, do your best to communicate your desired expectations to both parties, both in the request to your client and time suggestions for the prospect. You want to convey your openness and transparency while demonstrating to the prospect that you value and respect your clients' time.

Your client-reference policy should be flexible. There will always be opportunities that present exceptions to the rule, plus there is always potential value in connecting like-minded professionals.

Do your best throughout the sales process to build confidence and trust, and keep the feelings of both the prospect and your client in mind when faced with this final step.

The Proposal

Effective proposals demonstrate that you clearly understand your prospect's needs and goals, and have the knowledge and capabilities to positively impact their business. Here are six core elements of a powerful service proposal:

1. **The snapshot:** Also known as the executive summary, this is where accounts are won. In one or two pages, tell a powerful story that conveys your understanding of their business, identifies their challenges, defines how your agency is going to solve them, and establishes the benchmarks for how you will measure success.

    Forget the boring, technical jargon. Create a narrative that engages the prospect and builds their desire to work with you. They should be able to make a buying decision based on their experience with your agency to this point in the lead-nurturing process and the snapshot. The rest of the proposal exists to provide supporting information, and define the scope of the engagement.

2. **Discovery:** Share what you learned about the prospect through preliminary research. Include data and screenshots that demonstrate your capabilities, and how they apply to the prospect's business. Here are some specifics:

    - Run an initial keyword analysis to see how their website performs in search engines.
    - Compare their website to competitor sites using Website Grader.com.
    - Evaluate their social media presence, and identify opportunities for enhanced participation and engagement online.
    - Assess their competitors' content marketing strategy, and show how your services can make them more competitive.

- ○ Identify publicity opportunities by running editorial calendar searches through Cision or other PR-management platforms.
- ○ Suggest blog post topics that demonstrate your understanding of their markets and customers.

3. **Objectives:** Connect your services to measurable and meaningful outcomes. Define preliminary marketing objectives relevant to the prospect's campaigns, which will be used to guide campaign strategy and measure performance.

   Ideally you will benchmark all relevant data at the initiation of an engagement, and then provide monthly reports throughout the life of the relationship to continually monitor progress and adapt strategy. This is the section in which you define success factors as well, including metrics such as website traffic, inbound links, organic visits, social media reach, blog subscribers, lead volume, and content downloads.

4. **Activity center:** Establish the services, pricing, and timelines for the proposed engagement. If you are selling service packages or retainers, this section will be relatively standardized, but be sure to personalize it based on your prospect's unique needs.

5. **Appendix:** Share any additional information that is relevant to the prospect. This may include agency and account team profiles, sample experience, and client testimonials.

6. **Terms of agreement:** Include the contract to seal the deal. Your prospects are marketing professionals, just like you, so avoid using legal speak, and keep it simple and transparent. Consider elements such as: pricing structure, payment terms, reporting standards, expenses, and how add-on services are billed.

Choose the Right Clients

Commit your talent and energy to clients who will value your contributions to their business. Learn to trust your instinct, and watch for red flags, such as unrealistic expectations and a lack of respect for your time and talent during the discovery process.

Model agencies never appear desperate for new business, even if they are. They are willing to walk away from opportunities when their leadership team determines it is not in the best interest of the agency to pursue the engagement. At that same time, they demonstrate patience and a willingness to fight for the right clients.

CONVERSIONS AND TRANSITIONS

The assignment and integration of account teams is key to successful client conversions. It is advised to involve the account team as early in the sales process as possible.

Prospects quickly develop a rapport with strong salespeople, and they can assume that their representative will continue to work with them should they move forward. If you have the capacity and an account manager ready to go, then simply have that professional participate in discovery and proposal meetings, and build a relationship that makes for a smooth transition.

This is the ideal arrangement, because the account manager/ lead consultant, not the salesperson, should be dictating the preliminary strategic recommendations and appropriate service package or retainer that will be featured in the proposal. In essence, once the lead has been qualified into a prospect, the account team should begin to assume ownership of the opportunity, and the salesperson takes on more of a support and administrative role.

However, this can become a challenge when you have no idea who will be on the account team. Because most top agencies are continually functioning at or near capacity, large opportunities present challenges from the perspective of account management and workflow.

For example, let's say you are a $540,000 agency, and a $5,000/ month lead has blossomed into a highly qualified opportunity. If you can close the deal, this client would represent 10 percent of your average total revenue each month, which is fairly significant. Assuming your agency is already at or above its capacity, you may need to hire in order to deliver on what you are promising in the contract. However, no prospective client wants to hear that they will be the lucky recipient of a rookie account manager or team.

So what do you do?

Adjusting for growth is a great problem to have, but, unfortunately, there is no perfect solution. However, if you have put the proper forecasting and project-management systems in place, you can quickly identify experienced team members who can step in to lead the account, while grooming their successors and transferring management over the coming months.

Remember, your most efficient and profitable growth comes from your existing client base. So commit to clients from day one, and never stop proving to them why they chose you.

Chapter Highlights

- Every agency, no matter its size, can benefit from having a formal system in place to manage its new business development efforts.

- Concentrate on creating a sales system that meets your current needs for lead generation, and is scalable with your long-term growth goals.

- Agency leaders should have 24/7 access to lead volume and opportunities in order to effectively forecast workflow, staffing needs, and revenue.

- Agencies need a reliable CRM platform in which they can post activities, track opportunities/deals, and segment leads based on their position in the funnel.

- Selling is both an art and a science, which requires experience and education, as well as an intimate knowledge of the agency.

- You are always selling. You are selling an idea, vision, service, agency brand, personal brand, and belief that your firm is more capable and qualified than the next one.

- Your account teams are your most valuable salespeople. Their performance, behavior, and ability to build strong client relationships determine if an account stays or goes and whether clients provide referrals and testimonials.

- Tech-savvy agencies are able to gather and leverage lead intelligence at every stage of the funnel and use that information to enhance their nurturing efforts and dramatically improve conversion rates.

- Defining and building marketing and sales strategies around buyer personas enables agencies to better target communications and content, while improving lead generation and conversion.

- The agency that comes to the table more prepared and confident, and demonstrates a greater understanding of the lead's business, has an immediate advantage over the competition.

- You can consistently earn referrals by keeping your agency in the minds of current clients and building a reputation based on proven performance, loyalty, honesty, and innovation.

- Content marketing is the premier lead-generation strategy available to agencies today.

- Effective proposals demonstrate that you clearly understand your prospect's needs and goals and have the knowledge and capabilities to positively impact their business.

- The prospective account manager/lead consultant, not the salesperson, should be dictating the preliminary strategic recommendations and appropriate service package or retainer that will be featured in the proposal.

chapter **7**

Commit to Clients

All clients are not created equal.

BUILD RELATIONSHIPS AND LOYALTY

The strength and stability of your agency is directly related to your ability to retain and grow accounts. Loyal clients lead to higher retention rates, greater profit margins, more predictable cash flow, and stronger referrals.

Everything laid out in the Blueprint to this point—value-based pricing, hybrid services, top talent, a scalable infrastructure, an Inbound Marketing GamePlan, and a powerful sales funnel—puts your agency in the position to build loyalty. Now, it is time to commit to your clients, deliver on the promises you have made, and make a measurable impact on their businesses.

The need to build strong client relationships must be ingrained in an agency's culture. From day one of their training, agency professionals must understand the importance of each client and the financial impact retention has on sustainability. Employees should be 100 percent focused on the happiness and success of their clients.

Create Value

Push yourself and your agency to create as much value as possible for every client. Become indispensable through your hard work, insight, consultation, services, expertise, friendship, and professionalism.

- Treat them as partners, and take a passionate approach to their success.

- Hold your team to the highest standards of performance.
- Bring innovative ideas to the table.
- Publish and share blog posts relevant to your clients' challenges and opportunities.
- Commit your account team to continually advance their knowledge of clients' businesses and industries.

Take a Personal Approach

Create deeper connections with your client contacts. Do the little things that build relationships, and take the time to show them you care about their successes, both on the individual and organizational levels.

- Know what matters to them—family, hobbies, and personal interests—and never lose sight of the fact that they are real people, too.
- Recognize milestones in their lives with personal notes and handwritten cards.
- Use your agency's customer-relationship-management (CRM) system to keep track of calls, communications, meetings, and notes.
- Connect through social networks to stay in touch with what is going on in their businesses and their personal lives.
- Make every client feel like the most important client. Never appear too busy with other clients to help them.
- Keep your leadership team connected. Agency executives should regularly be thinking about and communicating with client contacts, especially if they are not involved in the day-to-day account management.
- Seek opportunities to make your client contacts look good, and help build their careers.
- Send personal communications to clients when you have published or found content of interest to them.

Be Open and Honest Your clients should trust you, and you should trust your clients. For this to happen, you must be genuine. Tell your clients when something is not working out, and let them know when things are going really well. If you communicate openly and honestly, they will be more likely to be open and honest with you.

Listen to Their Problems, and Respond When Appropriate   If clients are unhappy about something, listen to what is bothering them (even if it is not something you caused or have control over). Then, if you can, devise a solution to fix it. Sometimes, just being there to listen is enough to calm frustrations.

Do What You Say You Will Do   Keep your promises. There is nothing worse than thinking someone is going to do something, only to be disappointed. Be someone your client can count on.

Admit When You Are Wrong, and Apologize   Face it. Eventually one person in the relationship is going to make a mistake, no matter how hard you both try not to. If it is you, own up to it. Admit you were wrong, apologize, and make it up to them. Your client will appreciate that you took responsibility for your actions.

Go Out of Your Way to Make Them Happy   Show you care in your everyday actions. Keep the little things in mind with your clients. E-mail them interesting articles, wish them a happy birthday, take them out to lunch, or introduce them to like-minded people. Go above and beyond their expectations for customer service.

Stay on the Edge

Remain at the forefront of innovation and technology. As discussed in Chapter 2, marketing agencies that are immersed in technology are able to continually increase efficiency and productivity, evolve client campaigns, and make strategic connections of seemingly un-related information.

- Share technology news, trends, and innovations through your agency social networks.
- Publish content on your website demonstrating how advances in technology are impacting the marketing industry.
- Push your account teams to continually integrate new techno-logies and ideas into client campaigns.
- Tell your clients about technologies you think would be valu-able to their businesses.

Invest in Talent

The greatest value you can bring to clients is staffing their account teams with A players. These professionals are analytical, confident, creative, detail oriented, highly motivated, and strategic—all traits that consistently translate into success for your clients.

- Hire the best.
- Provide advanced training and education that accelerates their development.
- Build reward programs that recognize team over individual success, and put a premium on retention and growth of accounts.
- Develop professionals who are committed to efficiency and productivity.

Build Connections

Extend your reach and influence in the places that matter to your agency and your clients. Be proactive in creating and nurturing connections now for you and your clients. Do not go looking for new contacts when you have something to pitch or sell.

- Attend networking events.
- Join clubs and associations.
- Participate in Twitter chats and online forums.
- Share your expertise on Q&A sites, such as Quora, Focus, and LinkedIn Answers.

Diversify Your Relationships

Look for opportunities to expand your connections within client organizations. If you only have a single contact person, and that professional leaves, the account can be at risk. However, if you have built relationships with multiple contacts, then you have a far greater chance of retaining the account.

- Understand the organization's dynamics, including key decision makers and how agency partners are evaluated.
- Be willing to invest nonbillable time attending client events and participating in meetings, if it means you will have opportunities to make valuable connections.
- Seek opportunities to work with multiple divisions of larger companies.

The Client in Residence (CIR)

As your agency expands, account teams are pushed to their limits to deliver on expectations and priorities. At the same time, senior leaders, who bring invaluable knowledge and experience to accounts, are pulled away from client services to manage growth.

No matter how talented your account teams are, it becomes easy to lose sight of the big picture. Sometimes agencies can go days or even weeks without taking an objective look at their efforts, and considering things from the client's point of view. However, these sorts of insights can be essential to building stronger, more profitable relationships.

One possible solution is to create a client in residence (CIR)—a senior agency leader charged with assessing accounts from the client's perspective. These client advocates ask the difficult questions, challenge campaign strategies, push for improved results, scrutinize time and billings, assess the account team, and critically evaluate the agency's value and contributions—all so the client does not have to.

The CIR considers factors affecting the client each day—meetings, communications, management, budgets, staffing, expectations, and demands—and looks for ways to make their lives easier. In small agencies, it may be the CEO or president who functions part-time as the CIR, whereas, in large agencies, it may become a full-time position, overseeing dozens of accounts. Here is a look at possible CIR responsibilities:

- Sit in on client calls and internal strategy meetings.
- Monitor account activities to gauge efficiency and productivity.
- Review monthly client analytics reports to look for gaps in assessments.
- Lead internal brainstorming sessions to bring creative and innovative ideas to campaigns.
- Teach young professionals the inner workings of client businesses and cultures.
- Provide feedback on the style and tone of agency communications.
- Challenge account team members' strategic recommendations and thoughts.
- Question invoices and budgets.
- Explore opportunities to enhance service levels.
- Advocate for client interests and needs.

THE SIGNIFICANCE OF SYSTEMS

Prototype hybrid agencies, specifically disruptors, are driven by systems. They are built on adaptable infrastructures that enable them to evolve more quickly than their traditional agency brethren.

The systems create standards and stability, while providing autonomy to account teams and managers. They are designed to increase efficiency and productivity, encourage creativity, accelerate innovation, and push professionals to realize and embrace their potential, all of which produce higher performance levels and more satisfied and loyal clients.

In the following sections, we will examine three core systems that have significant impact on client loyalty: career path, account management, and agency management.

Career Path

As I have stated numerous times, talent is your greatest asset as an agency. Your ability to attract and retain A players directly affects your client loyalty. These professionals are highly motivated, career-focused individuals. They need a system that defines titles, responsibilities, pay scales, bonus structure, performance metrics, expectations, and opportunities.

Like everything else in your agency, career paths should be flexible and adapt as needed to maximize your talent and deliver the greatest value to clients. The career paths establish how your organizational chart is structured, and they lay the foundation for how you construct account teams. Therefore, they are essential for every marketing agency that plans to recruit and develop talent.

There are endless ways to build your agency's organizational chart, define your career paths, and construct your account teams, and they continue to change. For example, in June 2011, Interpublic Group-owned PR firm GolinHarris announced plans to do away with its traditional pyramid structure and introduce four new titles—catalyst, strategist, creator, and connector.[1]

According to the *New York Times*, "The reorganization is primarily meant to transition employees from working as generalists to being designated as one of four types of specialists."[2]

When I first developed PR 20/20's career path in 2005, I felt that clients too often left agency professionals out of high-level strategic discussions, and tended to view them more as practitioners. I wanted our professionals to be seen as strategists first, so I chose to move away from the standard "account executive/supervisor" titles.

Instead, I created a career path with three primary titles—associate consultant, consultant, and senior consultant.

As we grew, we added management positions responsible for the agency's operations and advancement, specifically in the areas of human resources, finance, and marketing, but these core client-service positions are still the basis for our career path.

Our account teams, whose primary responsibility is the retention and growth of core accounts, consist of group managers (senior consultants or higher), account managers (consultants or senior consultants) and support staff (associate consultants and consultants). We continue to tweak our system, but I hope that sharing the basic framework gives you some perspective on one approach that may be helpful in defining your career path.

Following is a snapshot of our primary positions.

Associate Consultant is an entry-level position, ideally suited for professionals with 0 to 3 years of industry experience. Associate consultants are primarily producers—meaning that their primary task is to provide revenue-generating services to clients—and students, developing the skills necessary to advance to the consultant level.

Associate consultants are forecasted to log 120 to 140 client-service hours per month, and are expected to invest significant time and energy outside regular business hours to advance their knowledge and capabilities.

Consultant is a midlevel position. Consultants generally have 3 to 7 years of industry experience, and have displayed the potential and desire to advance to senior-level positions. Consultants are primarily producers; however, they have increased account-management (manager) responsibilities, and they are actively involved with business development and agency initiatives.

Consultants have demonstrated advanced strategic planning and consultation competencies, and they have a proven performance track record. Consultants and senior consultants are usually the primary day-to-day contacts on core accounts. Consultants are forecasted for 100 to 120 client-service hours per month.

Senior Consultant is a senior-level position, commonly for professionals with more than seven years of industry experience. Senior consultants have demonstrated advanced competencies in all relevant areas, and they are viewed as builders, innovators, producers, managers, and leaders. Top senior consultants commonly fill management roles within the agency, so their forecasted client hours range from 80 to 100 per month.

Group Managers are senior consultants who manage a collection of accounts. They are responsible for the growth and management of all accounts and personnel within their group. Group manager responsibilities include:

- Complete monthly group client-hour forecasts.
- Conduct annual staff performance reviews.
- Conduct weekly group meetings to review accounts.
- Provide final approval on all phases of major projects, strategic decisions, client communications, monthly reports, campaign strategies, invoices, activity reports, and account dashboards.
- Determine workflow priorities.
- Construct and manage account teams.
- Run weekly TimeFox reports to analyze group performance and update forecasts as needed.

Assistant Vice President is a position for professionals who play an integral role in the agency's management and growth and who have more than five years of experience. Assistant vice presidents hold client-service positions of senior consultant, and may also function as group managers or group directors.

Vice President is a position of influence for the agency's most accomplished professionals. Vice presidents are heavily involved in the strategic decisions that guide the agency, and their compensation packages are directly influenced by the agency's performance. Vice presidents may also hold senior consultant positions and function as group managers or group directors.

Account Management

Account-management systems start with the right tools and processes. Time-tracking, project-management, and CRM solutions in particular play major roles in building effective systems that continually improve client services and increase loyalty.

Account Team Dashboards We maintain an account team dashboard for every campaign client. The primary purpose is to define ownership of activities for accounts with multiple team members.

The dashboards are simple Excel worksheets, but they give professionals a clear understanding of their roles as group managers, account managers, or support staff. The dashboard can be customized to include more granular-level activities, but the following items are part of every standard worksheet:

- Build and nurture strong client relationships.
- Complete monthly account forecasts.
- Deliver value and results every day.
- Develop and train supporting professionals.
- Engage with target audiences through social media and networking.
- Maintain target client hours.
- Manage workflow of supporting personnel.
- Participate in major strategic discussions and communications.
- Pursue the ongoing training and education needed to advance yourself and the agency.
- Conduct quarterly budget reviews of all campaign-based clients.
- Create, review, and approve invoices.
- Direct account development efforts.
- Direct all account strategy and function as the primary consultant.
- Manage partner-agency relationships.
- Immerse yourself in your clients and their industries.
- Keep Basecamp and Highrise updated with all account activity and communications.
- Monitor analytics, Google News Alerts, Twitter lists, and social-media activity.
- Maintain monthly activity reports and dashboards.
- Coordinate account contracts and renewals.

Group Meetings In addition to account dashboards, we hold group meetings every Monday to set the groundwork for the week and to discuss client campaigns in detail. Groups commonly consist of 3 to 5 professionals, managing up to a dozen campaign clients. Group meetings function as breakout sessions, enabling teams to concentrate on the unique needs and goals of their client base.

All professionals must come prepared to present on behalf of the accounts they manage. These meetings are not billable (for agencies still using billable hours). They should last 15 to 30 minutes and cover topics such as:

- Are monthly forecasts on target?
- Is account development time being invested in priority clients, or wasted on nonpriority accounts?
- Are proper resources allocated to priority clients?
- Are projects and campaigns on track? Are we exceeding time estimates or budgets? If so, why?
- Are we underdelivering on major projects or campaigns?
- Are there workflow issues? Are people taking on more than they can handle?
- How are professionals utilizing downtime?
- What are pros doing with professional development time?
- Are there any client issues or challenges we need to address as a team?
- Are clients happy?

Project Management   A comprehensive project-management solution, such as Basecamp, is one of the most essential components of an agency management system. In order to effectively manage workflow and give agency leaders visibility into the entire client network, agencies should maintain every project, task, and milestone in the same platform.

Project management tools can also be used to create dedicated client portals that enable clients to track campaign milestones, monitor agency tasks and progress, share files, view communications, and submit and read messages. This level of transparency helps build confidence and trust, which lead to loyalty.

We also use utilize the Highrise CRM system to track all important notes, calls, meetings, and e-mails. This gives managers and account teams real-time access to relevant client information and activities.

Client Exercises   Use nonbillable exercises to educate and train your team, which will enhance the value you deliver to clients. Give each team member the chance to complete the same assignment, and then meet as a group to review them and to talk about the strengths and weaknesses of each approach.

For example, pick one new client each month. Have the account manager start the project by presenting the team with an overview of campaign activities, successes, opportunities, and challenges to date. Each professional is then given five business days (and no more than three hours) to create a 1 to 2 page document outlining five strategies for increasing lead volume to the select client. They are then asked to present their recommendations to the group the following week.

This type of exercise offers tremendous professional development benefits, but, more important, it has the potential to identify actionable ideas that you can take to the client.

Agency Management

Agency management, as it relates to client loyalty, comes down to two things: intelligence and action. In order to take the actions necessary to retain and grow accounts, leaders have to have their finger on the pulse of the agency.

At all times, they need to know service-hour forecasts, client hours logged, capacity status, efficiency rates, and employee performance metrics. They have to be aware of opportunities and issues with core accounts and be prepared to bring new technologies and strategies to enhance the agency's value and performance.

Agency Manager As featured in Chapter 3, we use an Agency Manager dashboard (Figure 3.1) built into Microsoft Excel to view and edit monthly service-hour forecasts by client and employee. This tool enables us to balance workflow and allocate resources to the right accounts based on capacity and priority levels. We integrate TimeFox reports throughout the month to ensure that campaigns are on track with forecasts and that clients are receiving the proper levels of support.

Huddles We use brief, action-oriented meetings to start every Tuesday–Friday. The daily huddles are strictly for problem identification and prioritization of that day's activities, and should last no more than 15 minutes. They start promptly at 8:15 AM, and require participation from all attendees. The huddle agenda includes:

- Identification of any trends or topics relevant to the agency and its clients. These are posted continuously on Yammer throughout the day, and then curated each morning for the huddle.
- Discussion of any issues, conflicts, or challenges with accounts.
- Review of employees' top three priorities for the day.
- Discussion of events or meetings scheduled for the day.

Monday Morning Meeting (M3)   The Monday Morning Meeting (M3) is an enhanced version of the daily huddle that, as the name indicates, occurs every Monday in place of the huddle. It starts 15 minutes later at 8:30 AM to give everyone a chance to catch up from the weekend, and it is intended to last 30 to 45 minutes. Here is a look at the M3 agenda:

- **The good news:** Focus on positive results produced for clients and the agency during the previous week.
- **The numbers:** Brief check in on professional and agency data.
- **The agency:** Cover what is happening internally that week— initiatives, events, milestones, news, and updates.
- **The project center:** Run down the week's major projects by client. Also seek team input on any issues or barriers with clients.
- **Loyalty building:** Discuss what is happening with campaign clients to retain and grow their business.
- **The pipeline:** Who is hot in the sales pipeline? What is the conversion probability and action plan?
- **Priorities:** Employees share their top priorities for the day, just as they do in huddle.

Change Velocity Assessments   It seems like new technology companies, software solutions, and mobile apps are emerging every day that have the potential to impact your agency infrastructure and client services. Tech-savvy firms are constantly reviewing and assessing these advances, and looking for opportunities to improve efficiency and performance.

It is helpful to have a standard process to ensure assessments are consistently performed with the clients' best interests in mind. Here is a format that we use internally to evaluate potential solutions:

- **Snapshot:** One or two paragraphs describing the solution or company, and why we are assessing it. Think of this as a very brief executive summary.
- **Strengths:** Describe the value it offers, and how it may improve on our existing solutions.
- **Weaknesses:** Explain how it falls short. This may be pricing structure, feature sets, or limitations, such as seat licenses if it is a software product.
- **Use cases:** Detail how the agency would use the solution and how it would benefit clients.

- **Takeaways:** Outline the 3–5 key takeaways from the assessment.
- **Actions:** Define next steps, assign responsibilities, and set timelines.

Sharing assessments with clients, and/or turning them into blog posts, can be a great way to create additional value, and build loyalty.

PRIORITIZING AND EVALUATING ACCOUNTS

All clients are not created equal. Although agencies need to make every client feel valued, the reality is that some accounts are far more important to the stability and success of your agency, and they need to be treated different.

These priority accounts have a greater appreciation for your services, value your people, and treat your agency as a partner, not as a vendor. They pay bills on time (or early), have realistic expectations and reasonable timelines, and commit the time and energy needed to make the relationship work.

Evaluating existing clients is similar to how you assess and qualify leads. You are looking for the clients that are the best fit for your agency and have the greatest potential to contribute to your growth. However, unlike the sales process, you have actual experiences with these clients, which introduces a whole new set of factors into the equation. Let's take a look at some of the criteria your agency can use to prioritize accounts.

Ranking Factors

Our Agency Manager dashboard highlights two core factors for all clients—account status and income potential. Account status defines whether the clients are *project* or *campaign* clients and income potential establishes a 1 to 5 rating based on their forecasted annual revenue, with 1 being the highest potential accounts.

Since our Agency Manager is maintained in Microsoft Excel, this gives us the ability to sort the entire client portfolio by these two factors at any time. Although account teams are charged with retaining and growing all accounts, special attention is paid to campaign clients with high-income potential.

Agencies should be willing to invest nonbillable account-development time in these core clients. Although this can lead to below-average revenue-efficiency ratings in the short term, the lifetime-value potential dictates that you take a long-term approach to their development.

We use a simplified approach for real-time ranking, but there are many additional factors that go into valuating clients. Here is a collection of some of the more important elements to consider:

- **Efficiency:** The revenue-efficiency rate (RER) introduced in Chapter 1 measures how efficiently your agency turns one hour of service into X dollars in revenue, with X being the hourly revenue target (HRT). In the value-based pricing model, the goal is to deliver the service as close to 100 percent efficiency as possible in order to achieve your desired profits. Therefore, if your HRT is $100, you want every one hour of service to produce $100 in revenue.

  Although it is great, in theory, to get paid for every minute you invest in a client, it is not reality. Whether your agency chooses to invest nonbillable time through account-development activities or has to eat time due to budget shortages, accounts are rarely 100 percent efficient, even in a traditional billable-hour model.

  As you collect months, and even years, of time-tracking and billing data, you will be able to better analyze which accounts are the most efficient and, therefore, the most profitable. For example, you may have a client billing $100,000 per year, but if your firm is investing 2,000 hours to produce the revenue, it is very likely an anchor—an unprofitable account pulling down your agency's efficiency and productivity.

- **Financial stability:** Build your agency around clients with strong financial health and a history of on-time payments. Accounts that are regularly 15-plus days past due can cripple your cash flow, especially if they are core clients (accounting for large percentages of your monthly revenue) and you are in an early-growth phase.

  Consistent late payments are often a sign that clients are in financial trouble or that they have a blatant disregard for their service providers. Either way, it is not a good situation to be in. You have to be willing to walk away from this type of dysfunctional relationship before it is too late.

- **Expectations:** Realistic expectations of success are key to strong client-agency partnerships. Set reachable objectives at the beginning of the engagement, and evolve them as the campaign progresses.

- **Leadership support:** Agencies often need the freedom to experiment creatively and the time to see their strategic vision fully executed. These both require support and patience from your client's leadership team.

- **Synergy:** The most effective and rewarding partnerships have shared values and complementary cultures. It is important that your account teams feel respected by their clients and have a passion for seeing them succeed.

- **Commitment:** Consider their level of commitment to the agency. How long have they been clients? Have they maintained or increased budgets over time?

- **Growth opportunities:** The highest potential accounts have growth opportunities beyond the standard engagement. This may include chances to work with other divisions of the company, budgets for add-on projects, and the potential to consolidate agency relationships.

  For example, if your firm is building a website and providing SEO support, there may be a chance to also win the content marketing and social media business, which is being led by other firms right now.

- **Profile and platform:** If the client has a high profile and significant reach, there are ancillary benefits that come from having them on your client roster. Your agency can gain credibility and possibly enjoy access to contacts and networks you otherwise would not have.

- **Experience:** Clients who provide opportunities to expand your knowledge and capabilities in target niche markets can be very valuable.

- **Innovation:** Case studies are rarely made of conservative companies. Clients have to be willing to take risks, try new strategies, and give your agency some creative freedom.

THE MARKETING CONSULTANT LAWS

When PR 20/20 launched in November 2005, we set out on a journey to "lead and create leaders," as our mission states. My theory behind growing a wildly successful and influential firm was to hire talented, intelligent, and motivated professionals, provide them with the systems and infrastructure necessary to succeed, and then get out of their way.

We wanted to develop and retain the industry's premier marketing consultants: professionals whose services and expertise bring immeasurable value to our clients and directly contribute to the clients' growth and success.

The Marketing Consultant Laws were originally created in August 2008 and distributed as an internal document to give us (the consultants) direction and focus and to challenge us to become stronger and more valuable—individually and as a team.

I hope that the laws, which are featured in the following list, provide some sort of motivation or guidance to agency professionals who are looking to differentiate themselves, become leaders, and build loyal clients.

- **Deliver results:** Tasks, milestones, and activity reports are a means to an end. Our job is to deliver results. Chapter 8 is dedicated to this Marketing Consultant Law.
- **Pay attention to details:** Maintain a vigilant focus on details in all communications and projects. Never make mistakes that are due to lack of focus or effort. Always ask yourself, "Is this the best I can do?"
- **Be a proactive communicator:** Do not ever leave your clients or peers wondering. Anticipate their information needs and maintain a high level of communication at all times.
- **Challenge yourself to be great:** Always challenge yourself and those around you to improve. There is no limit to what you can achieve in business and in life.
- **Bring solutions:** "I don't know" is not an acceptable answer. Your clients and your peers rely on you for solutions. Use your experience and the endless resources available to you to find answers.
- **Maintain a career/life balance:** Your career affords you the opportunity to live a full and rewarding life, but do not let it consume you. Maintain balance among work, wellness, relationships, community involvement, professional associations, friendships, hobbies, and interests.
- **Grow your accounts:** The life-blood of every consultant is the client base. It is your job to retain and grow your accounts by maintaining an in-depth knowledge of your clients and their industries, building relationships, delivering results, and keeping a pulse on opportunities.
- **Be creative:** Show imagination in your strategic thinking, and bring creativity to every project.
- **Be an independent thinker and risk taker:** Do not get stuck in the rut of conformity. Look beyond traditional wisdom and

conventional solutions. Be willing to take calculated risks and make mistakes.

- **Strive for excellence:** Set high performance standards, and always strive toward personal and professional goals.
- **Think strategically:** Challenge yourself to see the big picture. Always be analyzing—perceptions, audiences, objectives, strengths, weaknesses, opportunities, and threats. Find connections in seemingly unrelated news and trends.
- **Hunger for knowledge:** Do not ever stop learning. Consume the wealth of information that is all around you, and share your knowledge for the betterment of your clients and peers.
- **Stay in the moment:** You will see and do things in your career others can only dream of. There will be highs and lows, victories and defeats. Cherish those moments, but do not dwell on them. Your job is to stay in the moment, and appreciate it for what it is.
- **Have fun:** Positive energy is contagious. Bring enthusiasm and passion to your work every day.

Chapter Highlights

- Loyal clients lead to higher retention rates, greater profit margins, more predictable cash flow, and stronger referrals.
- From day one of their training, agency professionals must understand the importance of each client and the financial impact retention has on sustainability.
- The greatest value you can bring to clients is staffing their account teams with A players.
- Be proactive in creating and nurturing connections now for you and your clients. Do not go looking for new contacts when you have something to pitch or sell.
- Agency systems are designed to increase efficiency and productivity, encourage creativity, accelerate innovation, and push professionals to realize and embrace their potential—all of which produce higher performance levels and more satisfied and loyal clients.
- Time-tracking, project-management, and CRM solutions play major roles in building effective systems that continually improve client services and increase loyalty.

(continued)

(*continued*)

- Agency management, as it relates to client loyalty, comes down two things: intelligence and action.
- Although agencies need to make every client feel valued, the reality is that some accounts are far more important to the stability and success of your agency, and they need to be treated differently.
- Agencies should be willing to invest nonbillable account-development time in the core clients. Although this can lead to below-average revenue-efficiency ratings in the short term, the lifetime-value potential dictates that you take a long-term approach to their development.
- Build your agency around clients with strong financial health and a history of on-time payments.
- The most effective and rewarding partnerships have shared values and complementary cultures.
- The highest potential accounts have growth opportunities beyond the standard engagement.
- Case studies are rarely made of conservative companies. Clients have to be willing to take risks, try new strategies, and give your agency some creative freedom.

Great chapter for analysis

chapter 8

Deliver Results

An agency's value is measured in outcomes, not outputs.

BECOME MEASUREMENT GEEKS

Marketing executives—your clients—are drowning in data. They have access to powerful tools that produce endless streams of information about prospects and customers. However, data without analysis is simply noise.

Marketing agencies from every discipline—advertising, PR, social, SEO, content, and web—have the opportunity to evolve, and play an integral role in bringing structure and meaning to the numbers. Your professionals can and should be extracting insight from the wealth of information available to businesses.

Leading marketing agencies turn information into intelligence, and intelligence into action. They build campaigns that consistently produce measurable outcomes, including inbound links, website traffic, leads, and sales. Hybrid agencies must shift away from arbitrary metrics, such as media impressions, reach, advertising equivalency, and PR value, and become measurement geeks who are obsessed with data-driven services.

Learn to Love Data

Elite agency professionals, the A players, have an insatiable desire for data. They are constantly seeking bits of information—click rates, downloads, referring traffic, leads, conversions, search rankings, sales—from which they can derive knowledge. They take a scientific approach to marketing, and develop processes to analyze data for insight that can increase efficiency and maximize ROI for clients.

Integrate Measurement Tools

You have to be a tech geek before you can become a measurement geek. Hybrid agencies are immersed in technology and continually testing and integrating the latest advances in monitoring and measurement. Use change velocity assessments, as discussed in Chapter 7, to keep your firm at the forefront of innovation.

From a measurement perspective, look for solutions that help you discover and interpret the metrics that matter most to your clients. For example, if your agency is evolving to meet the demand for digital services, you need platforms that can deliver online data, such as search rankings, blog analytics, website traffic sources, inbound links, shares, clicks, social reach, leads, and conversion rates.

Train Analysts

Turn your hybrid professionals into analysts. Teach them to make decisions based on logic and reason. Show them how to gain insight from information and how to use that insight to educate clients, build consensus, and drive action.

One of my favorite marketing-book lines of all time comes from Sergio Zyman in *The End of Marketing as We Know It*: "You've got to look everywhere and learn everywhere, because everything is connected."[1] Develop professionals who see the big picture and have the ability to make connections that result in actionable intelligence.

Practice on Your Agency

Learn on your time, not your clients'. If measurement and data analysis are new to your agency, experiment on yourself first. Like we talked about in the Inbound Marketing GamePlan, start with the basics:

- Install website analytics to enable real-time tracking of traffic, referrers, page views, and keywords.
- Build unique landing pages that enable you to track views and conversion rates for content downloads, event registrations, contact requests, and other calls to action.
- Track marketing events and milestones, and monitor how they correlate to spikes in website traffic, inbound links, leads, and sales.
- Assign a team member to monitor website analytics and social-media activity daily.

Once you have proven that you understand measurement and analysis, then look for opportunities to build it into your services.

Tie to Services

Every campaign should start with performance benchmarks—current lead volume, inbound links, website traffic, content downloads, blog subscribers, social media reach—and clearly defined success factors for how the client will measure your value and their ROI.

Challenge your agency to move beyond the arbitrary measurements of success used by traditional marketing firms, and push the conversation toward more meaningful outcomes that can be tracked in real time and directly connected to sales.

Dig into the Data

Anyone can pull charts and numbers and present the client observations and assumptions. Your agency has to go further. You have to find cause-and-effect relationships, not just correlations. You have to turn noise into insights, and find the answers to difficult questions.

- Why are e-mail click-through rates so low?
- Why has website traffic reached a plateau?
- Why are competitors outperforming your client on search engines for priority keywords?
- Why are pages per visit dropping on the website?
- Why does landing page A have a 20 percent higher conversion rate than landing page B?
- What is the best day and time to send an e-mail newsletter?
- What impact is blogging having on your client's business?

The answers are in the data. You just have to know where to look and how to make the connections that will produce results for your clients.

Every Agency Pro Should Take Google AdWords Training

Professionals do not become analysts overnight. Agencies have to provide the knowledge and training to develop and hone these skills. A great starting point is the Google AdWords Certification Program.

According to Google, "Professionals looking to update and demonstrate search skills to employers can study and certify to become individually qualified in Google AdWords. To gain qualification, exam takers must pass both the Advertising Fundamentals exam and one advanced-level exam."[2]

I feel so strongly in its value that we require all PR 20/20 consultants to take and pass the Fundamentals exam, despite the heavy time commitment involved. The AdWords Learning Center contains 21 lessons for the Advertising Fundamentals exam alone, totaling more than 400 pages of reading.

The exam tests your knowledge of Google AdWords tools, account management, analytics, and ad-optimization techniques. Although it focuses particularly on online advertising, it is an invaluable exercise for all marketing agency professionals. The exam fosters analytical thinking, refines budgeting skills, and expands knowledge of how search engines work.

Encourages Analytical Thinking   Being able to demonstrate your success through tangible factors, such as search engine rankings, website traffic, inbound links, leads, and sales, is essential in today's business environment. The Google AdWords exam forces you to think analytically, translate data into meaningful measurements, and adjust strategies based on results. All these skills are vital for marketing-agency professionals looking to demonstrate their value to clients and to manage successful campaigns.

Refines Budgeting Skills   An organization's ROI using Google AdWords does not necessarily relate to how much the organization spends; it is determined by how well their budget is used through keyword and bid selections, targeting, and optimization. These factors usually need to be tweaked, often based on past performance, in order to get the most benefit for your money.

This same logic can be applied to the financial aspects of managing any type of campaign. Hybrid professionals need to be able to work within a client's budget—choosing those activities that will have the strongest ROI—while simultaneously being able to determine when a larger budget is needed to achieve desired objectives. They also need to continuously review their current campaigns and budget allocations to determine if their existing financial distribution is optimal or if funds should be reallocated to better-performing activities.

Provides a General Understanding of Search Engines   In Chapter 2, we focused on content marketing as the greatest opportunity for agency growth. However, to optimize content for online audiences, professionals need a sound understanding of search engines and how they function.

The AdWords training program offers a general overview of Google paid and organic search. It also provides an in-depth lesson on keyword selection. Although most information has a paid-search focus, the knowledge derived can be applied to organic search as well. Having basic knowledge of how the search engines work can significantly impact the success of your client's online content.

Google Analytics Training

Google also offers a free online course that provides comprehensive training in Google Analytics implementation and data analysis, and is a great way to train your team. Completing the course prepares professionals to take the Google Analytics Individual Qualification (IQ) test. The fee for taking the Google Analytics IQ test is $50. Like the AdWords training, this is required learning for PR 20/20 professionals.[3]

USE ANALYTICS TO ADAPT

The most advanced hybrid agencies win with speed and agility. They draw on their experience to develop theories and strategies, and then use the science of analysis to adapt to changing business environments and evolve client campaigns in real time. They continually experiment, measure, analyze, and adjust.

Once your agency has the right tools and talent in place, concentrate on making analytics a part of your professionals' daily routines. In order to foster deeper thinking among your team, analytics needs to become second nature, rather than an afterthought. Following are some tips to get started:

- Review Google Analytics reports as part of your account teams' daily campaign management duties.
- Communicate insights to clients in real time.
- Build data analysis into daily, weekly, and monthly client reports.
- Talk about client analytics as part of your agency's daily meetings.
- Conduct internal analytics training sessions with senior consultants during which they demonstrate to associates how they process and interpret data.

- Assign exercises to challenge and develop associates' analytical skills.
- Share insights throughout the day on Yammer or through whatever internal social network your agency uses.

Services, Measurement, and Selective Consumption

As consumers tune out traditional, interruption-based marketing methods and choose when and where to interact with brands, agencies gain the ability to connect actions to outcomes. Let's look at selective consumption at work to better understand its power and the role of real-time analytics.

Assume the client, a B2B software company, wants to generate 100 leads next month. The company has solid brand awareness, but struggles to gain market share from the larger, more established competitors. Historically, it has invested heavily in industry publications, spending north of $10,000 per month on advertisements. Although the ads are creatively strong and are believed to have been influential in building brand awareness, there is no direct way to measure their impact on the client's success. This is what I would call the publish-and-pray approach, also known as outbound or interruption-based marketing. We will consider this option A.

Now your agency comes along with a few new ideas. You recognize that your client's leaders are some of the brightest minds in the industry, but they have been hidden away behind the bland corporate messaging that permeates their website and marketing campaigns. You see an opportunity to differentiate the client by creating value, and parlaying its personal brands into thought-leadership initiatives.

For the same $10,000 per month, you propose option B, which we will call the inbound-marketing approach: Publish a 3,000-word ebook on a custom-built landing page. Announce the ebook on the company blog, and consider doing a few guest blog posts on partner sites to promote it as well. Although there is no registration (lead form) required, there is a call to action to sign up for a webinar, featuring the client's affable lead engineer. The ebook and webinar are promoted through the client's database of 10,000 contacts, and they are also distributed through a media partner's database of 25,000 subscribers.

As a marketer, as much as I like to see nice full-page, full-color print ads, I am going to put my money on option B. Why? Because my experience tells me it has a far better chance of producing 100 leads. More important, even if it does not, I can measure every single element of the program—downloads, webinar registrations, landing page conversions, e-mail click-through rates, referring sources, blog-page views, new blog subscribers, social sharing, and inbound links. I will be able to monitor the campaign's performance in real time, and have actionable data to better spend my $10,000 next month.

The takeaway: In order to use analytics and constantly adapt to bring greater value to clients, your services must be measurable.

Real-Time Marketing and Monthly Scorecards

Change velocity and the availability of real-time data have created new demands and opportunities for agencies. Tech-savvy firms with fully integrated digital services and top-grade talent are more nimble in the planning and execution of client campaigns. They are capable of quickly adapting strategies and tactics based on insights into consumer behavior, and they are obsessed with improving performance and ROI. Analytics is the key to success with this agile approach to marketing.

At PR 20/20, we start all long-term client engagements with a customized Inbound Marketing GamePlan, as detailed in Chapter 5. Knowing how quickly things change, our general philosophy is, "less time planning, more time doing." The goal of the GamePlan is to set clear benchmarks and objectives, arrive at a consensus for a 12-month approach, and approve services for first-quarter activities. We plan tactically in quarters, and adapt daily based on campaign performance, changing market factors, and the client's business goals and priorities.

During the initial GamePlan development process, which usually lasts 30 days, we go through a relatively traditional discovery period. The discovery phase uses internal information and secondary online research to assess the following: organizational goals, buyer personas, market segments, SWOT (strengths, weaknesses, opportunities, and threats) analysis, competitors, brand positioning, website performance, products/services, pricing, historical marketing strategies, sales systems, marketing software, budgets, and timelines. This is also the time in which we evaluate existing analytics tools and determine the need for any additional monitoring and measurement support.

Our focus is on having the right solutions in place to gather and interpret data. We build monitoring and reporting into every client's daily campaign management, and then we rely on monthly scorecards for a full analysis and action plan. Here is a look at the monthly scorecard structure:

- **Section 1 — Snapshot:** The snapshot provides a dashboard overview of campaign performance, including results from all major activities completed during the previous month. The snapshot functions as an executive summary with key findings in the areas of website, social media, search marketing, content marketing, and PR.
- **Section 2 — Analysis:** This is where we dig into the data to look for actionable intelligence. We analyze website grade, site traffic, traffic sources, keyword performance, referring sites, inbound links, lead sources and quality, blog statistics, social-media reach and engagement, and customer conversions.

    This area is often customized based on client preferences. For example, marketing directors may use scorecard charts and key findings as part of their monthly executive meetings. In this case, we will tailor the design and content so it can be easily extracted and dropped into their presentations.
- **Section 3 — GamePlan:** Using the findings from section 2, we construct an updated GamePlan for the next month. Time and budgets are reallocated based on priority opportunities and evolving business goals.

Monthly scorecards are one way that agencies can use analytics to continually adapt and evolve client campaigns. They encourage transparency, demonstrate a commitment to results-driven services, and help to build confidence, trust, and loyalty.

ACTIVATE BUILDERS AND DRIVERS

I introduced the concept of *builders* and *drivers* in Chapter 1 as a key variable of value-based pricing. Builders are services designed to set the foundation for future success, whereas drivers are intended to produce short-term results. Your agency's ability to succeed and bring value to clients requires a balanced and strategic approach to both.

The Builders

Builders lay the groundwork. They create the necessary base on which you will develop your client's brand, differentiate them from competitors, and expand their reach and influence.

Builders are essential, but often not measurable (at least in the short term), which means many organizations have limited patience and budgets to do them well. As a result, businesses want to rush right into the marketing tactics. They expect immediate gratification and demand results, such as more Facebook page "likes," increased blog subscribers, media coverage, speaking engagements, and leads.

This is dangerous when engaging a marketing agency. Agencies can be a tremendous asset, but they can also be an enormous liability if expectations are not aligned from the beginning. Clients and prospects that do not understand or value the importance of builders will always be trouble. The model agencies get paid to do it right. They refuse to take shortcuts or give in to clients' desperate desires for quick fixes.

Remember, success is a process. Your clients will get the greatest return from an agency relationship if they have a realistic understanding of their current situation, and focus on builders first. Consider the following questions when assessing the need for builders in your clients' campaigns:

- **Market research:** Do they understand their market, and how they fit in the competitive landscape?
- **Brand positioning:** Have they defined what makes them different, and are they conveying their unique positioning in their marketing and sales materials?
- **Website development:** Is the website user-friendly with distinct calls to action, strong brand messaging, and lots of amazing content to keep people coming back?
- **Search engine optimization:** Has a keyword analysis been conducted to identify the most relevant words and phrases for the website? Is the website properly optimized for search engines, including page titles, URLs, headings, image ALT text, copywriting, and meta descriptions? Has an inbound link analysis been performed?
- **Copywriting:** Is the organization's copywriting strong, action oriented and buyer-persona focused? Does the website or marketing collateral need to be refreshed?
- **Social media:** Have they established profiles on all the major networks? Do they have existing reach and influence online? Are they engaging with the community or simply broadcasting content? Do they have a social media policy? Are they providing training and education to employees?

If you are working with larger, more established organizations, chances are their internal marketing teams or other agency partners, have already completed most of the foundational work. However, for many agencies, this is where your services begin.

It is also important to note how dependent the builders are on each other, because this demonstrates the ever-growing importance of the collaborative agency ecosystem. For example, consider the case of a website.

The strength and marketing effectiveness of websites is essential to your clients' success, but websites can no longer be designed in a vacuum by web-development firms. These are not brochure sites any more. They are, or should be, dynamic hubs for information and engagement, and the metaphorical front door to brands and businesses.

A powerful website requires professional design, strategic brand messaging, on-page optimization, social media integration, engaging copywriting, landing pages, lead forms, and volumes of original content. It has to enable real-time updates through an intuitive content-management system (CMS), and it needs to connect to a customer-relationship management (CRM) system to automate the collection and processing of online data.

Every agency in the ecosystem, from disruptors to soloists, has to understand that there are no more silos in marketing. Everything is connected. Success depends on the integration of services, and collaboration among firms.

The Drivers

Once the foundation is in place, it is time for drivers to make things happen. Drivers are marketing activities that generate traffic, create inbound links, produce quality leads, make connections, establish relationships, and grow your client's business.

Selective consumption dictates that drivers focus on value creation through web, search, social, content, and PR activities, including link building, case studies, ebook, e-mail newsletters, online videos, podcasts, webinars, mobile apps, social networking, and blogging.

Like builders, drivers must be unified. Clients will increasingly demand hybrid solutions from hybrid agencies. Consider the dependency of these core disciplines on each other:

- **Brand marketing:** Organizations are personified through the personal brands of their employees, creating deeper levels of engagement, trust, and loyalty. As we saw with the Matt Cutts example in Chapter 5, powerful personal branding requires content creation, social media engagement, and an adherence to the values and principles of the corporate brand.

- **Web development:** Websites without dynamic, optimized content become static corporate wastelands. Websites have to give visitors the desire to experience and share the site, and reasons to return, over and over again.

- **Content marketing:** Original content—ebook, blog posts, podcasts, case studies, reports, and videos—requires social distribution channels to be discovered and shared. Quality matters far more than quantity, so the copywriting must be exceptional. Corporations must view themselves as brand journalists, no longer relying on mainstream media to control their messages.

- **Public relations:** Next generation PR professionals—not the traditional flacks that have given the industry a bad reputation—build relationships and enhance communications with all core audiences. They use social media and content to create transparency and trust. They focus on personalized approaches to media and blogger relations in order to generate third-party validation that builds brand awareness and preference.

The Inevitable Convergence

To further validate the inevitable convergence of marketing disciples, let's consider what is happening in the SEO industry.

Search-engine optimization is evolving, in large part due to major algorithm changes from Google and other search engines that value content quality over quantity, greatly consider user experience, and are continually integrating social circles and recommendations into results. Therefore, effective search-engine optimization (SEO) increasingly requires high-quality original content, social sharing, and engaging site designs that capture and keep visitors.

Every two years, SEOmoz publishes a Search Engine Ranking Factors report in which it surveys the top SEO minds in the industry, and asks them to rank the different elements that go into search-ranking algorithms.[4]

Following is a breakdown of the highest-ranking factors for 2011, and the overall importance each has on a site's ability to rank on a search-engine result page (SERP), according to the experts. Note that I have consolidated different sections of the report to simplify the concepts.

Inbound Links—42 Percent of SERP Impact   Inbound links are continuously mentioned as a key marketing performance metric throughout this book. The SEOmoz report highlights their value to search engine rankings, and demonstrates the importance of agencies offering services that create inbound links.

The report indicates that the number of unique websites considered important by search engines—that is, have a high PageRank or mozRank—that link to a site or page is the highest-ranking factor when it comes to a website's ability to rank for a search query.

As we discussed in Chapter 2, the most effective way to continually generate high-quality inbound links is by publishing and sharing valuable content, including blog posts, videos, ebooks, and original reports. In other words, SEO requires copywriting and social media strategies in order to maximize its value.

Keyword Usage—26 Percent of SERP Impact Standard SEO on-page elements are still highly relevant to site performance in search engines. At the domain level, search engines look for keywords in the domain and subdomain of a website, and the order in which the keywords appear. For example www.keywordABC.com will likely rank better than www.ABCkeyword.com.

In addition to domain names, agencies have to take a strategic approach to other on-page elements, such as page title, internal-link anchor text, headings, and image ALT text.

The key here is that the more optimized pages a site has, the better its chances of attracting traffic and inbound links for specific keyword phrases. So again, it comes down to creating and optimizing content that people will want to share, and then taking actions to get that content found.

Social Media—7 Percent of SERP Impact The SEO experts agree that Twitter is the most important social network in regard to its impact on search engine algorithms, specifically the authority of a user tweeting links and the quantity of tweets to a page.

Other influential social media factors include Facebook shares; authority of the user who is sharing the links; votes on and comments about a site on social bookmarking sites, such as Digg, Reddit, and StumbleUpon; and authority and quantity of links shared on Google Buzz.

Agencies need to the take the initiative to get their clients active in social media, monitoring for discussion opportunities, sharing resources, and engaging audiences. Depending on the situation, including their internal resources and willingness to participate, your responsibility may be as a social media advisor or actually managing the accounts on their behalf.

Brand Popularity—7 Percent of SERP Impact   Brand popularity also plays a significant role in search engine rankings. According to the experts, some of the most important factors are search volume for a brand name; quantity of brand mentions on websites and social sites; citations for the domain in Wikipedia; and active accounts on Facebook, Twitter, and LinkedIn.

Other Important Factors to Consider   The SEO experts also called out the importance of unique, fresh content across the entire site, and the visitor bounce rate as tracked by the search engines; this refers to visitors who go to a site and then use the back button to return to the SERP. The lower the bounce rate, the better, so make the content worth reading and give them reasons to stick around for more.

The Case for Social Media

The SEOmoz report shows how social media is having an increasing impact on search engine results. Social media enables personalization based on a searcher's social graph, in addition to functioning as a publishing channel for your clients' original content.

Social media also offers marketing agencies the opportunity to build more meaningful relationships with media, bloggers, and analysts, and take a more personalized approach to PR. For example, by actively monitoring reporters' tweets or Facebook shares, you can get to know more about them than just their beats. As a result, you can tailor pitches to directly relate to their interests and needs, thus improving your chances for success.

Social media has transformed the way that people communicate and gather information online. With more than two-thirds of U.S. Internet users regularly using a social network,[5] individuals are more often turning to sites such as Facebook, Twitter, and LinkedIn to ask questions, share resources, and research products and services.

Through active social media participation, your clients can connect with qualified consumers online when they are actively looking for products, services, and information. According to a 2011 ForeSee report, "visitors to websites influenced by social media are more loyal and satisfied customers, and they spend more than visitors who were not influenced by social media."[6]

There is also correlation between social media involvement and financial performance. A 2009 study from Wetpaint and the Altimeter Group shows that of the 100 brands evaluated, those with the heaviest social media engagement grew company revenues by 18 percent from July 2008 to July 2009, while the least engaged companies saw revenues sink six percent over the same time period.[7] In addition, 2010 data from Chadwick Martin Bailey and iModerate suggest that individuals are more likely to buy from brands with which they are friends or followers on social networks.[8]

The Case for Content Marketing

Inbound marketing is powered by content. In order to grow smarter and faster than the competition, organizations must maintain powerful and informative websites and continually publish valuable content online.

Content can be used to connect with target audiences on an emotional level—something often lacking in business communications—by addressing consumers' pain points, thought processes, goals, and preferences. As we have seen, it also has the ability to establish your clients' professionals as industry thought leaders and trusted resources, which is especially valuable in business-to-business (B2B) marketing. This increases the likelihood that prospects and customers will turn to them for solutions.

According to a study of HubSpot customers, websites of companies that blog have 55 percent more visitors, 97 percent more inbound links, and 434 percent more indexed pages than the websites of companies that do not—signaling the importance of content to website strength.[9]

In addition, business-to-consumer (B2C) and B2B companies that blog generate more leads—88 percent and 67 percent, respectively—than their nonblogging counterparts.[10] Content has also been proven effective at helping move prospects through long sales cycles.

The Content Spam Epidemic   Despite all its tremendous potential, content marketing has a downside. The reality is that it is not easy to regularly produce interesting, high-quality content (thus the opportunity for marketing agencies to become content creators). However, as with anything in business, there are organizations that look for shortcuts and cheap solutions to compete.

They believe that any content is better than no content. Just as link spam infiltrated the SEO industry in the early days, the flood of content spam—low-quality content produced solely for search-engine rankings and traffic—has begun spewing from media organizations and corporations looking to cash in on the content rush.

The good news is that Google has a very public distaste for poor-quality content. In June 2011, Google released its Panda update 2.2, which, according to SEOmoz, "changed SEO best practices forever."[11] This, in turn, directly impacts content marketing. In essence, Google is continuing to evolve its algorithm to put a premium on websites that produce trustworthy, credible, high-quality content.

So, when strategizing drivers for your clients, steer clear of mass-produced, cheap content solutions. Although they may offer short-term benefits, the greater opportunity is constructing an integrated campaign powered by premium content that is worthy of inbound links and social sharing.

The Rise of Content Curation   Content curation has become a rising trend in the marketing world, and an essential component of content marketing strategies.

Rohit Bhargava (@rohitbhargava), award-winning author of *Personality Not Included*, published a blog post in 2009 titled "Manifesto for the Content Curator,"[12] in which he defined a content curator as "someone who continually finds, groups, organizes and shares the best and most relevant content on a specific issue online."

The term *content curation* stems from traditional museum curation—museum curators collect art and artifacts and identify the most relevant or important to be displayed in an exhibit for the public. Museum curators are subject-matter experts with higher levels of education that guide an organization's overall art collection. Curation has also, historically, referred to overseeing the care and preservation of precious collectibles.

With the overwhelming amount of content available on the Internet today, it is difficult for professionals to efficiently manage their daily reading activities as well as separate useful and accurate content from poor content. This is where content curation comes in, allowing individuals and businesses to provide a valuable service to their audiences by addressing their need for quality content and the lack of available time to find it.

Further, by sharing the most relevant, thought-provoking online content, curation can establish individuals and companies as authorities and thought leaders. Content curation enables your clients to stand out in the marketplace and influence buyer behavior during a time when everyone is fighting for recognition.

To date, curation has been a relatively time-consuming process because it requires significant energy to find, filter, and editorialize the best information. For example, at PR 20/20 we attempt to publish a curated post each week on our blog that highlights the week's most relevant marketing articles. The posts are usually 500 to 700 words, but commonly take one to two hours longer to prepare than a standard post.

Curation will take on increased importance in your clients' marketing strategies as software platforms emerge to make curation more intuitive and automated, so keep an eye on innovations in this space.

UNPLUG TO EXCEL

Efficiency and productivity have been recurring themes throughout this book. They are essential to an agency's profitability and the ability of your professionals to deliver results. However, there are barriers preventing professionals from reaching their potential and performing at their peaks.

We have become a society consumed with connectivity—much to our own detriment and that of our clients, coworkers, friends, and family. We are wasting time and money at alarming rates, instead of focusing our energy on what matters.

Unfortunately, although many of us think that we are increasing our value and productivity with our always-wired lifestyles, the inverse is more likely true, especially for marketing-agency professionals whose careers require both strategic and creative thinking.

We are so focused on meeting short-term demands for our time and attention that we have lost sight of the higher-priority outputs that will build our careers and businesses and make us better and happier people.

The Distractors

We suffer from channel and information overload. At any given moment during business hours (and often after), we are connected through an array of channels competing for our attention—Twitter, Facebook, Internet, TV, chat, e-mail, phone, text, internal social networks, and Skype—not to mention face-to-face time and meetings. In essence, we are always distracted or anticipating distraction, and, therefore, we are never performing at our peak and never achieving flow.

> People lived so deeply in the moment, and felt so utterly in control, that their sense of time, place, and even self melted away.
>
> —*Daniel Pink,* Drive: The Surprising Truth About What Motivates Us, *p. 115.*

These channels are important to our daily lives and our ability to consume information, communicate, produce, and grow. However, as author Dr. John Medina explains in *Brain Rules*, our minds are wired to work and think sequentially, not simultaneously. In other words, it is biologically impossible for us to give our full attention to more than one task at once.[13]

We cannot process Twitter alerts, e-mail notifications, instant messages, and texts and still efficiently produce outputs. Plus, research has shown that every time we are interrupted, our brains take up to 45 minutes to refocus and resume a major task.[14]

What is the trade-off? We use our personal time (nights, weekends, and vacations) to make up for lost productivity and poor efficiency.

The Six-Step Unplugged Plan

So what can we do about it? How can we improve our performance, achieve better balance, and deliver greater results?

I propose that marketing-agency professionals go unplugged. Set aside time each day to go off the grid in order to regain focus, improve productivity, create more value, and concentrate on what is most important in business (and life).

1. Unplug at Regular (Daily) Intervals For a minimum of four hours every workday, shut off every nonessential application, and focus all your energy and attention on priority tasks and projects. Obviously, you still need to be available for high-priority communications and meetings, but commit to an unplugged schedule as much as possible.

We instituted agency-wide productivity blocks (9–11 AM and 1–3 PM) at PR 20/20 in spring 2010 after reading *Rework* by Jason Fried (@jasonfried) and David Heinemeier Hansson (@dhh).[15] Those blocks serve as our standard unplugged sessions. They flex as needed, but committing to them has had an incredible impact on our efficiency and performance.

This can be a difficult thing in team environments when communications and ideas are constantly flowing; however, we have found that blocking off periods of our calendars each day as busy, and limiting interruptions such as instant messages and e-mails, enables us, individually and collectively, to be more creative and productive.

2. Create and Communicate in Bursts   Use the productivity blocks to create, and use the other times to communicate. This enables you to give people and projects the full attention they deserve, while using your time as efficiently as possible.

Hopefully you will unlock some stifled creativity along the way, and become a better listener.

3. Eliminate Channel and Sensory Overload   Be honest. How often do you check and respond to e-mails or take a quick look at Facebook or Twitter to distract yourself from work or delay pushing through a challenging project? I used to do it all the time—probably dozens of times per day.

Why? Because they were always open and accessible. It is like recess for the mind. Besides, 10 minutes here and there is harmless, right? Wrong! We are cheating ourselves, and anyone who relies on our production.

We have made it agency policy to shut off all desktop notifications, and set e-mail to autocheck every hour.

4. Get Lost to Find Answers   Adjust your routine a bit, and maybe seek out a change of scenery more often. Whether it is a local coffee shop, a golf course, or a road trip, we need to quiet our minds and be inspired to think and create.

5. Reset Expectations and Priorities   What percentage of communications, specifically calls and e-mails, are truly urgent? Of course, there are exceptions, but I guarantee the vast majority of those messages could wait an hour or two for a reply.

I know if I were paying a marketing agency for its creative work, I would rather they spent 60 uninterrupted minutes straight on my project than 60 minutes over three hours with calls, e-mails, tweets, and instant messages in between. Some agencies/consultants keep the meter running while allowing themselves to be constantly interrupted. That can be a costly situation when you are paying by the hour. I will take efficiency, with higher levels of creativity and attention, every time.

6. Remember What Matters   I am consumed by a passion for our agency. Since the day I launched it, I have cherished every waking second. The people and the moments have enriched my life, and I would not trade them for the world.

However, the agency does not define me. It is a means to a better life, for me and my coworkers. It affords us the opportunity to work with amazing people, build businesses, and do remarkable things. More importantly, it is our vehicle to create financial freedom so that we can enjoy our lives, improve the lives of those we care about, and affect the causes we believe in.

The more productive and efficient we are, the more time we have for the things that truly matter.

How Will You Know if Unplugging Works?

Simple really. Set goals, establish benchmarks, and measure metrics that matter to your business and life. For example, I track the number of blog posts I publish (goal: write more), hours working on nights and weekends (goal: spend more quality time with my family), and engagement in social networks (goal: build more relationships and create more value).

CHAPTER HIGHLIGHTS

- Leading marketing agencies turn information into intelligence, and intelligence into action.
- Look for measurement solutions that help you discover and interpret the metrics that matter most to your clients.
- Develop professionals who see the big picture and have the ability to make connections that result in actionable intelligence.
- Challenge your agency to move beyond the arbitrary measurements of success used by traditional marketing firms, and push the conversation toward more meaningful outcomes that can be tracked in real time and directly connected to sales.
- The most advanced hybrid agencies win with speed and agility.
- Make analytics a part of your professionals' daily routines in order to foster deeper thinking among your team.
- In order to use analytics and constantly adapt to bring greater value to clients, your services must be measurable.

(continued)

(continued)

- Builders are services designed to set the foundation for future success, whereas drivers are intended to produce short-term results.

- Drivers are marketing activities that generate traffic, create inbound links, produce quality leads, make connections, establish relationships, and grow your clients' businesses.

- Every agency in the ecosystem, from disruptors to soloists, has to understand that there are no more silos in marketing. Everything is connected. Success depends on the integration of services and collaboration among firms.

- We are so focused on meeting short-term demands for our time and attention that we have lost sight of the higher-priority outputs that will build our careers and businesses and make us better and happier people.

- Our minds are wired to work and think sequentially, not simultaneously. In other words, it is biologically impossible for us to give our full attention to more than one task at once.

chapter **9**

Embrace Failure

Never hesitate to head in a direction that others seem to fear.

IF YOUR MODEL IS BROKE, FIX IT

History is full of industry leaders and business pioneers who have become irrelevant because they failed to innovate and evolve. Maybe it is the result of conservative cultures, poor leadership, a lack of will and vision, or the systematic inertia that builds from years of complacency.

Or, possibly, they were just afraid. People fear the unknown. They resist taking the bold and decisive actions that are needed to survive because they do not want to fail. However, we learn from failure. It builds character, teaches us humility, shows us how to cope with adversity, and challenges us to continually test, revise, and improve.

Marketing agencies are no different. Agency leaders become comfortable in their positions. They learn to ignore their instincts for change, instead favoring status quo. They make decisions to avoid short-term risk and pain, often to the detriment of their agencies' long-term viability. Even worse, this tentativeness trickles down to employees and carries over into client campaigns.

Marketing agencies must take action to survive and thrive in the new ecosystem. They have to make difficult choices to break from traditional agency-centric pricing models, invest in technology, recruit and retain hybrid professionals, build scalable infrastructures, and transform their services. They have to be willing to make mistakes. They have to embrace failure.

> We can learn nearly as much from an experiment that does not work as from one that does. Failure is not something to be avoided but rather something to be cultivated. . . . All creative avenues yield the maximum when failures are embraced.
> —*Kevin Kelly, editor-at-large, Wired*[1]

THE DISRUPTOR ADVANTAGE

The unknown is one of the most exciting things about being an entrepreneur. It is the adrenaline rush that comes from taking chances and venturing down the road less traveled. That is the disruptor agency advantage. These organizations, by their very nature, are risk takers. They thrive on change, easily tire of tradition, and pride themselves on their agility.

These emerging firms have less to lose than their larger, more conservative competitors. They are building new, hybrid agency models from the ground up. They do not have the restrictions of legacy systems or the internal politics that hinder change. They have flexibility in their pricing, lower overhead costs, and more dynamic and versatile talent.

Disruptors need to be willing to take risks the established agencies cannot or will not. While traditionalists try to fix their models, you should be focused on continually reinventing yours.

Never hesitate to head in a direction that others seem to fear.

THE TRADITIONALIST OPPORTUNITY

I have watched some incredibly talented traditional firms fade or disappear in the last decade because they continued to do what was familiar. While revenues fell, and their staffs slowly churned, they would just put their heads down and keep grinding. Rather than getting to the root of the problem—a broken model—they would raise billable-hour rates, form a few strategic partnerships, and reach out to the same tired networks on which they built their firms.

Many of them suffered from what I call the Frodo syndrome. In the 2001 classic movie, *The Lord of the Rings: The Fellowship of the Ring*, Frodo Baggins, beaten down and scared, confides in Gandalf, "I wish none of this had happened." To which Gandalf, in his wizardry wisdom, replies, "So do all who live to see such times, but that is not for them to decide. All we have to decide is what to do with the time that is given to us."

Traditionalists, along with soloists and specialists, have to put their fears aside and confront the challenges ahead, just as Frodo did in *The Lord of the Rings*. They have to acknowledge something is wrong, be willing to fix what is broken, and return to the ideas and inspirations that made them great. They have to think and act more like start-ups. They have to become disruptors themselves.

Experiment with Services and Pricing

Although traditional firms may hesitate to make major overhauls to their services and pricing, they can start to progress by experimenting in niches or with select prospects.

For example, we released our first service packages in fall 2008. They were targeted at the specific needs and goals of HubSpot customers. Pricing ranged from $1,299 per month for the starter package, to $2,999 per month for the enterprise solution. These packages bundled services such as SEO analysis, on-page optimization, landing pages, blogging, and social media consulting.

These first service packages helped to differentiate the agency and bring in new business, but I would not consider them a financial success. The efficiencies and profitability were low, but that was part of the process. We had to take a chance and try something new in order to learn and evolve.

Trust Your Instinct

Trust your gut instinct when it comes to determining direction. Research and analyze your options, but only to refute what you already know to be the best choice. This can become challenging in larger agencies, but the most effective CEOs are adept at building consensus and support for their visions, no matter how unconventional they may be.

You should try to do things that most people would not.[2]
—*Larry Page, Google cofounder and CEO*

Deconstruct Your Brand

Be willing to deconstruct your brand and business model to remain relevant, and position yourself where the market is going. History means nothing if you have no future.

Maintain a Sense of Controlled Urgency

Some of the greatest inventions and advances in business have come in the face of adversity, but do not wait for desperate times to evolve. The best time to pursue opportunities and innovations is when you are prospering. Something or someone will eventually come along to disrupt your agency, so it might as well be you.

Look Beyond Tradition

Following tradition and conventional wisdom is easy, and boring. Take risks, be bold, and dare to fail.

Failing Forward: The Return and Revenge of Steve Jobs

In 1984 Steve Jobs was fired from Apple, the company he cofounded in 1976 out of a family garage. He went on to found NeXT, a computer company, which was acquired by Apple in 1996 for $429 million. Jobs returned to Apple as CEO in 1997, and he has since created some of the most transformational technology products in history.

SPEND LESS TIME PLANNING, MORE TIME DOING

Plans have their place in business and life, but I have found that they often serve as a convenient excuse to avoid action. We hold meetings, form committees, set goals, create proposals, assign responsibilities, and build task lists and timelines. We spend months agonizing over details and gaining approvals, only to have our strategies be outdated by the time they are finally activated.

Business moves too fast to watch from the sidelines. Technology is changing, consumer behavior is evolving, and competition is emerging. Marketing agencies have to become more agile. They have to focus less on thinking and talking and more on doing, both for themselves and their clients.

Venture into the Unknown

In January 2011, Seth Godin, best-selling author of *Linchpin*, took to the Helen Mills theater stage in New York to share his ideas on the new dynamics of publishing.

It was an intimate affair with 100 attendees, including myself. There were no PowerPoints, splashy parties, or corporate sponsors. We spent six hours listening, asking questions, and discussing what is next for the book-publishing industry. Although the event was targeted at authors and book publishers, the lessons learned apply to all marketers.

My favorite line of the day came when someone asked Godin how he so consistently innovates and creates remarkable content. To summarize his reply: "I practice staring into the abyss."

His message was that if you are not scared and unsure when creating content and pushing new ideas, then it is probably not worth pursuing. We have to challenge ourselves to tackle the unknown. We have to look into the dark to find the light.

Failing Forward: Beds, Breakfasts, and a Billion-Dollar Valuation

Founded in August 2008 by Brian Chesky (@bchesky) and Joe Gebbia (@jgebbia), Airbnb is a marketplace that connects people who have space to spare with those who are looking for a place to stay. The concept was created by accident, when Chesky, an industrial designer, moved from Los Angeles to San Francisco.

An international design conference was coming to San Francisco and all the hotels were sold out. The two eventual cofounders were trying to figure out how to make rent, so they decided to create an "airbed and breakfast" for one weekend during the conference. They ended up hosting three people, made some money, and had an amazing experience. The concept for Airbnb was born. They believed that, one day, people all over the world would do this.

However, the road was not that easy. According to Chesky, in a TechCrunch Disrupt NY 2011 interview, out of the 15 to 20 angel investors they met with in fall 2008, half did not return their e-mails, and the consensus was that it was an awful idea.

They got their break after meeting with Paul Graham (@paulg) of Y Combinator in January 2009. Graham thought the idea was terrible too, but invested in them because, as Chesky explains it, they were creative, smart entrepreneurs, and Graham figured they would eventually change their idea.

Well, it turned out that Chesky and Gebbia saw a market no one else could. As of June 2011, they had booked more than 1.6 million nights in 181 countries. In July 2011 they raised a Series B financing round of $112 million at a $1 billion-plus valuation.

(continued)

(*continued*)

When asked to explain how they had gone from a start-up no one wanted to invest in to one of Silicon Valley's hottest companies, Chesky said, "It was just something that seemed like obviously a bad idea, until one day it just seemed like obviously a good idea."[3]

Make it Safe for Employees to Fail

Innovation in agencies cannot always come from the top. Employees must feel empowered to contribute to the agency's advancement. Their ideas and inspirations should be nurtured and cultivated.

Although careless mistakes are unacceptable, professionals should not be afraid to miss or falter. It is easy to lose confidence and become conservative if you constantly fear your actions will be questioned and criticized. Agencies should build cultures that encourage and reward creativity and innovation.

If you don't make mistakes, you're not working on hard enough problems. And that's a big mistake.[4]

—*Frank Wilczek, 2004 Nobel Prize winner in physics*

Don't Make Promises That You Can't Keep

Sometimes when we are small, we make promises that are too big. Just remember, once you break a promise, there is no going back. Keep expectations in line with your ability to deliver at scale. Do not let desperation or a lack of perspective cloud your judgment and actions. Be ready for increased expectations as you grow and evolve.

Master the Art of the Unexpected

Give people something they did not know they wanted, and take them places they did not expect to go. Think Steve Jobs. No one does it better.

Apply this thinking to your content, business model, and personal brands. In order to capture and keep the attention of the crowds, we must take chances and be willing to go where others will not.

Always Fight Like the Underdog

It is more exciting when the odds are against you. Underdogs have passion and the intrinsic drive to keep fighting, no matter the odds or obstacles. They have purpose.

CHAPTER HIGHLIGHTS

- We learn from failure. It builds character, teaches us humility, shows us how to cope with adversity, and challenges us to continually test, revise, and improve.

- Marketing agencies have to make difficult choices to break from traditional agency-centric pricing models, invest in technology, recruit and retain hybrid professionals, build scalable infrastructures, and transform their services.

- Disruptor agencies do not have the restrictions of legacy systems or the internal politics that hinder change. They have flexibility in their pricing, lower overhead costs, and more dynamic and versatile talent.

- Traditionalists have to be willing to fix what is broken and return to the ideas and inspirations that made them great.

- History means nothing if you have no future.

- The best time to pursue opportunities and innovations is when you are prospering. Something, or someone, will eventually come along to disrupt your agency, so it might as well be you.

- Marketing agencies have to become more agile. They have to focus less on thinking and talking and more on doing, both for themselves and their clients.

- If you are not scared and unsure when creating content and pushing new ideas, then it is probably not worth pursuing.

- Employees must feel empowered to contribute to the agency's advancement. Their ideas and inspirations should be nurtured and cultivated.

- Give people something they did not know they wanted, and take them places they did not expect to go.

chapter **10**

Pursue Purpose

It is purpose, not profits, which defines an agency.

STAND FOR SOMETHING

Success is not about money, or at least it should not be. We all have basic financial needs that must be satisfied, but no amount of money, fame, or power will bring happiness. In fact, my experiences have shown me that they often have the opposite effect on people. In order to find happiness, we must be a part of something greater than ourselves, something that we truly believe in.

The same holds true for businesses. Although for-profit companies exist to make money, the most important organizations, the ones that have the potential to change industries and our world, are often started because the founders believe they have a higher calling.

They build, out of passion and an undying belief that they can create something of great and lasting significance, what others are not willing or able to. True entrepreneurs will never be satisfied with riches alone. They have to affect change and will risk everything to make their visions reality.

They had a great sense of purpose, which is a prerequisite for anyone who is nutty enough to want to start a company. That burning sense of conviction is what you need to overcome the inevitable obstacles.

—*David Vise*, The Google Story: Inside the Hottest Business, Media and Technology Success of Our Time, *p. 65.*

THE PURPOSE PYRAMID: A NEW PLANNING PARADIGM

We are programmed to set revenue goals, target growth rates, and measure our importance and value based on financial returns. We compare ourselves to industry benchmarks, flaunt our client lists, and tout our awards because they create the perception of success and make us feel good about ourselves.

There is nothing wrong with having financial goals and achieving milestones, but these are simply means to an end. If you believe that your agency exists solely to make money, then you likely are falling short of your potential and cheating your employees of opportunities to realize theirs.

It is purpose, not profits, which defines an agency.

What Is Our Agency's Purpose?

Have you ever stopped to ask yourself or your employees this question? You will not find the answer in the *Blueprint*, or any other book for that matter. Purpose comes from within, often originating with the founder, and is perpetuated through the agency's actions and professionals.

An agency's purpose may be innate and unspoken at first, residing in the minds of its leaders. However, over time it becomes essential to involve employees. Purpose evolves as the agency and its employees mature, and their perspectives and priorities change.

To recruit and retain top professionals, you must instill in them a belief that their time and energy is contributing to the pursuit of a greater goal that transcends standard business measurements and personal achievements and enriches their lives.

> The most successful people . . . often aren't directly pursuing conventional notions of success. They're working hard and persisting through difficulties because of their internal desire to control their lives, learn about their world, and accomplish something that endures.
>
> —*Daniel Pink*, Drive: The Surprising Truth About What Motivates Us, *p. 60.*

Finding Purpose: A Personal Journey

I started PR 20/20 with aggressive growth goals and a grand vision. I do not think that, at the time, I understood the agency's purpose, but I had a business plan and the freedom to find my way. Everything seemed so perfect. Then life happened, and it turned my world upside down.

In a 20-month span, two of the most important people in my life tragically passed away. I quickly realized that our personal and business lives are inextricably bound. For me, nothing has been the same since. The future I thought I knew changed. My life began to take on new meaning, and so did the agency.

These personal experiences have had a direct and lasting impact on my goals for the agency, the people that I choose to surround myself with, and the decisions that I make every day on where to focus my time and energy.

My situation is not unique. We all have our challenges. Our priorities and perspectives change, and that affects how we view the world, our careers, and our businesses.

Planning for Purpose

In September 2010, I found myself looking for direction. PR 20/20 was on pace for a record year as we approached our five-year anniversary, and I was about to be honored with an Innovation in Business Rising Star Award from *Smart Business*. It was an incredible time with tremendous promise for the future.

We had assembled a remarkable team of talented and amazingly driven professionals, and had achieved so much together, but something was missing. I was beginning to feel that somewhere along the road, I had lost my way. I had gotten so caught up in pricing, services, staffing, infrastructure, growth, and profits that I had forgotten to focus on what really mattered.

In an effort to organize my thoughts, I wrote, "The Pursuit of Purpose" on my dry erase board, and sketched a pyramid with five levels—pursuit, people, process, performance, and purpose.

At the time, I had no idea what I would use it for, other than as a daily reminder to remember why the agency existed, and to keep my priorities straight. As I wrote the *Blueprint*, the pyramid started taking on new meaning for me. I realized that it was the missing, intangible piece to building an agency that truly matters.

Figure 10.1 is a snapshot of how the pyramid works, and how the five levels support and build on each other.

Pursuit   The first level of the pyramid is pursuit. This is where you define your agency's vision, mission, and values, and establish the financial metrics and growth goals that will enable your agency to recruit and retain talent. You look internally to determine if you truly have the passion and drive to succeed, and you make a commitment to be great.

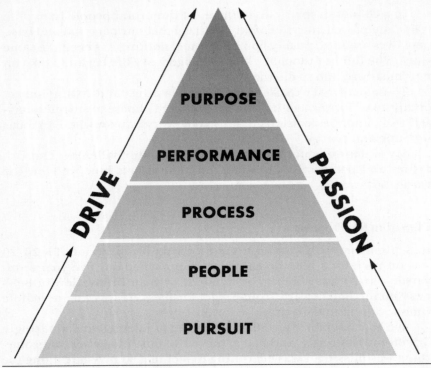

Figure 10.1   The Purpose Pyramid

This is also an opportunity for agency leaders to define their personal goals. What are you willing to sacrifice? How will you find balance in your life to remain focused and continuously bring the positive energy needed to motivate and inspire your team?

Why try for greatness? If you're doing something that you care that much about, and you believe in its purpose deeply enough, then it is impossible to imagine not trying to make it great.

—*Jim Collins,* Good to Great: Why Some Companies Make the Leap . . . and Others Don't, *p. 208.*

People   This is possibly the most important level in building an agency, and it is the focus of Chapter 3. Once you know where you are going, you can better identify the type of people it will take to get there. This includes employees, strategic partners, clients, advisors, and any other professionals who will influence your agency and its ability to succeed.

To create an enduring brand, you need to assemble a team of talented and intrinsically motivated employees, build partnerships with like-minded organizations, and surround your agency with clients who value your professionals and services.

> Together, we had built a business that combined profits, passion, and purpose. And we knew that it wasn't just about building a business. It was about building a lifestyle that was about delivering happiness to everyone, including ourselves.
>
> —*Tony Hsieh, CEO of Zappos.com and author of* Delivering Happiness[1]

> Great organizations . . . are filled with people who are absolutely determined to see the organization succeed, whatever the odds against it.
>
> —*Alan Murray,* The Wall Street Journal Essential Guide to Management: Lasting Lessons from the Best Leadership Minds of Our Time, *p. 82.*

Process   Much of the *Blueprint* has focused on process, which in large part determines your agency's efficiency, productivity, and profitability. It is the systematic way in which you construct and manage your agency.

I tend to segment process into logical business units—operations, human resources, finance, technology, and marketing—but it includes elements such as pricing, services, hiring, training, marketing strategy, sales systems, and client services.

Success itself is a process. It requires persistence, perseverance, and an uncommon drive to achieve remarkable things. There are no shortcuts, and no guarantees. You have to be able to find satisfaction and motivation in incremental progress over days, weeks, months, and years. You have to be willing to outwork your peers and competitors. It is not about rewards or recognition; it is about an internal burning desire to improve.

If you are not putting in the time and energy to succeed, someone else will, and you have no right to complain when they take what was yours. It is acceptable to be mediocre, but if that is the path you choose, then alter your expectations about what life will give you in return. Success is not easy, but things worth achieving never are.

Performance   These are the outcomes that fuel growth and success. Performance is the achievement of business objectives such as lead volume, customer conversions, client loyalty, employee advancement and retention, efficiency, productivity, revenue, and profits.

People and process drive performance, which enables agencies to focus on their purpose.

Purpose   The truly transformational agencies, the ones that will thrive and lead in the new marketing services ecosystem, will pursue purpose. Think of purpose as your agency's compass. Purpose is not necessarily measureable, but it provides direction and meaning. Every action and decision should align with this ultimate pursuit.

Purpose eases the pain of the long hours and gives you the fortitude to fail. It makes menial tasks meaningful, and serves as the pivotal piece of your employee recruitment and retention strategy.

Purpose is aspirational and, in most cases, something that is never fully realized. In other words, the pursuit itself is the end game.

Purpose is:

- Steve Jobs of Apple, in 1983, famously saying to John Sculley, then president of PepsiCo, "Do you want to sell sugar water for the rest of your life or do you want to come with me and change the world?"[2]

- Brian Halligan and Dharmesh Shah of HubSpot building a software company to disrupt and transform the marketing industry to match the way consumers shop and learn.

- Larry Page and Sergey Brin of Google and their unending desire to create the perfect search engine that understands exactly what you mean and gives back exactly what you want.[3]

- Facebook's Mark Zuckerberg and his commitment to make the world more open and transparent, in order to create greater understanding and connection.[4]

- My mom, Judy Roetzer, starting a cookie bouquet franchise because a bouquet she sent as a gift had brought a smile to the face of a terminally ill friend. After 20-plus years as a preschool teacher, she ventured into the unknown because she believed that her purpose was to bring that same happiness to others.

If you're going to do something, do something that matters.

—*Fried and Hansson*, Rework, *p. 32.*

FATE, DESTINY, AND THE BUSINESS OF LIFE

Life is full of joy and pain, opportunities and obstacles. This is what we are given. It is our fate. Many people choose lives of fate, dwelling on what they have lost and living within the limitations that they believe control their existence. However, life also gives us choice. It gives us free will to create our destiny.

If you want to keep good people, work needs to provide them with a sense they are doing something important, that they are fulfilling their destiny.

—*Alan Murray*, The Wall Street Journal Essential Guide to Management: Lasting Lessons from the Best Leadership Minds of Our Time, *p. 28.*

Everything that we are given, and everything that we create, can be taken away in the blink of an eye. That is what unites us—our mortality. It is the decisions we make and the actions we take in the time we are given that define who we are and what we will be.

Life Lessons of an Entrepreneur

I leave you with a collection of life lessons I have learned along the way. I hope they play a small part in helping you discover and pursue your agency's purpose:

- Fate is what we are given. Destiny is what we make. It is up to you which path you choose.
- Our business and personal lives are inextricably bound. Finding balance is the key.
- We live life in days, weeks, months, and years, but we remember it in moments. Seek to create, embrace, and cherish them.
- Everyone has a story, a unique set of circumstances and experiences that make them who they are. Take the time to listen and understand before you judge.
- Your energy is best invested in positive people whom you trust and respect and who challenge you to be a better person and professional.
- Negativity will destroy relationships and ruin the chemistry and culture within companies. Build your personal network and business around positive people.

- Loyalty and trust are invaluable traits of friends, employees, and coworkers.
- Integrity takes a lifetime to build and a moment to lose.
- We all need to be inspired. Discover the people, places, events, books, and music that inspire you.
- We are all mortal. Money, fame, and power mean nothing in the face of death.
- Get out of your comfort zone. Some of the most memorable experiences in life happen when you let go of your fears and anxieties.
- Life is full of noise, interruptions, and distractions. It will pass you by if you let it. Take the time to quiet your mind, and find your direction and purpose.

CHAPTER HIGHLIGHTS

- In order to find happiness, we must be a part of something greater than ourselves, something that we truly believe in.
- Purpose comes from within, often originating with the founder, and it is perpetuated through the agency's actions and professionals.
- In order to create an enduring brand, you need to assemble a team of talented and intrinsically motivated employees, build partnerships with like-minded organizations, and surround your agency with clients who value your professionals and services.
- Success itself is a process. It requires persistence, perseverance, and an uncommon drive to achieve remarkable things.
- If you are not putting in the time and energy to succeed, someone else will, and you have no right to complain when they take what was yours.
- People and process drive performance, which enables agencies to focus on their purpose.
- Purpose eases the pain of the long hours and gives you the fortitude to fail. It makes menial tasks meaningful, and serves as the pivotal piece of your employee recruitment and retention strategy.

Conclusion

Hybrid firms will rule the modern age of marketing services.

THE TRANSFORMATION

Change is not always easy, but it is inevitable. In the coming years, the marketing-services industry will be transformed.

Traditional firms, who are unable or unwilling to evolve, will fade and a new category of disruptive hybrid agencies will rise to prominence. These emerging firms are tech savvy, offer integrated services, hire and retain versatile talent, and profit from diversified revenue streams. They thrive on change, and continually apply shifts and advances in technology to strengthen their businesses, evolve their services, and deliver greater value to clients.

Your agency has the opportunity to prosper in the coming age of marketing services, but you must make the choice to disrupt or you will be disrupted.

The three primary catalysts of transformation—change velocity, selective consumption, and success factors—will drive the need for a new breed of agencies, functioning within a more open and collaborative ecosystem.

If you are a rising star in a traditional firm, you too have a choice. Life and business are about the pursuit of purpose. Push for change now before it is too late. Do not give all of your time and energy to a hopeless cause. Know when it is time to walk away and go to an organization where your effort and vision are valued. Alternatively, take a risk, venture into the unknown, and build your own hybrid firm. There has never been a better time.

CORE CONCEPTS

Inefficiency Is the Enemy of Success

Pricing strategy is a key component to disruption. Agencies motivated to change will shift away from the inefficient legacy system of billable hours and move to more results-driven, value-based models. This presents the opportunity for agencies and independent consultants to disrupt the industry with lower prices and potentially higher profit margins.

- The traditional billable-hour system is tied exclusively to outputs, not outcomes, and assumes that all agency activities— account management, client communications, writing, planning, consulting, and creative—are of equal value. It is a broken model.
- The amount professionals are paid does not have a direct correlation to the quality or value of the services they provide.
- There are countless factors that can affect a professional's efficiency, but distractions, time tracking, and motivation are three of the biggest culprits.
- The guiding principle in hybrid marketing agency pricing is that it must be value based, meaning prices are determined based on perceived and actual value rather than the number of billable hours something takes to complete.

A Real-Time World Demands Real-Time Agencies

The rate of change, continually accelerated by technology innovations, has created growing demand for tech-savvy, forward-thinking firms. Specifically, trends and shifts in consumer behavior, business processes, software, data analysis, communications, and marketing philosophies have affected the need for evolved services and consulting.

Although change velocity presents challenges, it also provides significant advancement opportunities. Technology has made it possible to create remarkably efficient agency management and client-services systems that lower operating costs while increasing productivity and profitability.

- Hybrid agencies are able to build more scalable models that largely operate in the cloud, capitalize on advances in online communications and mobility, and rely on their social graphs to create a more open and collaborative agency ecosystem.

- Agencies that understand technology trends and innovations are able to more readily adapt their own business models, continually increase efficiency and productivity, evolve client campaigns, and make strategic connections of seemingly unrelated information.
- You must have the willingness and ability to change your agency's services, processes, and infrastructure to accommodate market shifts.
- Your agency's future depends on its ability to adapt, deliver measurable and meaningful results, and develop professionals who are capable of providing consulting and services across multiple disciplines.
- The market is moving fast, with growth opportunities everywhere, but do not come into it unprepared and try to sell services you are not qualified to deliver.
- The marketing agency ecosystem, which consists of disruptors, traditionalists, softservers, specialists, connectors, and soloists, is client centric. This means agencies must continually evolve to meet client needs and demands.

Talent Cannot Be Replicated

Model agencies are constructed one employee at a time. They do not allow market demand or outside expectations to dictate their growth, and they do not sacrifice the quality of their hires to satisfy short-term needs. They take a controlled, almost methodical, approach to expansion. They develop talent from within and construct teams based on shared values, innate abilities, and complementary character traits.

- Constructing an agency filled with top talent establishes a distinct and formidable competitive advantage.
- Although intelligence and experience are key, their character, internal drive, personality, and innate abilities are the intangibles that truly differentiate great candidates from good ones.
- Hybrid agencies are built on a culture of we, succeeding and failing as one. Professionals are passionately loyal to the agency and to each other.
- Client acquisition and retention must be driven by the collective strength, reputation, and capabilities of the firm.
- Professionals who are unmotivated or who fail to live up to their potential can negatively impact the team's performance,

but more important, they drag down the morale and momentum of peers and leadership.

- Professionals are given unparalleled opportunities for career advancement and encouraged to build strong personal brands.
- The top firms, which will lead industry transformation and deliver the most value, are built from within. In order to excel and continually differentiate, agencies must have a solid strategy to recruit, advance, and retain emerging talent.
- Hybrid professionals are trained to deliver services across search, mobile, social, content, analytics, web, PR, and e-mail marketing. They provide integrated solutions that historically required multiple agencies and consultants.

The Best Plan Is to Prepare for Perpetual Change

Change velocity principles dictate that trying to plan for anything beyond three years is an exercise in futility. Have a vision for the long-term, but make infrastructure decisions based on current and short-term realities.

- Success is an iterative process.
- Hybrid agencies are built on a stable operational foundation with nimble management systems that enable them to execute and adapt faster than the competition.
- Making decisions too far ahead of the growth curve can cost you valuable resources now, but not planning for the contingencies of growth can be detrimental to your ability to profitably build your business in the future.
- Marketing agencies are bound by the limitations of human resources.
- Cloud applications offer rapid deployment, often without professional IT support. They enable agencies to build more agile systems that are capable of adapting quickly to changing business environments.

Doing Is the Key to Differentiation

The marketing world is full of thinkers, talkers, and self-proclaimed gurus, but after awhile they all start to sound the same. What we need are more doers—agencies and professionals that drive change by practicing what they preach.

- A hybrid agency is defined by the collective strength of its employees' personal brands. Your job as an agency leader is to clearly establish the agency brand, and then give your team the freedom and support to build and evolve theirs.

- Treat your agency website with the same care and attention that you do your clients' websites. Continually analyze, track, and monitor its success through inbound links, traffic, referrers, and website visits by keywords, among other metrics.

- When building your agency marketing strategy, be sure to think beyond prospects.

- Agencies have the ability to reach and influence audiences directly at the exact moment they are searching online. In essence, they are granting you permission to market to them, but you have to be there, and provide value.

- Social media is about listening, learning, building relationships, and bringing value to the communities relevant to your agency.

- Content marketing enables you to differentiate your agency while driving acquisition (leads) and retention (loyalty). It requires that you understand your audiences and continuously publish compelling, multimedia content.

- Public relations is about listening to your audiences, sharing your unique story, creating connections, gaining influence, and building loyalty in a measurable and meaningful way.

Everything Is Sales

You are always selling. You are selling an idea, vision, service, agency brand, personal brand, and belief that your firm is more capable and qualified than the next one.

However, in a professional service firm, sales happens at every level of the company. It is often the account executives that have the most direct client contact, and, therefore, regardless of whether they are charged with it, they function as the agency's primary salespeople. They are the ones whose performance, behavior, and ability to build strong client relationships determine if an account stays or goes and whether clients provide referrals and testimonials.

- Selling is both an art and a science that requires experience, education, and an intimate knowledge of the agency.

- Concentrate on creating a sales system that meets your current needs for lead generation and that is scalable with your long-term growth goals.

- When building your sales system, your most valued asset is your team. No one individual sales or business development manager can possibly deliver the value and lead volume that you can create through a collective and strategic effort.

- Sales processes help define responsibilities, set performance expectations, give professionals the knowledge and resources to excel, and connect actions to business goals.

- In order to maximize the lead-generation and nurturing process, and increase the probability of conversion, it is important to understand how organizations make marketing-services buying decisions.

All Clients Are Not Created Equal

Although agencies need to make every client feel valued, the reality is that some accounts are far more important to the stability and success of your agency, and they need to be treated different.

These priority accounts have a greater appreciation for your services; they value your people and treat your agency as a partner, not as a vendor. They pay bills on time (or early), have realistic expectations, and reasonable timelines, and they commit the time and energy needed to make the relationship work.

- The need to build strong client relationships must be ingrained in an agency's culture. Employees should be 100 percent focused on the happiness and success of their clients.

- Become indispensible through your hard work, insight, consultation, services, expertise, friendship, and professionalism.

- Do the little things that build relationships, and take the time to show clients that you care about their successes, both on individual and organizational levels.

- The greatest value you can bring to clients is staffing their account teams with A players. These professionals are analytical, confident, creative, detail oriented, highly motivated, and strategic—all traits that consistently translate into success for your clients.

- Use nonbillable exercises to educate and train your team while enhancing the value you deliver to clients.

- Agency management, as it relates to client loyalty, comes down to two things: intelligence and action. In order to take the actions necessary to retain and grow accounts, leaders have to have their finger on the pulse of the agency.

An Agency's Value Is Measured in Outcomes, Not Outputs

Leading marketing agencies turn information into intelligence, and intelligence into action. They build campaigns that consistently produce measurable outcomes, including inbound links, website traffic, leads, and sales. Hybrid agencies must shift away from arbitrary metrics, such as media impressions, reach, advertising equivalency, and PR value, and become measurement geeks who are obsessed with data-driven services.

- Marketing agencies from every discipline—advertising, PR, social, SEO, content, and web—have the opportunity to evolve and play an integral role in bringing structure and meaning to the wealth of information available to businesses.

- Take a scientific approach to marketing, and develop processes to analyze data for insight that can increase efficiency and maximize ROI for clients.

- Turn your hybrid professionals into analysts. Teach them to make decisions based on logic and reason. Show them how to gain insight from information, and how to use that insight to educate clients, build consensus, and drive action.

- Every campaign should start with performance benchmarks, including current lead volume, inbound links, website traffic, content downloads, blog subscribers, and social media reach.

- *Builders* are services designed to set the foundation for future success, while *drivers* are intended to produce short-term results. Your agency's ability to succeed and bring value to clients requires a balanced and strategic approach to both.

Never Hesitate to Head in a Direction That Others Seem to Fear

Disruptors need to be willing to take risks that established agencies cannot or will not. While traditionalists try to fix their models, you should be focused on continually reinventing yours.

- Failure builds character, teaches us humility, shows us how to cope with adversity, and challenges us to continually test, revise, and improve.

- Marketing agency leaders have to make difficult choices to break from traditional agency-centric pricing models, invest in technology, recruit and retain hybrid professionals, build scalable infrastructures, and transform their services.

- Traditionalists, along with soloists and specialists, have to put their fears aside and confront the challenges ahead. They have to think and act more like start-ups. They have to become disruptors themselves.
- Be willing to deconstruct your brand and business model to remain relevant, and position yourself where the market is going.
- Do not wait for desperate times to evolve.
- If you are not scared and unsure when creating content and pushing new ideas, then it is probably not worth pursuing.
- Give people something they did not know they wanted, and take them places they did not expect to go.

It Is Purpose, Not Profit, Which Defines an Agency

We are programmed to set revenue goals, target growth rates, and measure our importance and value based on financial returns. We compare ourselves to industry benchmarks, flaunt our client lists, and tout our awards, because they create the perception of success and make us feel good about ourselves.

There is nothing wrong with having financial goals and achieving milestones, but these are simply means to an end. If you believe that your agency exists solely to make money, then you are likely falling short of your potential and cheating your employees of opportunities to realize theirs.

- In order to find happiness, we must be a part of something greater than ourselves, something that we truly believe in.
- True entrepreneurs will never be satisfied with riches alone. They have to effect change, and they will risk everything to make their visions reality.
- Purpose evolves as the agency and its employees mature and as their perspectives and priorities change.
- To create an enduring brand, you need to assemble a team of talented and intrinsically motivated employees, build partnerships with like-minded organizations, and surround your agency with clients who value your professionals and services.
- Success requires persistence, perseverance, and an uncommon drive to achieve remarkable things. There are no shortcuts and no guarantees.

- The truly transformational agencies, the ones that will thrive and lead in the new marketing-services ecosystem, will pursue purpose.

Thank You

Thank you for reading *The Marketing Agency Blueprint*. I wish you and your agency success. Please visit us at www.MarketingAgency Insider.com to learn more, join the agency community, and help lead the industry transformation.

Resources

VISIT MarketingAgencyInsider.com

The Marketing Agency Blueprint presents 10 rules for building tech-savvy, hybrid agencies that are more efficient, influential, and profitable than traditional firms. This book was written as a practical and candid handbook to help agencies and consultants:

1. Build tech-savvy, hybrid firms.
2. Generate more qualified leads.
3. Win clients with value-based pricing.
4. Secure more long-term retainers.
5. Create diverse and recurring revenue streams.
6. Develop highly efficient management systems.
7. Construct more effective account teams.
8. Recruit and retain top talent.
9. Deliver greater results and value to clients.
10. Increase client loyalty.

However, the book is just the beginning. We have launched a website and online academy dedicated to building a more open and collaborative agency ecosystem. MarketingAgencyInsider.com is the hub for marketing agency news, information, resources, training, education, and engagement. The site features include:

- **Marketing Agency Insider Blog:** The Marketing Agency Insider blog serves up a mix of original and curated content, industry news, interviews, case studies, change-velocity assessments, and more. I invite you to subscribe, and send us your thoughts and ideas about topics you would like to see included in upcoming posts.

- **Marketing Agency Academy:** The Marketing Agency Academy is an education and training program designed to accelerate industry transformation.

  The Academy curriculum mirrors and expands on *Marketing Agency Blueprint* concepts and processes through live and on-demand webinars and original content. Visit Marketing AgencyInsider.com to register for upcoming events.

- **Resources:** Check out the resource center on MarketingAgency Insider.com for access to management templates, guides, how-to videos, software recommendations, affiliate/VAR program opportunities, and relevant industry links. The resource center is continually updated with the following audiences in mind:
  - Advertising agencies.
  - Brand-development agencies.
  - Content-marketing firms.
  - Copywriters.
  - Digital/interactive marketing agencies.
  - Graphic design shops.
  - Inbound marketing agencies.
  - Marketing-communications firms.
  - Marketing consultants.
  - PR agencies.
  - SEO firms.
  - Website development firms.

- **Community:** Join the community. You can connect through MarketingAgencyInsider.com, or visit us directly on Twitter, LinkedIn, and Facebook.
  - Twitter: @AgencyIn.
  - Book Hashtag: #AgencyBlueprint.
  - LinkedIn Group: Search "Marketing Agency Insider."
  - Facebook Page: www.Facebook.com/MarketingAgencyInsider

Notes

INTRODUCTION

1. Tim O'Reilly, "Create More Value Than You Capture," O'Reilly Media, Inc., www.slideshare.net/oreillylearning/create-more-value-than-you-capture-1597291 (accessed July 5, 2011).

CHAPTER 1   ELIMINATE BILLABLE HOURS

1. Clayton Christensen, "Key Concepts," http://claytonchristensen.com/disruptive_innovation.html (accessed July 5, 2011).
2. Rupal Parekh, "Top New York Advertising Creatives Charge $750 per Hour," *AdAge*, last modified October 1, 2009, http://adage.com/article/agency-news/4a-s-top-york-advertising-creatives-charge-750-hour/139409/.
3. StevensGouldPincus, "PR Agency Industry 2009 Best Practices Benchmarking Report," www.stevensgouldpincus.com/images/SGP_2009_Benchmarking_Report.pdf (accessed July 5, 2011).

CHAPTER 2   TRANSFORM INTO A HYBRID

1. "HubSpot Inbound Marketing Marketplace," HubSpot, http://services.hubspot.com/ (accessed July 5, 2011).
2. Mark Suster, "What Should You Do With Your Crappy Little Services Business?" TechCrunch, last modified April 24, 2011, http://techcrunch.com/2011/04/24/what-should-you-do-with-your-crappy-little-services-business/.

3. Amit Singhal and Matt Cutts, "Finding More High-Quality Sites in Search," Google, last modified February 23, 2011, http://google blog.blogspot.com/2011/02/finding-more-high-quality-sites-in .html.

4. Amit Singhal, "High-Quality Sites Algorithm Goes Global, Incorporates User Feedback," Google, last modified April 11, 2011, http://googlewebmastercentral.blogspot.com/2011/04/high -quality-sites-algorithm-goes.html.

5. Amit Singhal, "More Guidance on Building High-Quality Sites," Google, last modified May 6, 2011, http://googlewebmaster central.blogspot.com/2011/05/more-guidance-on-building-high -quality.html.

6. Bradley Johnson, "Tweet This: Agencies Get 28% of Revenue from Digital," *AdAge*, last modified April 25, 2011, http://adage .com/article/agency-news/tweet-agencies-28-revenue-digital /227164/.

7. Shar VanBoskirk, "Interactive Marketing Spend Will Near $77 Billion By 2016," Forrester, last modified August 25, 2011, http://blogs.forbes.com/forrester/?p=231

8. David Segal, "The Dirty Little Secrets of Search," *New York Times*, last modified February 12, 2011, www.nytimes.com/2011/02/13 /business/13search.html.

9. Paul Roetzer, "7 Key Elements of Great Business Content," HubSpot, last modified June 21, 2010, http://blog.hubspot.com/blog /tabid/6307/bid/6120/7-Key-Elements-Of-Great-Business-Content .aspx.

10. "The 1M/1M Deal Radar: crowdSPRING, Chicago, Illinois," Deal Radar, last modified February 8, 2011, www.sramanamitra.com /2011/02/08/the-1m1m-deal-radar-crowdspring/.

11. Paul Roetzer, "Top PR Firms Fail to Make the Grade Online," PR 20/20, last modified June 17, 2009, www.pr2020.com/page /top-pr-firms-fail-to-make-the-grade-online.

CHAPTER 3   THINK TALENT AND TEAM

1. Bradford D. Smart, *Topgrading: How Leading Companies Win by Hiring, Coaching, and Keeping the Best People* (New York: Penguin, 2005), 6.

2. Daniel H. Pink, *Drive: The Surprising Truth About What Motivates Us* (New York: Penguin, 2009).

3. Maureen Morrison, "Left to Fend for Themselves, Employees Feel No Loyalty to Agencies," *AdAge*, last modified March 8, 2011, http://adage.com/article/special-report-4as-conference/andrew-benett-offers-bleak-talent-management-stats/149297/.

4. David H. Maister, *Managing the Professional Service Firm* (New York: Simon & Schuster, 1993).

5. Bradford D. Smart, *Topgrading: How Leading Companies Win by Hiring, Coaching, and Keeping the Best People* (New York: Penguin, 2005).

CHAPTER 4   BUILD A SCALABLE INFRASTRUCTURE

1. Brian Halligan, "Transforming the Marketing Services Industry," HubSpot, last modified February 18, 2010, www.hubspot.com/blog/bid/5618/Transforming-The-Marketing-Services-Industry

2. Olafur Ingthorsson, "The Growing Impact of Cloud & Mobility Solutions," Data Center Knowledge, last modified May 23, 2011, www.datacenterknowledge.com/archives/2011/05/23/the-growing-impact-of-cloud-mobility-solutions/.

CHAPTER 5   DEVISE AN INBOUND MARKETING GAMEPLAN

1. "comScore Releases May 2011 U.S. Search Engine Rankings," comScore, last modified June 10, 2011, www.comscore.com/Press_Events/Press_Releases/2011/6/comScore_Releases_May_2011_U.S._Search_Engine_Rankings.

CHAPTER 6   CONTROL THE SALES FUNNEL

1. Steve W. Martin, "Seven Personality Traits of Top Salespeople," *Harvard Business Review*, last modified June 27, 2011, http://blogs.hbr.org/cs/2011/06/the_seven_personality_traits_o.html.

2. Dave Kurlan, *Baseline Selling: How to Become a Sales Superstar by Using What You Already Know About the Game of Baseball* (Bloomington, IN: AuthorHouse, 2005).

CHAPTER 7   COMMIT TO CLIENTS

1. Rachel Kaufman, "GolinHarris 'Prevolves', Gets Rid of Account Executives," MediaBistro, last modified June 15, 2011, www.mediabistro.com/mediajobsdaily/golinharris-prevolves-gets-rid-of-account-executives_b7325.
2. Stuart Elliot, "Account Executive Is Antiquated. Consider Yourself a Catalyst," *New York Times*, last modified June 14, 2011, www.nytimes.com/2011/06/15/business/media/15adco.html?_r=2.

CHAPTER 8   DELIVER RESULTS

1. Sergio Zyman, *The End of Marketing As We Know It* (New York: HarperCollins, 1999).
2. "Demonstrate AdWords Skill with Individual Qualification," Google, www.google.com/adwords/professionals/individual.html (accessed July 9, 2011).
3. "Get Smarter with Google Analytics," www.google.com/analytics/education.html (accessed July 9, 2011).
4. "Search Engine Ranking Factors," SEOmoz, www.seomoz.org/article/search-ranking-factors (accessed July 9, 2011).
5. "100 Awesome Marketing Stats, Charts, & Graphs [Data]," HubSpot, last modified May 20, 2011, http://blog.hubspot.com/blog/tabid/6307/bid/14416/100-Awesome-Marketing-Stats-Charts-Graphs-Data.aspx.
6. Danielle Leitch, "Impact of Social Media on Website Traffic," *Social Media Today,* last modified April 18, 2011, http://socialmediatoday.com/dleitchmorevisibilitycom/287238/impact-social-media-website-traffic.
7. "New Study: Deep Brand Engagement Correlates with Financial Performance," Altimeter Group, last modified July 20, 2009, www.altimetergroup.com/2009/07/engagementdb.html.
8. "Social Fans More Likely to Buy," eMarketer, last modified March 6, 2010, www.emarketer.com/Article.aspx?R=1007568.
9. Rick Burnes, "Study Shows Small Businesses That Blog Get 55% More Website Visitors," HubSpot, last modified August 17, 2009, http://blog.hubspot.com/blog/tabid/6307/bid/5014/Study-Shows-Small-Businesses-That-Blog-Get-55-More-Website-Visitors.aspx.

10. "100 Awesome Marketing Stats, Charts, & Graphs [Data]," Hub-Spot, last modified May 20, 2011, http://blog.hubspot.com/blog/tabid/6307/bid/14416/100-Awesome-Marketing-Stats-Charts-Graphs-Data.aspx.

11. Aaron Wheeler and Rand Fishkin, "How Google's Panda Update Changed SEO Best Practices Forever—Whiteboard Friday," last modified June 23, 2011, www.seomoz.org/blog/how-googles-panda-update-changed-seo-best-practices-forever-whiteboard-friday.

12. Rohit Bhargava, "Manifesto for the Content Curator," Influential Marketing Blog, last modified September 30, 2009, http://rohitbhargava.typepad.com/weblog/2009/09/manifesto-for-the-content-curator-the-next-big-social-media-job-of-the-future-.html.

13. John Medina, *Brain Rules: 12 Principles for Surviving and Thriving at Work, Home, and School* (Seattle, WA: Pear Press, 2009).

14. Jonathan B. Spira and Joshua B. Feintuch, "The Cost of Not Paying Attention: How Interruptions Impact Knowledge Worker Productivity," Basex, September, 2005.

15. Jason Fried and David H. Hansson, *Rework* (New York: Crown, 2010).

CHAPTER 9   EMBRACE FAILURE

1. Alok Jha, "We Must Learn to Love Uncertainty and Failure, Say Leading Thinkers," *The Guardian*, January 15, 2011, www.guardian.co.uk/science/2011/jan/15/uncertainty-failure-edge-question.

2. David A. Vise, *The Google Story: Inside the Hottest Business, Media and Technology Success of Our Time* (New York: Bantam Dell, 2005).

3. Sarah Lacy, "Airbnb Has Arrived: Raising Mega-Round at a $1 Billion + Valuation," TechCrunch, May 30, 2011, http://techcrunch.com/2011/05/30/airbnb-has-arrived-raising-mega-round-at-a-1-billion-valuation/.

4. Tim Ferriss, *The 4-Hour Workweek: Escape 9-5, Live Anywhere and Join the New Rich* (New York: Crown, 2007), 278.

CHAPTER 10   PURSUE PURPOSE

1. Tony Hsieh, *Delivering Happiness: A Path to Profits, Passion, and Purpose* (New York: Business Plus, 2010).

2. "Triumph of the Nerds: The Transcripts, Part III," PBS, http://to .pbs.org/leLIeI.

3. "Our Philosophy," Google, www.google.com/about/corporate /company/tenthings.html (accessed July 9, 2011).

4. "Facebook Principles," Facebook, www.facebook.com/princi ples.php (accessed July 9, 2011).

About the Author

Paul Roetzer (@paulroetzer) is founder and CEO of PR 20/20, a Cleveland-based marketing agency specializing in public relations, content marketing, social media, and search marketing. PR 20/20 was the first marketing agency in HubSpot's value-added reseller (VAR) program, which now includes more than 500 certified firms. A graduate of Ohio University's E.W. Scripps School of Journalism, Roetzer spent six years at a traditional PR firm prior to launching PR 20/20 in November 2005. In 2010, he was recognized by *Smart Business* with an Innovation in Business Rising Star Award.

Index

Absolute capacity, 65
Account growth opportunities, 161, 164
Accounting solution, 85
Accounting systems, strategic approaches to, 88
Account loss, variables leading to, 24
Account management system, 154–57
Account manager/lead consultant, 143, 145
Accounts
  growing, 162
  prioritizing, 206
  prioritizing and evaluating, 159–61
  ranking, 164
  retaining and growing, 14, 147
Account status, 159
Account team dashboards, 154–55
Account teams, 143, 144
Action-oriented content, 37
Actions, bold and decisive, 8
Activities, tracking, 115–16
Activity center element, of a proposal, 142
Advanced service level, 20, 21

Advancement plans, 75
Advisors, reliable, 87–88
Advisory board, 94
AdWords. *See* Google AdWords training
Affiliate programs, 28, 52–53
Agencies
  campaign-based, 65
  factors facing, 60–61
  positioning as thought leaders, 54
  prepared and confident, 144
  productive and efficient, 64
  stability of, 147
  as thought leaders, 50
  value of, 207
Agency audiences, inbound marketing influence on, 104–7
Agency blog editor, 112
Agency brand, approach to presenting, 100–101
Agency capabilities, pricing, 19
Agency capacity, breakdown of, 64–65
Agency competencies, standard, 49
Agency culture, 55, 56
  dynamic, 62
Agency founders, 56
Agency functioning, 78

Agency inefficiencies, charging for, 17
Agency leadership, 77
Agency life, speed of, 61
Agency management, 164, 206
Agency-management models, 27
Agency management system, 157–59
Agency manager dashboard, 157
Agency Manager Template, 65, 66
Agency model, transforming, 15
Agency partnerships, 49–50
Agency professionals, personal branding of, 101–2
Agency purpose, defining, 194
Agency salespeople, evaluating and training, 126–27
Agency sales system
  core elements of, 124–35
  questions concerning, 121–24
Agency services
  changing, 34
  mysterious nature of, 14
Agency systems, 163
Agency training programs, components of, 68–72
Agency transformation
  catalysts fueling, 44
  role of immersion in, 31–33
  role of integration in, 33–34
Agency value, understanding, 89
Agency VAR partners, 28. *See also* Value Added Reseller (VAR) program
Agency website
  monitoring, 205
  success of, 103
Aggressive growth model, 87
Ahead-of-need triggers, 67
Airbnb, 189
All-in-one software, 92
All Things Digital, 32
American Association of Advertising Agencies (4A), 8–9
Analysis
  critical, 57
  in the monthly scorecard structure, 172

Analysts
  developing, 207
  training, 166, 167–69
Analytical insights, sharing, 170
Analytical thinking, 168
Analytics, 129
  lead-intelligence, 132
  using, 116
  using to adapt, 169–72
Anchor accounts, 160
Angel investors, 89
A players
  competencies and traits of, 57–59, 77
  retaining, 67–68
Apologizing, for mistakes, 149
Appendix element, of a proposal, 142
Apple, 32, 188
Assistant vice president position, 154
Associate consultant position, 153
Audiences
  connecting with, 110
  inbound marketing influence on, 104–7
  listening to, 114
  reaching and influencing, 109, 205
  selecting, 51
Awareness stage, of the buying cycle, 135

Balance, between work and life, 57–58
Bank lending, 89
Basecamp, 34, 84, 92, 156. *See also* 37Signals' Basecamp project-management system
Baseline Selling—How to Become a Sales Superstar by Using What You Already Know about the Game of Baseball (Kurlan), 126
Basic service level, 20, 21
Belzer, Frank, 126
Bhargava, Rohit, 179
Billable-hour formula, 17
Billable-hour quotas, 13
Billable hours
  eliminating, 7–25

mysterious nature of, 14
for variable-scope services, 23
Billable hours practice, 1–2
Billable-hours system, 25, 202
 failure of, 8–14
 practical application of, 11–12
Blog editor, 112, 118–19
Bloggers, 178
 pitching content to, 114
 benefits of, 37
Blog post abstracts, 113
Blog-post writing, 71
Blogs, launching, 35
Blog subscribers, increase in, 117
Books, as training tools, 68–69
Brand awareness, building, 108–9
Brand-centric content, 37–38
Brand definition, 62
Brand marketing, 174
Brand popularity, SERP impact of,
 177
Brand positioning
 as a builder, 173
 for lead generation, 137–38
Brands
 deconstructing, 187, 208
 defining and differentiating, 97,
 99–100, 118
 enduring, 208
 third-party endorsements of, 109
Brin, Sergey, 198
Budgeting, 119
Budgeting skills, 168
Budgets, 114–15
 dynamic, 97
Builders, 207
 activating, 172–74
 interdependence of, 174
 questions related to, 173
Builder vs. driver variable, 20
Bundled services, 15, 28
Business content, 112
Business copywriting, core elements
 of, 37–38
Business development, as a loss
 leader, 20
Business development management
 system, 121, 144

Business practices, reputable, 35
Business problems, solving, 91–92
Business-savvy writers, 112
Business-to-business (B2B)
 organizations, 3
Business-to-consumer (B2C)
 organizations, 3
Buyer persona(s), 111
 example of, 130–31
 profiling, 129–30
Buyer-persona content, 38
Buying cycle, 135–37

Campaign management solution, 84
Campaign objectives, 97
Campaigns
 consumer-oriented, 33
 planning and executing, 171
 shifting to, 65
 starting with performance
 benchmarks, 167
 timelines for, 97
Candidate grading system, 63
Candidate interviews, 62
Candidate pipelines, building,
 62–63
Capacity breakdown, 64–65
Capital reserves, 88
Caputa, Peter, 29
Career, commitment to, 60
Career advancement, 56
Career/life balance, 162
Career path, defining, 62, 73
Career path system, 152–54
Career professionals, hiring, 67
Case studies, as marketing/sales
 tools, 16
Cash flow
 monitoring, 90–91
 realities of, 88–91
Cash-flow crunches, 88
Challenges, confronting, 208
Change, pushing for, 201
Change velocity, 2–3, 10, 27, 48, 201,
 202
 assessments of, 158–59
 infrastructure planning and, 80
 relentless nature of, 83

Channel overload, 180–83
  eliminating, 182
Chesky, Brian, 189–90
Christensen, Clayton, 7
Client acquisition, 56
Client-agency relationship,
  14–15
Client analytics, 169
Client case studies, 140
Client-centric agencies, 44
Client contact, 205
Client conversions, 143
Client development, long-term
  approach to, 164
Client exercises, 156–57
Client experience, 161
Client-hour capacity, 64–65
Client in residence (CIR), creating,
  151
Client online reviews, 140
Client-reference policy, 141
Client-reference requests, 140–41
Client relationships, 206
Clients
  bringing value to, 163
  caring for, 149
  choosing, 142
  commitment to, 147–64
  creating value for, 147–48
  differentiating, 170
  evaluating, 159–61
  importance of, 163
  inbound marketing influence on,
    106–7
  innovative, 161
  listening to, 149
  personal approach to, 148–49
  ranking factors for, 159–61
Client-service hours, 18
Client-services models, 27
Cloud, operating in, 27
Cloud applications, 28, 94, 204
  integrating, 91–93
  integration plans for, 92
  risks and challenges related to,
    92–93
Cloud-based management
  platforms, 49

Cloud companies, risk associated
  with, 93
Cloud computing, 91
Collaboration, 48–50, 54
  focus on, 118
Collins, Jim, 196
Comfort zone, going beyond, 200
Commitment, 60, 77
  of clients, 161
  to contracts, 20
  to inbound marketing success, 99
Communicating, in bursts, 182
Communication
  open and honest, 148
  via social media, 177
Competencies
  of A players, 57–59, 77
  assessing, 74
Competitors, inbound marketing
  influence on, 104
Comprehension, building, 108–9
Conferences, 32, 71
Confidence, 58
Connections
  building, 150
  creating and nurturing, 163
Connectivity overload, 180–83
Connector agencies, 44, 46
  characteristics of, 43
ConstantContact, 53
Consultant position, 153
Consulting, billable hours for, 23
Consumer behavior, evolution of, 95
Consumers, control of purchasing
  processes, xiii–xiv
Content
  buyer-persona-driven, 112
  focus on, 36
  as a growth opportunity, 37–38
  pitching to reporters and bloggers,
    114
  sharing, 71
Content curation, 179–80
Content-driven website, 97
Content-management systems
  (CMSs), 27, 47, 129
Content marketing, 46–47, 111–13,
  145, 175, 178, 205

integrated marketing and, 112
  for lead generation, 138
  strategy for, 113
Content publishing, 37
Content quality, assessing, 33
Content spam epidemic, 178–79
Contract base, building, 24
Contracts
  client commitment to, 20
  long-term, 24, 25
Controlled urgency, 187–88
Copywriting
  as a builder, 173
  effective, 37–38
  importance of, 103
Core brand messages, 111–12, 118
Core competencies, focus on, 48–49
Core concepts, 202–9
Core service businesses, problems
    impacting, 31
Core systems, impact of, 152–59
Cost considerations, 19
Costs, realities of, 88–91
Creating, in bursts, 182
Creative content, 38
Creativity, 58, 162
Critical infrastructure lessons, 82–88
  build through trusted solution
      providers, 83–86
  create a funding runway, 88
  find reliable advisors/mentors,
      87–88
  prepare for perpetual change, 82–83
  understand your limits, 87
CRM platform, 144. See also Cus-
    tomer relationship manage-
    ment (CRM)
CRM solutions, 70, 84–85, 163
crowdSPRING, 24, 43
"Culture of we," 56
Current needs, accommodating,
    80–81
Customer Happiness Index (CHI)
    score, 28
Customer relationship management
    (CRM), 27, 128. See also CRM
    entries; Highrise CRM system;
    SugarCRM

Cutts, Matt, 36
  personal branding snapshot of,
      102–3

Data
  analyzing, 167
  desire for, 165
  extracting insight from, 165
Deal Radar, 44
Debt servicing, 89–90, 94
Decision making
  basis for, 204
  for growth goals, 79–88
Decisions, desperation-driven, 36
Decision stage, of the buying cycle,
    136–37
Delegating, 76
Destiny, 199
Details
  attention to, 58
  focus on, 162
Dialogue, clear and open, 61
Digital agencies, 53
Digital capabilities, 53–54
  building, 35
Digital division/group, 34–35
Digital Due Diligence Advisors, 36
Digital marketing services, shift to,
    60
Digital services, 1, 53
  demand for, 34–38
  expanding, 29
  tips for building, 36
Direction, finding, 200
Discovery element, of a proposal,
    141–42
Discovery process, 132–33
Disruptive agencies, valuation of,
    89
Disruptive business characteristics,
    8
Disruptive hybrid agencies, 201
Disruptive innovation, 7–8
  partnerships and, 29
Disruptor advantage, 186
Disruptor agencies, 44, 45, 46, 68
  building, 47–48
  characteristics of, 39–40

Distractions
 disadvantages of, 25
 for marketing agency
  professionals, 12–13
 productivity and, 180–81
Diversification, of revenue streams,
  50–53
Doers, need for, 95, 118
Doing
 importance of, 204–5
 vs. planning, 188–91
Draft, building through,
  59–61
Drive, evaluating, 74
Drivers, 207
 activating, 174–75
Dynamic culture, 62

Earnings Before Interest, Taxes,
  Depreciation, and Amortization
  (EBITDA), 89
ebooks, 170
Economies of scale, achieving, 15.
  See also Scalable entries
Ecosystem, understanding your role
  in, 38–48
Ecosystem diagram, 44–46
Ecosystem partners, for lead
  generation, 138
Editorial calendars, 113
Education
 creating recurring revenue
  through, 50
 for salespeople, 123
 stagnation of, 2
Education programs, 56
Efficiency
 as the driver of success, 21
 improving/increasing, 15, 34,
  180–83
 of service delivery, 160
 system-wide, 56
Effort, importance of, 77
Eloqua, 53, 123
Elway, John, 75
E-mail marketing, 35
Emerging Marketing Agency
  Ecosystem, 45

Employee brands, 205
Employee confidence, 56–57
Employee failure, 190
Employees
 inbound marketing influence on,
  105
 online behavior of, 106
 supporting, 63
 value of, 13
End of Marketing as We Know It,
  The (Zyman), 166
Energy, investing, 199
Engadget, 32
Entrepreneurs
 helping, 5
 as mentors, 87–88
Environmental factors, 44
Estimated hours, 17–18
Ethical practices, maintaining, 36
Evaluation metrics, 74
Evaluations, connecting to
  performance, 74–75
Evaluation stage, of the buying
  cycle, 136
Evernote, 34
ExactTarget, 53
Excellence, striving for, 163
Excel worksheets, 154–55
Executive summary, 141
Exit strategy, 91
Expectation levels, failure to deliver,
  14
Expectations
 realistic, 160
 resetting, 182

Facebook, 32, 176
Facebook page, using, 100
Failure, embracing, 185–191
Fair market value, 19
Fate, 199
Finance systems, strategic
  approaches to, 88
Financial forecasts, for PR 20/20
  agency, 81
Financial health
 of clients, 164
 deceiving signs of, 90

Financial performance, social media and, 177–78
Financial stability, of clients, 160
Financial strength, in partnerships, 49–50
Financing, from friends and family, 94
Firms
  building from within, 59
  change velocity of, 2–3
  as tech firms, 27–34
  See also Marketing firms; PR (public relations) firms; Professional service firms; Tech-firm transformation; Technology-driven service firms; Tech-savvy firms; Tech-savvy hybrid firms; Traditional firms
Fishkin, Rand, 46
Flat-rate billing, 8
Focus, 58
Forecasting/reporting model, 65
Forrester, 34
Free agents, 61, 77
Fried, Jason, 181
Friends and family network, focus on, 89
Frodo syndrome, 186
FunctionFox, 84
Funding
  from friends and family, 89
  realities of, 88–91
Funding runway, creating, 88

Gadgets, Google & SEO blog, 102
GamePlan, in the monthly score-card structure, 172. *See also* Inbound Marketing GamePlan
Gebbia, Joe, 189
GigaOM, 32
Gizmodo, 32
Global cloud computing market, 91
Goals, for inbound marketing, 99
Godin, Seth, 188–89
GolinHarris, 152
Google, 32–33
  webspam and, 102–3

Google AdWords training, 167–69
Google Analytics reports, 169
Google Analytics training, 169
Google Buzz, 176
Google Panda, 32–33
Google Panda update 2.2, 179
Google search results, protection of, 36
Google training courses, 71
Google Webmaster Help Youtube Channel, 102
GoToMeeting, 34, 86, 135
GoToWebinar, 86
Graham, Paul, 189
Gross profit, 22
Group dynamics, 110
Group exercises, 71–72
Group manager position, 154
Group meetings, 155–56
Growth
  adjusting for, 143
  balanced, 121
  contingency planning for, 80
  controlled, 79–80
  driving, 48
  investing in, 88–91
  relationship to infrastructure, 87
Growth goals, decisions for, 79–88
Growth opportunities, 35
Guest articles/posts, 114

Halligan, Brian, 28, 89, 198
Hansson, David Heinemeier, 181
Happiness, finding, 193
Heavy Hitter book series (Martin), 125
High-growth agencies, 88
High performers, 57
High-profile clients, 161
Highrise CRM system, 34, 70, 84–85, 123, 128, 156. *See also* Customer relationship management (CRM)
Hiring, timing of, 64–67
Hiring decisions, 65, 78
Hiring mistakes, avoiding, 61
Hiring standards, 56
Historical timesheets, referencing, 17
Honest communication, 148

Hourly-rate contingency, 23
Hourly-rate formula, 10–11
Hourly revenue target (HRT), 17, 18–19, 21, 160
Hour quotas, 13
Hours, forecasting, 23
Hsieh, Tony, 197
HubSpot, xiii, xiv, 53, 85, 123
    philosophy of, 3
    relationship with, 34
HubSpot Inbound Marketing University, 71
HubSpot Services Marketplace, 24, 28–29
HubSpot VAR program, xv, 28
    insight into, 29–30
    See also Value Added Reseller (VAR) program
Huddles, 157
Human resource duties, 72
Human resources, limitations of, 87, 94
Hybrid agencies, xiv, xv, 27–54, 56, 118
    personal branding and, 103
    PR firms as, 46–47
    prototype, 129
    rules for building, 211
    use of analytics, 169–72
Hybrid professionals, 68
    hiring, retaining, and advancing, 61–72

iContact, 53
Immersion, role in agency transformation, 31–33
Inbound candidates, 62, 78
    capturing, 62
Inbound links, 117
    generating, 176
    SERP impact of, 175–76
Inbound marketing, xv, 170
    influence on agency audiences, 104–7
    power of, 118
    shift to, 95–96
    strategies and tactics of, xiv, 99, 109–16

value of, 116–17
Inbound marketing campaigns, results of, 96
Inbound Marketing GamePlan
    customized, 171
    football visual representing, 97–99
    foundation of, 99–103
    objectives of, 107–9
    origins of, 96–99
    steps in, 96–97
Inbound marketing service package, xiv–xv
Income potential, 159
Independent thinking, 162–63
Inefficiency (inefficiencies), 7
    absorbing, 22
    cost of, 11–12
    as the enemy of success, 202
    factors in, 12–14
Influencers, following and engaging, 32
Information
    how audiences consume, 113
    turning into intelligence, 165
Infrastructure, 79. *See also* Scalable infrastructure
Infrastructure as a Service (IaaS), 91
Infrastructure decisions, 204
    risks associated with, 83
Infrastructure investments, 80
Infrastructure planning, 80–81, 94
Innovation
    immersion in, 149
    lack of, 2
    See also Disruptive innovation
Innovative solutions, testing, 83, 94
Innovators, as leaders, 8
Insight mobile app, 84
Inspiration, 200
Instinct, trusting, 187
Integrated campaigns
    building, 97
    marketing strategies of, 109–16
Integrated campaign strategy, 118
Integrated marketing, content marketing and, 112
Integrated marketing platform, 30

Integration, role in agency transformation, 33–34
Integrity, 200
Interactive marketing spending, 34
Intermediate service level, 20
Internal analytics training sessions, 169
Internally driven professionals, 60
Internal marketing team, xiii
Internal social networks, 70
Internal social network solution, 85–86
Internet marketing solution, 85. *See also* Online entries; Web- entries
Internet operations, 27
Interruption-based marketing, 170
Interviews, informational, 62
Intuit, 85
Invoices, scrutinizing, 14
"It" factor, 58, 64

James, LeBron, parable of, 75–76
JCPenney link-building scam, 35–36
Jive Software, 85
Job candidates, inbound marketing influence on, 105
Jobs, Steve, 188, 198

Kelly, Kevin, 186
Keyword phrases, relevant, 107
Keyword usage, SERP impact of, 176
Knowledge, consuming, 163
Knowledge transfer, 70
Kurlan, Dave, 126
Kurlan & Associates, 126–27

Landing pages, unique, 166, 170
Leaders
    responsibility of, 56
    talent identification by, 61
Leadership, 75–77
    importance of, 78
    support from, 160–61
Lead-intelligence analytics, 132
Lead management, 132
Lead qualification, 129–31
Leads
    gaining intelligence into, 123

    gathering information about, 132–33
    generating, 96, 107, 118, 137–39, 206
    monthly, 122, 137
    nurturing, 124, 129, 139–42, 206
    ranking and prioritizing, 123
    responsibility for, 123
    scoring, 129, 132
    tracking, 123
Lead sources, 137
    identifying, 121–22
Lead survey question, 133–34
Lead volume, access to, 144
Legacy systems, 27
Life, business of, 199–200
Life/career balance, 162
Life lessons, of an entrepreneur, 199–200
Limits, understanding, 87
LinkedIn, thought leadership through, 110–11
Listening, 58
    to clients, 149
Logoworks, 24
Long-tail keyword phrases, 36
Long-term client relationships, 23
Long-Term Locke, 130–31
Loss leaders, 20
Lower prices, industry disruption via, 8
Low-quality work, 14
Loyalty, 200
    to the agency, 56
    building, 96, 107, 118, 147–51
    of clients, 163

Mad Men marketing methodology, xiii
MAD-R (money, authority, desire, response) characteristics, 139
MailChimp, 53
Maister, David H., 71
Management books, 68–69
Managing the Professional Service Firm (Maister), 71
"Manifesto for the Content Curator," 179

Marketing, scientific approach to, 207
Marketing agencies
  avoiding, xiii
  challenges facing, 29
  changes in, 1
  evolution of, 207
  sales and, 124–25
Marketing Agency Academy, 212
Marketing Agency community, 212
Marketing agency contacts, xv
Marketing agency ecosystem, 203
Marketing Agency Insider blog, 211–12
MarketingAgencyInsider.com, 5, 209, 211
Marketing Agency Insider community, 5
Marketing-agency model, 1–2
Marketing agency profiles, 39–44
  connectors, 43
  disruptors, 39–40
  softservers, 41–42
  soloists, 43–44
  specialists, 42–43
  traditionalists, 40–41
Marketing agency professionals, speed of, 60–61
Marketing Agency resources, 211–12
Marketing agency services, affordable, 15
Marketing books, 68–69
Marketing campaigns, 4
Marketing consultant laws, 161
Marketing efforts, impact of, 97
Marketing events, tracking, 116, 166
Marketing firms, success factors for, 4
Marketing guidelines, 30
Marketing models, fixing, 185
Marketing plans, 22
Marketing services buying decisions, understanding, 135–37
Marketing services ecosystem, 54
  agency classifications in, 38–44
  visualizing, 44–46
Marketing-services industry
  changes in, xv

disruptive innovation in, 7
transformation of, 1, 201
Marketing software, 123
Marketing strategies, 144
  building, 118
Marketing support, affordable, 24
Marketing tactics, rushing into, 173
Marketo, 53, 123
Market research, as a builder, 173
Martin, Steve W., 125
Measurement
  experimenting with, 166–67
  importance of, 165–69
Measurement tools, integrating, 166
Media, inbound marketing influence on, 105
Media relations, billable hours for, 23
Meetings, action-oriented, 157
Mentors, reliable, 87–88
Methodologies, testing, xiv
Milestones, tracking, 115–16, 166
Mistakes, apologizing for, 149
Model agencies, 55–57, 77
  calculated investments of, 93
  capabilities of, 95
  constructing, 203–4
Models, reinventing, 207–8
Monday Morning Meetings (M3s), 158
Money, budgeting, 114–15
Monthly forecasts, 65
Monthly scorecards, 171–72
Motivation
  intrinsic, 58
  to work efficiently, 13–14
Motivation level, maintaining, 74
Multimedia content, publishing, 33
Multimedia content services, 54
Multitasking, 12
Murray, Alan, 197

Negativity, 199
NetSuite OpenAir, 92
Networking, for lead generation, 139
New financial model, building, 15
News, creating, 114
Niche markets, for lead generation, 138–39

Nonbillable hours, investing, 14
Nonrevenue-generating time, 9

Objective Management Group
    Salesperson's Self-Assessment
    system, 126
Objectives
    defining, 51
    of inbound marketing, 99
    of the Inbound Marketing
        GamePlan, 107–9
Objectives element, of a proposal,
    142
Offline networking, 63
Ondercin, Larry, xvii
Online behavior, guidelines for, 106.
    See also Internet entries;
    Web-entries
Online career survey, 62
Online content, results-driven, 37
Online meeting solution, 86
Online presence, 62
Online portfolio, sharing, 140
Online services directory, 28–29
Online surveys, 132–33
Online training courses, 71
Open communication, 148
Opportunities
    for marketing agencies, 8
    project-based, 24
    researching and evaluating, 51
Options, exploring, 89
O'Reilly, Tim, 5
Outbound marketing, xiii–xiv, 170
Outlaw agencies, 32
Outsourcing, 48–50, 54
Overstaffing, 64

Page, Larry, 187, 198
Panda algorithm, 32–33
Pardot, 123
Partners, inbound marketing
    influence on, 104–5
Partnership programs, 53
Partnerships, 49–50
    effective, 164
Passion, importance of, 99
Patience of potential, 60

Peak efficiency, 17
Peers, inbound marketing influence
    on, 104
People, as sales system core
    elements, 124–28
Perceived value, 19
    pricing on, 21
Performance, 197–98
    in partnerships, 49
    unplugging and, 180–83
Performance benchmarks, 207
    starting campaigns with, 167
Perpetual change, preparing for,
    82–83, 204
Personal approach, to clients, 148–49
Personal branding
    example of, 102–3
    tips concerning, 103
Personal brands
    as drivers of awareness and leads,
        125
    for lead generation, 138
    power of, 101–2
Personal experiences, impact of, 195
Personal goals, defining, 196
Perspective, lack of, 60
Pierce, Doug, 36
Pink, Daniel, 181, 194
"Pivoting the agency," 82
Planning, vs. doing, 188–91
Plans, as loss leaders, 20, 25
Platform as a Service (PaaS), 91
Platform redundancies, limiting, 92
Platforms, user permissions and
    access across, 93
Portfolio, well-balanced, 24
Positioning, enhancing, 108
Positive cash flow, 90, 91
Positive energy, 58
Postpurchase behavior stage, of the
    buying cycle, 137
PowerPoint, 135
Power shift, in the marketing-
    services industry, 7
PR 20/20 agency, xiv–xv. See also
    Public relations (PR)
    start-up of, 81–82
    2x–3x scale for, 80–81

PR 20/20 career path, 152–54
PR 20/20 curated posts, 180
PR 20/20 lead survey questions, 133–34
Predictive data, 65
Preference building, 108–9
Premium content, producing, 37
Presentation process, 134–35
PR firms, 46–47
Pricing
  experimenting with, 187
  market demands and, 19
  in partnerships, 49
  value-based, 15–24
Pricing model, value-based, 17
Pricing strategy, for lead generation, 137
Pricing strategy, 8, 202
Priorities, resetting, 182
Priority accounts, 159–61, 206
Proactive communication, 162
Process(es)
  in partnerships, 49
  as sales system core elements, 129–35
Process building, 25
Product business, challenges of becoming, 30–31
Product innovations, 83
Production/delivery costs, 19
Production rate, 9
Productivity
  increasing, 180–83
  system-wide, 56
Productivity blocks, 181, 182
Professional reviews, 72–75, 78
  goals of, 73
Professionals
  assessing competencies and traits of, 74
  commitment, perspective, and speed of, 60–61
  developing, 35
  insight and guidance from, 87
  intrinsically motivated, 55
  key findings concerning, 126–27
  positioning and placement of, 51–52

  unmotivated, 56
  See also Hybrid professionals
Professional service firms, sales and, 124–25
Profitable business, building, 88–89
Profit goals, achieving, 18
Profits, options for increasing, 10
Program integrations, customizing, 93
Project-based services market, 24
Project management, 156, 163
Project management solution, 84
Project revenue-efficiency rate, calculating, 21–22
Project work, growing demand for, 24
Promises, keeping, 149, 190
Proposal process, 134
Proposals, effective, 141–42, 145
Proprietary product development, 30–31
Prospects, 122, 139–42, 205
  convincing, 139–40
  inbound marketing influence on, 106
  rapport with salespeople, 143
  sources for, 62
  See also Leads
Prototype agencies, expansion in, 79–80
Prototype hybrid agencies, 129
Publications, technology-related, 32
Publicity, for lead generation, 139
Public relations (PR), 113–14, 175, 205. See also PR entries
Publish-and-pray approach, 170
Publishing, creating recurring revenue through, 50
Purchasing processes, consumer control of, xiii–xiv
Purpose
  finding, 200
  as a personal journey, 194–95
  planning for, 195
  pursuing, 193–200, 208–9
Purpose pyramid, 194–98
  levels of, 195–98

Quality content, 33
Quality leads, 122
  identifying and prioritizing, 137
Quickbooks Online, 85, 92

Ranking factors, for clients, 159–61
Reach, *vs.* influence, 108
Real-time agencies, 202–3
Real-time marketing, 171–72
Real-time sharing, 70
Recruiting, 78
Recruitment strategy, 60
Recurring revenue, 24
  creating, 33, 50
Redundancies, reducing, 92
Referrals
  earning, 144
  for lead generation, 138
Relationships
  building, 58–59, 147–51
  diversifying, 150
  establishing and strengthening, 107–8
Reliable advisors/mentors, finding, 87–88
Reporters, pitching content to, 114
Requests for proposals (RFPs), 2, 20
Resources, 211–12
  allocating, 115
Results
  delivering, 162
  focus on delivering, 15
  product/services delivery of, 16
Results-driven content, 38
Retainer limits, 13
Retainers, traditional, 11
Return on investment (ROI), 168
  client expectations concerning, 14
  maximizing, 30
Revenue calculations, 18–19. *See also* Recurring revenue
Revenue-efficiency rates (RERs), 21–23, 160
Revenue-generating time, 9
Revenue goals, 88
Revenue growth, 117
Revenue streams, diversifying, 50–53
Review meetings, 73

Rework (Fried & Hansson), 181
Risk(s)
  calculated, 34
  expansion and, 88
  mitigating, 24
  tolerance for, 8
Risk taking, 59, 162–63, 207–8
Roberge, Rick, 126–27
Roetzer, Judy, 198
Roetzer, Paul, xiv–xv
Role playing, 71

Sacrificing, in the early years, 47–48
Salary multiple formula, 9
Salary-rate fallacy, 9–11
Sales efforts, efficient and effective, 124
Salesforce, 32, 53, 123, 128. *See also* Salespeople
Sales funnel, controlling, 121–45
Salespeople
  evaluating and training, 126–27
  prospect rapport with, 143
  training and educating, 123
  See also Successful salespeople
Sales process(es), 206
  core areas of, 129–35
Sales strategies, 144
Sales system
  building, 205–6
  creating, 144
Sales system tools, 128–29
Sales team, value of, 125
Scalable infrastructure. *See also* Economies of scale
  building, 79–94
  example of, 80–81
Scalable models, 202
Scalable technology infrastructure, considerations related to, 86
Schmitz, Christina Capadona, xvii
Scott, David Meerman, 4
Search engine optimization (SEO), 46, 175
  authentic, 36
  as a builder, 173
  for lead generation, 138
  See also SEOmoz entries

Search-engine-optimized content, 38
Search Engine Ranking Factors
    report, 175
Search-engine rankings, 32, 35
  boosting, 107
Search-engine result page (SERP),
    175
Search engines, understanding,
    168–69
Search marketing, 109–10, 118
Search stage, of the buying cycle,
    135–36
Selective consumption, 3–4, 10, 48,
    28, 170–71, 174, 201
Selective hiring, 63
Self-analysis, 72–73
Self-challenging, 162
Selling, 144. *See also* Marketing
    entries; Sales entries
Senior consultant position, 153
Senior executives, inefficiencies of,
    10
Sensory overload, eliminating, 182
SEOmoz, 30, 46, 53, 175. *See also*
    Search engine optimization
    (SEO)
SEOmoz report, 176, 177
Service businesses, problems
    impacting, 31
Service-level costs, 20–21
Service marketplaces, for lead
    generation, 138
Service offerings, expanding and
    integrating, 3
Service packages, bundling and
    promoting, 29
Service/pricing guide, 82
Service proposals, core elements of,
    141–42
Services
  adapting and integrating, 33
  defining the scope of, 15
  experimenting with, 187
  measuring, 170–71
  in partnerships, 49
  results-driven, 4
  standardizing, 15
  technology-driven, 28–29

Service standardization, 25
Set fees, value-based, 23
Set pricing, 15
Shah, Dharmesh, xiii, xiv, 198
Sharing, solutions for, 70
Shortcuts, avoiding, 173
Shortsighted thinking, 13
Silicon Valley Insider, 32
Site quality, assessing, 33
Skype, 34, 135
Smart, Bradford D., 57, 72
Snapshot element, of a proposal, 141
Snapshots, in the monthly scorecard
    structure, 172
Social bookmarking sites, 176
Social candidates, 62, 78
  monitoring and engaging, 63
Social media, 118, 205
  as builders, 173
  impact of, 177–78
  personal branding and, 101
  SERP impact of, 176
Social media consulting, 35
Social media participation, 46, 62
Social media policy, establishing,
    105–6
Social media strategy, 110
Social web savvy, 59
Soft capacity, 64
Softserver agencies, 44, 45–46
  characteristics of, 41–42
Software
  all-in-one, 92
  value-adding, 91
Software as a Service (SaaS), 91
Software-as-a-service platforms, 3
Software development, 50
Software platforms, 34
Soloist agencies, characteristics of,
    43–44
Solution providers, building
    through, 83–86
Solutions
  delivering, 162
  evaluating, 92
  format for evaluating, 158–59
  outgrowing, 93
  specialized, 92

Speakers' packet, 51
Speaking engagements, 114
Speaking events
    evaluating, 52
    preparing for, 52
Speaking strategy, steps for
        building, 50–52
Speaking topics, 51
Specialist agencies, 44
    characteristics of, 42–43
Stable business, building, 88–89
Standardized presentations, 134–35
Standardized proposals, 134
Standardized services, case-study
        example of, 16
Standard measurement systems, 2
Strategic content, 37
Strategic discovery process, 132–33
Strategic plans, as loss leaders, 20
Strategic thinking, 163
Strategizing, 59
Strong proposals, 134
Success
    as a process, 197
    realistic expectations of, 160
Success factors, 10, 201
    for marketing firms, 4
    setting, 107–9
Successful salespeople
    core competencies of, 127–28
    traits of, 125–26
SugarCRM, 123, 128. *See also*
        Customer relationship
        management (CRM)
Sullivan, Danny, 46
SurveyMonkey, 62, 132
Suster, Mark, 31
SXSW Interactive conference, 71
Synergy, in partnerships, 161
System building, 25
Systems, significance of, 152–59

Talent
    assembling a team of, 197
    attracting/recruiting and retain-
        ing, 48, 55, 61, 152
    evaluating, 63, 72–75
    importance of, 77, 203–4

investing in, 149–50
    motivated, 67
    personalized approach to, 73–75
Target net profit margins, 9
Team(s)
    constructing, 55
    value of, 206
Team leadership, 76
Team players, 59
Team video, 100
Teamwork, in inbound marketing,
        99
TechCrunch, 31, 32
Tech-firm transformation, 31–34
Technically sound content, 38
Technology
    advancement opportunities and, 3
    benefits of, 202–3
    investment in, 53
Technology-driven service firms,
        common elements in, 31–34
Technology-driven services, 28–29
Technology immersion, 149
    value of, 32
Technology industry, knowledge
        about, 31–32, 53
Technology infrastructure
        providers, 83–86
Technology partners, 94
Technology trendsetters,
        monitoring, 32
Tech-savvy agencies, 128, 144
Tech-savvy firms, 158
Tech-savvy hybrid firms, 53
Tech-savvy professionals, 59
Terms-of-agreement element, of a
        proposal, 142
Third-party software integration, 30
37Signals, 84
37Signals' Basecamp project-man-
        agement system, 49. *See also*
        Basecamp
Thought leaders, 50, 54
Thought leadership, 108
    through LinkedIn, 110–11
Thought-leadership content, at
        HubSpot, 30
Tiered-rate billing model, 8–10

Time, budgeting, 114–15
TimeFox, 65, 84, 92
TimeFox reports, 157
Timesheets, historical, 17
Time tracking, 13, 163
    accurate, 18, 25
Time-tracking software, 65
Time-tracking solution, 84
Time-tracking system, 19
Tools, as sales system core elements,
    128–29
Topgrading (Smart), 72
Top lead sources, identifying,
    121–22
Top-performing professionals,
    59–60
Tradition, looking beyond, 188
Traditional agencies
    alternative to, 82
    failure of, 8, 27
Traditional firms
    focus of, 2
    opportunity for, 186–88
Traditionalist agencies, 44, 46
    characteristics of, 40–41
Traditional marketing techniques,
    xiii
Traditional networking, 63
    for lead generation, 139
Traditional services, 53
Training
    of analysts, 166, 167–69
    of salespeople, 123, 126–27
    stagnation of, 2
Training programs, 56, 68–72
Traits
    of A players, 57–59, 77
    assessing, 74
    of successful salespeople, 125–26
Transformation
    accelerating, 4
    forces fueling, 2–4
    of the marketing-services
        industry, 201
Transformational agencies, 198, 209
Transparency
    power of, 14–15
    in pricing, 25

Trust, 200
Trust building, with transparency,
    15
Trusted solution providers, building
    through, 83–86
TweetDeck, 34
Tweets, varying, 110
20/20 Standard service/pricing
    guide, 82
Twitter, 32, 176
Twitter lists, 63
Tyre, Dan, 116

Underdogs
    fighting like, 191
    as leaders, 8
Underperforming professionals,
    transitioning, 56
Unexpected, mastering the art of,
    190
Unknown, venturing into, 188–89
Unplugging
    performance and, 180–83
    six-step plan for, 181–82
Unqualified leads, 122

Value
    creating, 147–48
    focus on delivering, 15
    product/services delivery of, 16
Value-added reseller (VAR)
    partnerships, 52
Value Added Reseller (VAR) pro-
    gram, xiv. *See also* HubSpot VAR
    program; VAR entries
Value-based pricing, 15–24, 202
    testing and revising, 18
Value-based pricing model, 25
    variables in, 17
Value-based set fees, 23
Value imperative, 5
Variable-scope services, billable
    hours for, 23
VAR partnerships, 4. *See also* Value
    Added Reseller (VAR) program
VAR program partners, 28
VAR programs, 28, 52
VAR relationships, 52

Vendors, inbound marketing
    influence on, 104
Venture capitalists, 89
VerticalResponse, 53
Vice president position, 154
Vise, David, 193
Vision
    setting and pursuing, 48
    turning into reality, 81–82

Web development, 175. *See also*
    Internet entries; Online entries;
    Website development
Webinars, 32, 68
    promoting, 170
Webinar solution, 86
Webmaster Central Blog, 33
Website analytics, 116, 166
Website careers page, 62
Website development, 103
    as a builder, 173
    See also Web development

Website grade, 117
Websites, 47
    content-driven, 97
    as dynamic hubs, 174
    enhancing, 140
    maintaining, 178
    See also Agency website
Website traffic, 117
Web spam, 102
    Google and, 102–3
Wired, 32
Work-life balance, 57–58
Writers, business-savvy, 112
Writing skills, 59
Wu, Jordyne, 29

Yammer, 34, 70, 85
Young professionals, 56
    developing/molding, 68, 77, 78

Zuckerberg, Mark, 198
Zyman, Sergio, 166

USPs. Our marketing and web development teams work together, combining design, developer and on-line marketing knowledge making us more adaptable to change, enabling us to constantly adapt & change as a company

Specialize - we are specialists in e-commerce marketing, design, development. and have For specialising enables us to focus solely on one discipline, emersing ourselves in the latest trends, changes in the marketplace, technologies enabling us to be ahead of the game, to react just

Magento - we have chosen the magento e-commerce platform. A world leader in...
our developers are magento coding experts, enabling us to build our own functionality, known as magento modules, which we then sell to other developers & web design agencies. Continuing.

our marketing team are also specialists in magento marketing. Not only are we made fully aware of the emerging functionality of magento our marketing team continually test the usability of all of our websites using customer behaviour analysis software.

Using the results from we can work closely with the design teams to not only inform the design of new websites for optimum usability and ROI but also to improve continuously & monitor the websites of nedi existing clients.

Each platform has its own intrecacies & our SEO & PPC specialists know the magento platform & all of its quirks.

Results driven services

meaningful outcomes - inbound links search
engine ranking, click-through rates,
website traffic, landing page conversions,
content downloads, blog subscriben +
leads - that can be tracked in real
time + directly correlated to sales

- how firms should be judged:
= superior knowledge + capabilities.
Agencies that understand technology
trends + innovations are able to more
readily adapt th

technology immersion - pretty geeky stuff
constantly adapt + interprate service,
Immersed in the tech industry -
from Designers through to marketers
not just the developers - th what we
chat about, pretty geeky stuff

Content.

measurement geeks. Learn to love data
plus we take a scientific approach to
marketing and have developed a process
for analysing data that can increase
efficiency + max roi

continually testing + intergrating the
latest advances th monitoring + measurec

Decisions based on logic + reason

Tentative : lengley

Tags. IPad. Homepage. Thumbnails.
bottom rail (could be to do with the speed)
Slider bar on 'shop by' is not working
on the IPAD.

Final. flash dropping the
subcategory. doesn't specifically
on iPad.

Flash white.

personalised whips - date
to list.